Response to Intervention

The Guilford Practical Intervention in the Schools Series

Kenneth W. Merrell, Series Editor

This series presents the most reader-friendly resources available in key areas of evidence-based practice in school settings. Practitioners will find trustworthy guides on effective behavioral, mental health, and academic interventions, and assessment and measurement approaches. Covering all aspects of planning, implementing, and evaluating high-quality services for students, books in the series are carefully crafted for everyday utility. Features include ready-to-use reproducibles, lay-flat binding to facilitate photocopying, appealing visual elements, and an oversized format.

Recent Volumes

Helping Students Overcome Depression and Anxiety, Second Edition: A Practical Guide
Kenneth W. Merrell

Inclusive Assessment and Accountability:
A Guide to Accommodations for Students with Diverse Needs
Sara E. Bolt and Andrew T. Roach

Bullying Prevention and Intervention: Realistic Strategies for Schools
Susan M. Swearer, Dorothy L. Espelage, and Scott A. Napolitano

Conducting School-Based Functional Behavioral Assessments, Second Edition:
A Practitioner's Guide
Mark W. Steege and T. Steuart Watson

Evaluating Educational Interventions: Single-Case Design
for Measuring Response to Intervention
T. Chris Riley-Tillman and Matthew K. Burns

Collaborative Home/School Interventions:
Evidence-Based Solutions for Emotional, Behavioral, and Academic Problems
Gretchen Gimpel Peacock and Brent R. Collett

Social and Emotional Learning in the Classroom:
Promoting Mental Health and Academic Success
Kenneth W. Merrell and Barbara A. Gueldner

Executive Skills in Children and Adolescents, Second Edition:
A Practical Guide to Assessment and Intervention
Peg Dawson and Richard Guare

Responding to Problem Behavior in Schools, Second Edition: The Behavior Education Program
Deanne A. Crone, Leanne S. Hawken, and Robert H. Horner

High-Functioning Autism/Asperger Syndrome in Schools: Asessment and Intervention
Frank J. Sansosti, Kelly A. Powell-Smith, and Richard J. Cowan

School Discipline and Self-Discipline:
A Practical Guide to Promoting Prosocial Student Behavior
George G. Bear

Response to Intervention, Second Edition: Principles and Strategies for Effective Practice
Rachel Brown-Chidsey and Mark W. Steege

Response to Intervention

Principles and Strategies
for Effective Practice

SECOND EDITION

RACHEL BROWN-CHIDSEY
MARK W. STEEGE

THE GUILFORD PRESS
New York   London

© 2010 The Guilford Press
A Division of Guilford Publications, Inc.
72 Spring Street, New York, NY 10012
www.guilford.com

Printed in the United States of America

This book is printed on acid-free paper.

Last digit is print number: 9   8   7   6   5   4   3   2   1

Library of Congress Cataloging-in-Publication Data

Brown-Chidsey, Rachel.
   Response to intervention : principles and strategies for effective practice / by Rachel
Brown-Chidsey and Mark W. Steege. — 2nd ed.
      p. cm. — (The Guilford practical intervention in the schools series)
   Includes bibliographical references and index.
   ISBN 978-1-60623-923-0 (pbk.: alk. paper)
   1. Remedial teaching.   2. Slow learning children—Education.   I. Steege, Mark W.   II. Title.
   LB1029.R4.B76 2010
   371.9′043—dc22

                                                                            2010019042

About the Authors

Rachel Brown-Chidsey, PhD, NCSP, is Associate Professor and Coordinator of the School Psychology Program at the University of Southern Maine in Gorham. She is a nationally certified school psychologist and a licensed psychologist and has consulted with schools, districts, and state departments of education to support implementation of response to intervention. Dr. Brown-Chidsey's research areas include curriculum-based measurement, response to intervention, and scientifically based reading instruction methods. She is the editor of *Assessment for Intervention: A Problem-Solving Approach* and coauthor (with Louise Bronaugh and Kelly McGraw) of *RTI in the Classroom: Guidelines and Recipes for Success.*

Mark W. Steege, PhD, NCSP, is Professor of School Psychology at the University of Southern Maine in Gorham. He is a licensed psychologist, a nationally certified school psychologist, and a Board Certified Behavior Analyst–Doctoral. Dr. Steege is the coauthor (with T. Steuart Watson) of the first and second editions of *Conducting School-Based Functional Behavioral Assessments: A Practitioner's Guide* and has published numerous articles and book chapters focusing on assessments and interventions for persons with disabilities.

Preface to the Second Edition
Moving Forward with Responsive Intervention

Be careful what you wish for, you just might get it!

In the years since the publication of the first edition of this book (2005), response to intervention (RTI) has become a well-known phrase in most classrooms and schools across the United States. When we wrote the first edition, we were not sure exactly what level of interest the book would attract. We now know that RTI has taken off as a national educational initiative. Data collected by Spectrum K12 School Solutions indicate that, as of 2009, 70% of respondents were implementing RTI practices in their schools. There are now many more books and other resources about RTI—indeed, more than we can reference in this second edition. Our goal in revising this book was to provide updated resources and examples that support RTI at the school, district, and state levels. Since RTI is a scientifically based initiative, we have updated the references to provide recent examples of the evidence supporting RTI practices. One of the most significant changes in this second edition is the inclusion of information about RTI for behavioral interventions. Recent work done in the area of positive behavior interventions and supports has shown that all the gains we have seen in student academic performance can be achieved for behavior as well when preventive and integrated instruction are provided by using a multi-tier RTI model. It is our hope that this second edition supplies educators at all levels with the theoretical, empirical, and practical information needed to implement and support RTI in schools.

Contents

12. Frequently Asked Questions: Some Answers about RTI 185

References 191

Index 205

List of Boxes, Figures, Tables, and Forms

BOXES

FIGURES

TABLES

FORMS

CHAPTER 1

Introduction
What Is Response to Intervention?

Consider the case of Sean. Sean is a first grader who has not yet developed important prereading skills that he will need if he wants to succeed in school, graduate, go to college, or get a well-paying job in the future. His parents, his teacher, his principal, and the superintendent of his school district want him to learn how to read. So, Sean keeps plugging away in school, sitting attentively when his teacher reads to the class, pointing to pictures in books when his parents read to him at home, and "borrowing" answers from other student's worksheets when completing class assignments. At the end of Sean's first-grade year, he takes a test to show what he has learned during the year. The test shows that he knows his colors and shapes, but he still cannot read.

Sean's teacher places a note about his reading problems in his file before it is sent on to the second-grade teacher. When Sean starts the second grade, his teacher is already concerned about his reading difficulties, and she works with him closely for several weeks. By the end of October she concludes that Sean must have a learning disability; so, she refers him for evaluation. In early January an individualized education plan (IEP) meeting about Sean is held. At the meeting, results from the evaluation are reported. These results show that Sean scored at the low end of the average range on both academic achievement and cognitive (IQ) testing—but *within* the range. As a result of these highly consistent scores, Sean's parents are told that their son does *not* have a learning disability. The parents are relieved to hear that, but then they ask, "Who will help our son learn to read?" The assistant principal who is chairing the meeting regretfully tells Sean's parents that, because his school does not have Title I funding and Sean did not qualify for special education, he will have to keep "trying" to learn to read in his current class. Sean's mom starts to cry, and his dad stands up and shouts angrily, "This is crazy! Our son cannot read, but you won't do anything to help him! We're leaving and I'm calling the superintendent."

When we first conceived the described scenario, response to intervention (RTI) was still very new to U.S. classrooms. Since then, many schools have set up intervention support systems to provide help to students like Sean (Spectrum K12 School Solutions, 2009). The student's experience is sometimes known as a "waiting-to-fail" model, because Sean may

> **There is no one right way to set up RTI practices. Every school needs to plan, set up, and evaluate its own RTI plan.**

eventually qualify for special education—but only if he continues to lag behind in reading and is unable to engage in or participate meaningfully in reading-based classroom activities. The tragedy of this model is that by the time Sean meets the criteria for special education eligibility the optimal years for teaching him to read will have passed (Snow, Burns, & Griffin, 1998). If Sean had received responsive intervention in kindergarten or first grade, the preceding scenario might well have been averted altogether (Denton, Fletcher, Anthony, & Francis, 2006).

The good news for students like Sean is that the instructional methods and educational policies needed to get him the reading (or math, writing, or behavior) instruction that he needs *are available*. The instructional methods and assessment procedures most likely to benefit students like Sean can be provided through a system known as *response to intervention*. RTI is an assessment and intervention model that enables schools to deliver sound instructional methods to students like Sean who might otherwise "fall through the cracks" (Barnes & Harlacher, 2008). This book is designed to provide the requisite knowledge, skills, and resources for using RTI methods successfully in schools.

RTI is a relatively new term for a very commonsensical approach to understanding and addressing students' school difficulties. In the interest of being clear in this book, let's look at the following definitions.

Response

1. The act of responding
2. An answer or reply

Intervention

1. The act of intervening; interposition
2. Any interference that may affect the interests of others, especially of one or more states with the affairs of another; mediation

Another word for intervention is *instruction*, and in some states RTI is known as *response to intervention and instruction*, or just *response to instruction*. See Box 1.1 to learn how instruction and intervention are really very much the same thing. Essentially RTI is a way of looking at the cause–effect relationship(s) between academic or behavioral *intervention* and the student's *response* to the intervention. For example, a student's *response* to a specific reading instruction *intervention* can be measured by using oral reading fluency indicators, examples of which are now widely used in schools throughout the United States (Hardy, 2008; VanDerHeyden, Witt, & Gilbertson, 2007).

When the core terms *response* and *intervention* are combined in the phrase *response to intervention*, a more general set of educational practices and procedures may be defined.

BOX 1.1. Instruction and Intervention? What's the Difference?

Most models of RTI use the word *intervention* to reflect the activities used to help students. Other models use the word *instruction*, so that it's *response to instruction* that's meant by RTI. Some uses put the two together and call it RTII or RTI² (e.g., the Alaska and California departments of education). *Intervention* is really just another word for *instruction*. Traditionally, the word *intervention* has been used to refer to instruction of a more specific and intensive nature, especially in medical settings. The interventions referred to as part of RTI are really just types of instruction matched to students' learning needs. Technically it does not matter whether we call them interventions, instruction, or anything else. What *does* matter is that we use scientifically based teaching practices that respond best to students' needs. In this way, it's the teachers—not the students—who are doing the responding! Whether we call the work we do to support students *instruction* or *intervention* or *activities*, we need to match that instruction to their learning needs and check on their progress regularly to see how they respond in turn. As school psychologist Dave Tilly is fond of reminding us, what RTI actually means is *really terrific instruction*.

Such practices include providing a specific *intervention* for one or more students and measuring the students' *response* to the intervention. Put more succinctly, RTI is a systematic and data-based method of identifying, defining, and resolving students' academic and/or behavior difficulties. While RTI methods may be used for both academic and behavioral interventions, most of the early research about RTI has focused on reading improvement. Recently more work has been done to show how to use RTI to support students' behavior needs as well (Nelson et al., 2009; Sprague, Cook, Wright, & Sadler, 2008). Since robust research outcomes have shown that RTI methods can prevent reading problems, the most recent version of the Individuals with Disabilities Education Improvement Act (IDEA, 2004) included significant changes related to the identification of learning disabilities. While RTI data can be used as part of the process in identifying a specific learning disability (SLD), RTI activities are fundamentally part of general education instruction (Moore & Whitfield, 2009). In fact, *all* educators in schools are using RTI methods (Graner, Faggella-Luby, & Fritschmann, 2005). As this widespread use of RTI has implications for many aspects of education, this second edition focuses on what both general and special education teachers need to know most about RTI. RTI is largely designed to take the guesswork out of helping students who are struggling to learn.

> **A great resource for planning RTI steps is the school-level RTI blueprint (discussed in Chapter 9).**

HISTORY

The components that make up RTI methods have been used in schools for many years but had not previously been organized into the system now called RTI. For example, teachers always have provided help to students who are struggling. Likewise, teachers have reported on student progress at regular intervals. What makes RTI different from these prior means of helping students is that the assessment and instruction practices have now been pulled into one data-based system with built-in decision stages (Glover & DiPerna, 2007; Marston, 2005). RTI is different from past models of student assessment. Prior to RTI, students were assumed to be performing satisfactorily unless identified otherwise (Fletcher, Coulter, Reschly, & Vaughn, 2004). In RTI, all students are screened and monitored for specific educational outcomes, and those needing additional assistance are provided targeted intervention that is monitored regularly. In essence, RTI brings together high-quality teaching and assessment methods in a systematic way so that students who are not successful when presented with one set of instructional methods can be given the chance to succeed by using other practices.

> **RTI did not just "fall out of the sky." Rather, it represents the culmination of many years of effort to provide effective education for all students.**

KEY FEATURES OF RTI

As described in the RTI definition above, two main components distinguish RTI from other teaching and assessment practices, namely, *systematic* and *data-based* activities. Figure 1.1 depicts an updated version of our RTI model, one significantly different from that presented in the first edition of this book. In the first edition, the triangle was "upside down," largely reflecting the early work done by Elizabeth Deno and others in describing a "cascade of services" for students with learning needs (Deno, 1970). The revised figure still includes a triangle with three sections, which reflect three tiers of intervention in RTI. In addition to inverting the triangle, we have now added features that emphasize that RTI supports both academic *and* behavior (social) skills equally. Tier 1 is now at the bottom of the figure and reflects the general education curriculum. This tier is provided to *all* students (at least initially) in each grade level. Tier 1 is comprehensive and universal. As will be discussed in detail in later chapters, Tier 1 activities are selected on the basis of effectiveness demonstrated in scientific studies (Stanovich & Stanovich, 2003). About 80% of students are able to be successful with Tier 1 instruction alone. For the roughly 20% who are not successful with Tier 1 alone, Tier 2 interventions are *added*. It is important to note that Tier 2 is provided *in addition to* Tier 1 as those students who are struggling the hardest in school generally require more instruction to attain their learning goals.

Importantly, in our figure, data are the only connecting point, or pathway, between each tier. About 15% of students, on average, require Tier 1 *plus* Tier 2 interventions to be successful. Tier 3 interventions are reserved for the small subset of students (roughly 5% overall) who do not respond well enough to the interventions provided in Tiers 1 and 2 to succeed in reaching the requisite educational goals. Tier 3 activities include comprehensive evaluation to identify whether a student has a specific disability and/or meets the criteria for special education. Sometimes a student's data indicate partial success with Tier 1 plus Tier 2 interventions, but the amount of time needed each day to achieve this level of success is so large (i.e., more than 2 hours per day per subject area) that Tier 3 instruction becomes

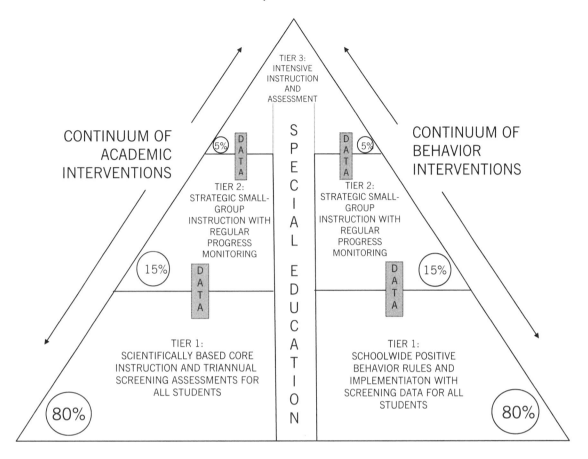

FIGURE 1.1. RTI model.

advisable. While a comprehensive evaluation is being conducted, students in Tier 3, typically about 5% of all students, receive intensive instruction daily, sometimes supplanting portions of their Tier 1 or Tier 2 instruction.

Notably, special education in our model is spread throughout all three tiers. This approach reflects the reality that students with disabilities who need special education normally participate in a combination of both general and special education instruction each day. The blend of general and special education varies for each student, and thus there are typically students with and without disabilities in the same classroom. In our model, Tier 3 is *not* special education; instead, it is the time when additional data are gathered and decisions about the instruction that a struggling student needs are made. If the student is found to be eligible for special education, an IEP is developed that specifies what instruction the student needs across all three tiers of interventions. If the student does not qualify for special education, there is still a need to find the right solution for the student, and ongoing problem solving continues while the student participates in Tier 3 intensive instruction. It is important to note that several different RTI models are being used in schools. Researchers have looked at how many Tiers are needed and while most models have three tiers, some have four (Marston, 2005). In four-tier models, the fourth tier is special education. Others have argued that Tier 3 can be special education (Fuchs & Fuchs, 2008). What is common among all models is that there are multiple tiers of support for all students (Glover & DiPerna, 2007).

As noted earlier, our own model of RTI is built upon previous work related to supporting students who are struggling in school. Deno's "cascade" model of special education service delivery (Deno, 1970) was an early precursor to the current multi-tier approach. In this model, Deno conceptualized students' educational progress as "developmental capital" that could yield dividends in response to appropriate instruction in the least restrictive environment. Deno's "cascade" featured increasingly small instructional groupings matched to the individual student's specific needs. Deno's model was used as a core framework for the implementation of special education regulations during the 1970s and 1980s (Brown-Chidsey, Seppala, & Segura, 2000). While this model helped to make special education a reality for many students, one of the problems seen in special education, starting in the 1980s, was the rapid increase in students identified as having learning disabilities (McBride, Dumont, & Willis, 2004; Ysseldyke, 2005).

In part to address the rapid increase in special education placements, several programs and initiatives have been implemented to address the needs of students before they are given special education services. The first of these, developed during the 1980s, was known as the regular education initiative, or REI (Hallahan, Keller, McKinney, Lloyd, & Bryan, 1988; Jenkins, Pious, & Jewell, 1990). This federal policy focused on having as many students as possible remain in "regular" education (Ackerman, 1987). Drawing on Deno's cascade model, the idea was to focus on determining what constituted the *least restrictive environment* for students with disabilities. Instead of assuming that all students with disabilities would need separate specialized teaching, the REI pushed teachers and administrators to keep as many children in their original classroom as possible (McLeskey & Skiba, 1990).

The REI was criticized from its earliest days, with concerns ranging from a purported lack of teacher training (Coates, 1989; Semmel & Abernathy, 1991) to alleged violation of student rights (Bryan, Bay, & Donahue, 1988; Chisholm, 1988). Jenkins et al. (1990) observed that the REI was chiefly an attempt to rationalize the regular and special education continuum (Drame, 2002). Subsequent analysis showed that the REI was not very effective in reducing the number of students receiving special education services (D'Alonzo & Boggs, 1990; National Center for Education Statistics, 2004; Peltier, 1993). Soon after REI measures were put into place, a second major push to reform special education was begun. Known as "inclusive education," this movement had longer-lasting effects than the REI (Fuchs & Fuchs, 1994; Kubicek, 1994). This effort to change special education policies and practices was focused more on establishing the rights and needs of students with disabilities than reducing the overall number of students receiving special education services (Kavale, 2002). The inclusion movement led to much greater examination of how special education services were being provided (Evans, 1990). As with the REI, many researchers suggested that additional training was needed by general education classroom teachers (Murphy, 1996; Taylor & Richards, 1997). Data showed that educators were reported to be philosophically supportive of special education but not adequately trained to meet the needs of students with disabilities in inclusive classrooms (Villa & Thousand, 1996).

Although the inclusion movement has not totally disappeared, recent efforts to address the large number of students in special education have shifted to using RTI methods as the primary mechanism of change. Additionally, some recent efforts are now squarely focused on reducing the number of students identified with specific learning disabilities rather than consciously setting out to pare special education enrollments overall. Kavale and Forness (2000) have suggested that the reason why both the REI and inclusion movement failed to bring about the desired changes in general and special education is that they neglected to focus sufficiently on the empirical evidence underlying effective practices, preferring instead to concentrate on philosophical issues associated with the moral imperative to educate all children. Related to the overly philosophical focus was the lack of professional development programs to implement both the REI and inclusion efforts (Cummings, Atkins, Allison, & Cole, 2008).

Seeking to gather comprehensive data on the status of and prospects for special education, President George W. Bush created the President's Commission on Excellence in Special Education (PCESE) in October 2001 through Executive Order 13227. This commission was specifically instructed to report on all issues relating to special education and provide recommendations for improving instruction for students with disabilities. The commission's final report, titled *A New Era: Revitalizing Special Education for Children and Their Families*, was published on July 9, 2002 (President's Commission on Excellence in Special Education, 2002). The findings were significant for the future of RTI because the report emphasized the joint roles of both general and special education in meeting the educational needs of all students. In the report's executive summary, the commission listed nine key findings, the second of which stressed the need for greater use of preventive and universal instructional methods:

> The current system uses an antiquated model that waits for a child to fail, instead of a model based on **prevention and intervention.** Too little emphasis is put on prevention, early and accurate identification of learning and behavior problems and aggressive intervention using research-based approaches. This means students with disabilities do not get help early when that help can be most effective. Special education should be for those who do not respond to strong and appropriate instruction and methods provided in general education. (PCESE, 2002, p. 7)

The PCESE report was an important catalyst for subsequent changes in special education law. Congress responded to the report with key changes in the Individuals with Disabilities Education Act. Renamed the Individuals with Disabilities Education Improvement Act, the new law enacted in 2004 included language that encourages the use of RTI methods and allows school districts to use RTI data as part of the process of identifying an SLD. The federal regulations for IDEA 2004 specifically detail how RTI data can be used to determine whether a student exhibits an SLD (see Chapter 2 for more information about how RTI connects the general and special education systems).

When reviewed as a successor to the REI and the inclusion movement, RTI might look like just another attempt to make special education less expensive. Now that RTI has been implemented in countless schools across the United States, it's clear that it is much more than that. Although RTI has certain origins in special education policies and practices, it is now clearly a general education initiative and practice. As noted in the PCESE report, all students who receive special education are also, first and foremost, general education students. And the practices that IDEA 2004 allows for incorporating RTI must originate in general education. Due to RTI's general education focus, it is significantly different from the REI and the inclusion movement. For example, unlike the REI and inclusion, RTI is by definition data-driven; so, no decisions are made without evidence to support them. Most important, RTI is not simply one intervention or method. It is a set of scientifically based procedures that can be used to make decisions about educational programs. In light of the history of efforts to improve educational outcomes for all students, it is important that such current and future initiatives not get bogged down in rhetoric (Kavale, Kauffman, Bachmeier, & LeFever, 2008). As emphasized by Hart and Risley (1995), early intervention has a remarkable impact on long-term outcomes. For this reason, this book focuses on

> RTI models vary in how many "tiers," or levels of instructional supports, they feature. Whether it is a two-tier, three-tier, or four-tier system, the key thing is that it must include scientifically based instruction of increasing intensity.

RTI as a system intended to aid *all* students enrolling in general education. It is designed to be a handbook and implementation manual for those seeking to use RTI in their general education teaching practices on a regular and ongoing basis.

RTI AND PROBLEM SOLVING

By their very nature, RTI methods are problem-solving activities. Although many students and teachers in schools may not perceive their daily experiences as "problems," they do engage in ongoing assessment and reflection. In the course of daily events, teachers (and students) are generally pleased when teaching and learning activities go as expected. Under such circumstances, no major "problems" are evident. When a teacher notices that a student's work is not what was expected, a different reaction is likely to occur. If the teacher finds the student's work to be exemplary, he or she may offer additional praise. If the teacher finds the work to be below expectations, he or she may believe that a learning problem is present. Such a problem could involve academic skills such as reading, writing, or math, or it could relate to behavioral expectations such as whether the student is able to stay seated, stand in line, or play with others at recess. Regardless of the event, teachers and students tend not to notice school problems until they occur, and then they suddenly are very apparent. As a result of efforts to help all students be successful in school, researchers have developed specific problem-solving methods designed to assist teachers and specialists when school difficulties arise (Brown-Chidsey, 2005a; Deno, 2002; Tilly, 2008).

RTI methods are closely linked with problem-solving models for school difficulties. In this volume, Deno's five-step data-based problem-solving model will be used as part of the

RTI stages and activities (Deno, 2005). A summary of the problem-solving model is found in Table 1.1. This model includes (1) problem identification, (2) problem definition, (3) designing intervention plans, (4) implementing the intervention and progress monitoring, and (5) problem solution. As shown in Table 1.1, each of these steps is aligned with specific assessment and instructional activities designed to reduce or eliminate a student's school difficulties. This model is designed to be used continuously and interactively. As one step ends, the next begins. In some cases, not all steps will be implemented. In other cases, each step will be utilized multiple times to help identify the best way to help a student be successful in school. An important feature of this problem-solving model is that it recognizes that schools cannot be problem-free. Instead, it offers a way of dealing with problems when they happen so that the long-term negative impact is minimized.

Step 1: Problem Identification

The first step begins with problem identification activities. Such activities include any and all moments when a student's school difficulties are initially identified. To help explain this step and the other steps of the model, the metaphor of radar will be used. Problem identification may be likened to the moment when something is first detected on a radar screen. Those monitoring the screen do not know what's causing the "blip" on the screen, but they know it needs to be addressed. A number of different people may participate in problem identification activities. Teachers, parents, students, administrators, bus drivers, and/or cafeteria staff may help to bring problems to greater attention and put them on the "radar screen." Problem identification is not an end unto itself. Instead, this first step activates a process by which more data about a student's school difficulties can be collected.

TABLE 1.1. A Data-Based Problem-Solving Model

Problem-solving steps	Assessment procedures	Evaluation decisions
1. Problem identification	Observing/recording student performance	Does a problem exist?
2. Problem definition	Quantifying the perceived discrepancy	Is the problem important?
3. Designing intervention plans	Exploring alternative goals and solution hypotheses	What is the best solution hypothesis?
4. Implementing the intervention and progress monitoring	Monitoring fidelity of intervention and data collection	Is the solution attempt progressing as planned?
5. Problem solution	Requantifying the discrepancy	Is the original problem being solved through this attempted solution?

Note. From Deno (2005, p. 25). Copyright 2005 by The Guilford Press. Reprinted by permission.

Step 2: Problem Definition

The second step of the problem-solving model is problem definition. This step includes evaluating the nature and magnitude of the problem and determining whether the problem requires an intervention or might resolve itself on its own. This process is similar to what seafarers and aviators must do in order to determine whether the radar signal is from a large attack ship or a small unarmed private vessel. How the pilot responds will be based on the nature of the object identified by the radar. In the same way, educators can help students by defining the nature of the student's problem. Problem definition activities include evaluating the student's skills in certain areas and comparing them to what is expected. Such definitions include measurements such as reading fluency, frequency of on-task behaviors, and rate of homework completion. Only once a student's current behaviors have been identified is it possible to know the magnitude and importance of the problem identified in Step 1. Some problems may be very small and likely to resolve on their own over time. Alternatively, other problems may be of immediate concern. If the difference between a student's current performance and what is expected is large, that student is likely to have a serious school problem that needs to be resolved.

Step 3: Designing Intervention Plans

The third step of the problem-solving model includes putting in place specific activities and procedures designed to reduce significantly the difference between what a student can currently do and what he or she is expected to do. The development of such intervention plans is similar to how a pilot of a boat or plane might respond to information concerning the source of a radar signal. If the captain of a small sailboat is charting a course and finds that he or she is steering toward a much larger vessel, changing course is the prudent thing to do, especially if the larger ship is an aircraft carrier or oil tanker. Educators can help students to chart a new course by designing ways to improve their skills so that they can be successful in school. As will be discussed in Chapter 4, all interventions need to be empirically validated with evidence of effectiveness in school settings. Effective interventions include methods such as direct instruction of specific skills, positive behavior interventions and supports (PBIS; Albrecht, 2008; Eber, Breen, Rose, Unizycki, & London, 2008), and peer-assisted learning strategies (PALS; Calhoon, Al Otaiba, Cihak, King, & Avalos, 2007; Kroeger & Kouche, 2006). A specific time frame and plan for implementing the intervention, what personnel will be involved, and how data will be collected provide crucial links to the next steps of the problem-solving process.

Step 4: Implementing the Intervention and Progress Monitoring

This step of the model has two major components, implementation and progress monitoring. The intervention (i.e., instruction) should be implemented as planned and intended. If a well-designed intervention is put into action incorrectly, it may be impossible to know whether it could have worked. For this reason, the intervention plan should include some form of verification to document whether the plan was implemented as intended. If an intervention is implemented as planned but does not work, it can be changed, but information about initial ineffectiveness is needed in order to design effective alternatives. If some portions of the intervention did work, these might be retained and used with additional new components. The only way to know if an intervention works is to collect data. This task is the critical second component of problem-solving Step 4. From the first moment that an intervention is put into place, data concerning the outcomes must be collected. This requirement is no different from a ship pilot's monitoring the radar screen as well as other sources of information to verify that the threat posed by a larger vessel is reduced as a result of changing course. Data collection methods can include recording the frequency, rate, accuracy, duration, and intensity of a behavior or skill (Steege & Watson, 2009). Determination of what type of data recording procedure to use is based on the specific nature of the problem. Students who are often off-task can be monitored by tracking the frequency of on-task behaviors. Students with reading difficulties can be monitored by checking and recording oral or silent reading fluency (Brown-Chidsey, Davis, & Maya, 2003). Progress monitoring also involves ongoing data analysis. Typically, single-case experimental designs (e.g., Brown-Chidsey, Steege, & Mace, 2008) are used in the analysis of these data.

Step 5: Problem Solution

As mentioned earlier, the problem-solving model is organized in such a way that it can be used to solve a wide range of school problems. It is set up to account for the reality that there will always be problems in schools. Thankfully, many school problems are solvable, and this model has an identifiable end step that documents when a problem is resolved. The specific way that each school problem will be solved will always differ according to the strengths and needs of each child. The important aspect of the fifth, and final, step of the model is that it allows for recognition of success by noting when certain preset criteria for success are met. Just as the captain of a boat lets out a sigh of relief when a new course results in being out of harm's way, students and their support teams can determine a given performance level that will indicate success and celebrate when it is met. As noted above, the problem-solving model is set up to be used continuously, as needed. For some students, one intervention may be all that it takes to achieve the problem's resolution. For others, the problems may be greater in size and number, and multiple problem solution parties may need to be shared on the pathway to greater success. Importantly, problem solution provides all members of the school team with the chance to identify what has been successful and build upon it when developing new goals and plans.

RTI AND SPECIAL EDUCATION

As described at the beginning of this chapter, RTI methods share a common tradition with prior efforts to improve special education programs. It is impossible to separate RTI completely from special education because RTI activities occur in a sequence along a continuum

(Cummings et al., 2008). When empirically validated interventions are used, it is expected that most students' school progress will be appropriate. Still, RTI methods include steps to be taken for students who continue to struggle in school despite attempted interventions. For some students, RTI activities will result in evaluation and eligibility for special education services. Indeed, as described in detail in Chapter 2, RTI methods have been included in the most recent reauthorization of the IDEA. Such methods also fit with other recent education policies such as the No Child Left Behind Act (NCLB, 2001) and related state programs. Importantly, RTI methods were developed with the goal of spreading a wide net for the identification of students having difficulties in school. This net is designed initially to identify a larger number of students who need help than will end up in special education (Brown-Chidsey, 2007; O'Connor, 2003). The goal is to provide students at risk of or already experiencing school difficulties with interventions that prevent additional problems (Compton, 2003; Speece, Case, & Malloy, 2003; Moore & Whitfield, 2009).

An example of the wide-net approach included in RTI is the Texas Primary Reading Instrument (TPRI). This instrument is part of a statewide effort to identify and define the needs of students at risk of reading problems (Center for Academic and Reading Skills, 1999). It is organized such that scores on the TPRI yield a list of students who may have reading problems. This list is used to design and implement reading interventions that are monitored over time. It is expected that most students will show reading improvement as a result of the intervention. Those students who do not show improvement are provided with additional interventions that are developed in response to the data collected during the earlier program. Students who consistently struggle to learn to read despite multiple empirically based reading interventions are evaluated to determine whether they are eligible for special education services. Similar programs also have been used in Iowa and Massachusetts. Data from early reading RTI programs in Iowa showed that fewer students were ultimately placed in special education programs after RTI methods were used than before (Tilly, 2003).

RTI AND GENERAL EDUCATION

The success of RTI as a means of reducing the number of students who receive special education services is important for those concerned about too many students being identified as disabled. The more important aspect of RTI data is how many students have found greater success in school as a result of data-based educational programming. Yes, fewer students have been labeled as "disabled;" however, and more significantly, these same students have developed critical basic skills that increase the likelihood they will be successful in school and life. For this reason, RTI is really a general education initiative. RTI activities begin and end in general education. They may serve as a pathway for "child find" activities for some students, but they provide systematic data-based decision making for far more general education students. Some researchers have noted that general educators were not initially prepared for the instructional techniques and data analysis skills that are required for implementing RTI methods (Fletcher, 2003; Fletcher et al., 2002; L. Fuchs, 2003; Kovaleski,

2003; Vaughn & Fuchs, 2003). Nevertheless, there is evidence that RTI methods are very effective as part of general education, and the U.S. Department of Education's recently concluded Reading First grant program was organized according to several RTI principles (Good, Simmons, & Kame'enui, 2001; U.S. Department of Education, 2008, 2009). Data reported by the Kansas Department of Education showed that statewide student scores on the Kansas state assessment improved significantly after a statewide data-based system of interventions (i.e., RTI) was put into place (Kansas Department of Education, 2009).

In order for RTI to continue to improve students' educational outcomes in general education, teachers, administrators, and specialists need to work on how best to implement and interpret RTI methods and data. Some teachers still may not have received much, if any, training in data analysis. Others may worry that RTI is another "add-on" to what they are already doing and fear that there are not enough hours in the school day to incorporate RTI practices. Importantly, RTI does not require "adding on" to what is already being done in the classroom. Instead, it involves reviewing current classroom practices to identify those that yield evidence of effective instruction as well as those that do not. RTI methods call for teachers to *replace* those practices that do not yield student improvement with those that do. RTI depends on general education teachers as the most important element accounting for students' school success.

RTI AND PUBLIC POLICY

RTI has already become part of several educational policies and is likely to be incorporated into future programs as well. The rationale for having RTI as a central focus of public education policy is that it is a population-based system for determining which students need more assistance. Population-based decision making comes from the field of public health (Doll & Haack, 2005). Examples of population-based policies already widely in place include mandatory immunization of all school children, review and recall of food products by the U.S. Department of Agriculture, and warnings about alcohol use on beer, wine, and liquor labels. All of these polices are designed to protect the public health and welfare through systematic procedures, recalls, and warnings. Although population-based decision making has been widely used in health, food, and safety policies for many years, it has been less utilized in school settings. RTI represents a major application of population-based policy in education because it calls for screening of the entire school population for identification of possible school difficulties (Coyne, Kame'enui, & Simmons, 2001, 2004; Coyne, Kame'enui, Simmons, & Harn, 2004).

Just as there are many public welfare benefits from immunizations, meat recalls, and alcohol labels, RTI applications in schools are likely to yield important gains for all students. The universal nature of RTI methods means that all students are reviewed regularly to determine whether school problems are present (Biglan, Mrazek, Carnine, & Flay, 2003). This screening prevents students from "slipping through the cracks." Those students who need additional assistance are provided with interventions previously shown to be effective, just as physicians use treatments validated in research studies. The data-driven nature of RTI means that decisions about school practices are derived from students' actual performance in class. New interventions are provided only as needed when data show that existing practices are not working. In the end, RTI is designed to enhance *all* students' educational outcomes by providing continuous progress monitoring of all students and specialized assistance to those who need it.

BIG IDEAS ABOUT RTI

There are three main components to RTI: high-quality instruction, frequent assessment, and data-based decision making (see Table 1.2). Each of these components connects to a "big idea" about educational policy. High-quality instruction is based on the idea that all children deserve effective instruction that leads to the development of functional skills. Frequent assessment is based on the idea that continuous assessment leads to skill improvement. Instructional decision making relates to the idea that adjustments to instruction must be based on data. When the three components of RTI are put together with the problem-solving assessment model, decisions about a student's progress toward education goals are much easier to make.

The remaining chapters of this book provide detailed information about each component of RTI and how to use each to foster positive academic and behavior outcomes for all students. Chapters 2 and 3 provide information about the policy framework around which RTI procedures can be used. Chapter 4 includes a review of scientifically based educational practices and evidence-based instruction. Chapter 5 describes single-subject research designs and how they can be used in RTI practices. Chapters 6 and 7 detail the individual steps in RTI methods and show how they are applied in cases involving academic as well as behavior difficulties. Chapter 8 covers the use of RTI with students from diverse backgrounds. Chapter 9 describes the importance of long-term planning for effective RTI implementation, whether at the school, district, or state level. Chapter 10 provides case examples of RTI methods in action, while Chapter 11 further elaborates by providing samples of various RTI reports. Finally, Chapter 12 answers some frequently asked questions (FAQs) about RTI and speculates about future directions. In sum, readers should come away from this book with the requisite knowledge and skills to design, implement, and evaluate RTI methods effectively in their own school settings.

TABLE 1.2. "Big Ideas" about RTI Methods

RTI component	"Big idea"
High-quality instruction	All children deserve effective instruction that leads to the development of functional skills.
Frequent assessment	Continuous assessment leads to skill improvement.
Data-based decision making	Adjustments to instruction must be based on data.

A NEW VISION FOR SEAN

This chapter began with a scenario of Sean, a student for whom past educational practices were not helpful. Here is a different vision for Sean:

> Sean is a first grader who has not yet developed important prereading skills that he will need if he wants to succeed in school, graduate, go to college, or get a well-paying job in the future. His parents, his teacher, his principal, and the superintendent of his school district want him to learn how to read. Sean did not attend kindergarten, but when he enrolled in first grade his school conducted universal screening of all students in the fall. The screening data showed that Sean was significantly behind his peers in key prereading skills. As a result of Sean's risk level, he participated in a supplementary reading group for 30 minutes each day in addition to the 90-minute reading instruction his classroom teacher provided. All of the reading instruction Sean received was scientifically based, and he participated in weekly progress measures that showed his reading growth. By the middle of first grade, Sean was on his way to becoming a reader. By the end of first grade, Sean had caught up with his classmates and was eager to practice his emerging reading skills over the summer.

This book is designed to ensure that students like Sean have every chance to be successful readers, students, and citizens.

CHAPTER 2

Using Scientifically Based Instruction
NCLB, IDEA, ARRA, and RTI

POLICIES SUPPORTING SCIENCE-BASED PRACTICE

Chapter 1 included information about the social and historical context in which RTI research and programs have evolved. Importantly, RTI is part of a larger effort to improve access to educational opportunities for all students. One of the core elements of RTI that is a very recent advance in the field of education is scientifically based practice (Brown-Chidsey, 2005c). Scientifically based practice refers to those instructional methods and pedagogical approaches that have been verified by numerous research studies. The scientific basis of education practice also has been referred to in a number of places as *evidence-based* practice (Kratochwill & Stoiber, 2002). The meaning intended by referring to certain educational methods as evidence-based or scientifically based is to help all educators understand the importance of scientifically based data in validating instructional practices (Stanovich & Stanovich, 2003). Although educational research has been conducted for many, many years, the use of such data to inform and change instructional practices is much more limited (Burns, Peters, & Noell, 2008; Pressley, Duke, & Boling, 2004; Sweet, 2004).

Thanks to research advances in the area of reading, there now exists a strong body of evidence about typical and atypical reading development (Lyon, Shaywitz, & Chhabra, 2004; McCardle & Chhabra, 2004; National Reading Panel, 2000; Shaywitz, 2003). The consistency and high quality of the research produced about reading led a number of policymakers and researchers to push for heavier emphasis on a scientific basis for any and all instructional methods used in schools (Carnine, 1997a). Three relatively recent U.S. educational programs have incorporated requirements for scientifically based practices, namely, the NCLB of 2001, the IDEA reauthorization of 2004, and the American Recovery and Reinvestment Act of 2009 (ARRA). Additionally, there were requirements for an evidence basis for instructional and assessment conducted as part of the Reading First grant program, which was a subpart of NCLB. When reviewed as a set, these legislated programs include language that sets up a policy framework in which scientifically based, data-driven RTI methods are expected to be an essential feature of educational practice throughout the United States. These legislative policies will be reviewed in turn.

> **RTI is really a way of thinking about and doing instruction. It is a mindset that recognizes that all children can learn and that a classroom teacher's job is to find the instruction that works best for each child.**

RTI COMPONENTS IN NCLB

No Child Left Behind

No Child Left Behind is the name of the 2001 reauthorization of the Elementary and Secondary Education Act (ESEA), first passed in 1965. ESEA was the first major U.S. federal legislation to provide funding to public schools. The thrust behind the 1965 act was a group of policies and programs collectively known as the "Great Society" (Halperin, 1979; Sweet, 2004). Begun during the Kennedy administration and completed by the Johnson administration, these programs sought to harness knowledge gleaned from research to address major social problems. The Great Society initiative sought to eradicate poverty by providing better housing, education, and employment opportunities for low-income families. While ESEA has been updated a number of times since 1965, the 2001 reauthorization (NCLB) included requirements for states that are much more specific than earlier versions. Specifically, NCLB put a very heavy emphasis on evidence-based practices. For example, here is an excerpt from *No Child Left Behind: A Desktop Reference*:

> **NCLB is the latest version of the Elementary and Secondary Education Act (ESEA) that was first passed in 1965.**

> All states must submit plans to the Secretary of Education that include *evidence* that they have content and achievement standards and aligned assessments, school report card procedures, and statewide systems for holding schools and districts accountable for the achievement of their students. (U.S. Department of Education, 2002b, p. 10)

In the example above, the evidence focus is on states' assessment systems. However, it sets the stage for specifications in states' federally funded programs that require evidence-based practices. For example, among the requirements for programs to be funded under NCLB is evidence of effectiveness, which was described as "programs that have been found through scientifically based research to significantly improve the academic achievement of participating children or have strong evidence that they will achieve this result" (U.S. Department of Education, 2002b, p. 45). In addition, language in NCLB implementation materials required that states continue to monitor student progress during program implementation. Thus, NCLB set up a set of requirements whereby states must implement scientifically based instruction and monitor student progress to verify that the programs are effective. NCLB guidance stated that

Activities must be based on a review of scientifically based research that shows how such interventions are expected to improve student achievement. This means that there must be reliable and valid research evidence that the program activities are effective in helping teachers to improve student academic achievement. (U.S. Department of Education, 2002b, p. 53)

In contrast to earlier versions of ESEA, NCLB included numerous references to evidence-based and scientifically validated instructional practices designed to improve learning outcomes for all students (Kavale et al., 2008). The focus on improving the performance of all students harkens back to the original focus of ESEA in 1965, when the goal was increasing performance of the poorest and most at-risk students. Greater specificity about program elements and targets for students to meet was included in certain portions of NCLB, including the Reading First, Early Reading First, and Even Start subsections.

Reading First

Thanks to the availability of excellent and conclusive research about the nature and course of reading difficulties (Foorman, 2003; Shaywitz, 2003), NCLB includes large sections specifying the exact features and components to be included in states' reading improvement programs. Specifically, states must submit evidence of how they will use evidence-based practices to teach and assess students' reading skills across the five reading domains identified by the National Reading Panel (2000). NCLB proposal guidance required that each state

[use] scientific evidence to enhance children's reading skills. Professional development, instructional programs, and materials used by a state education agency (SEA) or school district must focus on the five key areas that scientifically based reading research has identified as essential components of reading instruction—phonemic awareness, phonics, vocabulary, fluency, and reading comprehension. (U.S. Department of Education, 2002b, p. 24)

By having states and local school districts integrate scientifically based reading instruction methods, the Reading First portions of NCLB focused on increasing the likelihood that students at risk for reading difficulties will receive instruction previously shown to be effective in helping such students (U.S. Department of Education, 2002a).

> **Schools participating in the federal Reading First grant program may note that many Reading First activities are similar to aspects of RTI and thus may benefit in preparing for RTI.**

States were allowed to use different outcome measures to document student performance; so, the effects of Reading First outcomes across all 50 states and U.S. territories cannot be directly compared. Nevertheless, a review of aggregated Reading First data for each state revealed that there were significant improvements in student reading performance in most states (U.S. Department of Education, 2008). These data show how systemic efforts to improve students reading skills that utilized scientifically based reading instruction methods resulted in much better reading performance for students in grades 1–3. The Reading First data have implications for RTI because they align strongly with evidence from other research that has shown that when a combination of Tier 1 scientifically based core reading instruction and Tier 2 additional small-group instruction is provided, student reading skills improved (Al Otaiba & Torgeson, 2007).

Early Reading First

Another subsection of NCLB focused on evidence-based reading instruction was Early Reading First. This grant program provided funding for early childhood and kindergarten reading instruction. Again, the thrust for this program came from extensive scientific research that showed how early intervention for students identified as at risk has yielded impressive results by fostering critical prereading skills (Gettinger & Stoiber, 2007; Snow et al., 1998). For example, students as young as 3 years old were found to benefit from instruction to boost overall vocabulary knowledge.

> New research illustrates the importance of the intellectual competencies of young children and suggests specific ways to support learning through the use of strategies such as explicit and scaffolded instruction (in which adults build upon what children already know to help them accomplish a complex task by providing support where needed). An extensive body of evidence is now available stressing the importance of early reading skills, including phonological awareness and vocabulary development. Early Reading First is designed to improve these skills. (U.S. Department of Education, 2002b, p. 27)

Congress included Early Reading First in NCLB because of the persuasive evidence that early intervention works. Notably, the inclusion of early intervention in NCLB points to the importance of preventive efforts to support students in learning the precursors known to contribute to later reading development. A notable component of the Reading First and Early Reading First sections of NCLB that stands out is the way in which the legislation "requires programs to use scientifically based research to teach children cognitive and language skills. Programs must base their activities, services, and professional development on scientifically based reading research" (U.S. Department of Education, 2002b, p. 27). These criteria include emphasis on systematic, data-driven, and scientifically based practices for all levels and stages of each student's education (VanDerHeyden & Snyder, 2006).

Data from Early Reading First implementation sites have shown that providing early reading intervention to preschool students at risk for reading problems had a significant effect on their prereading skills (U.S. Department of Education, 2009). These results confirm similar findings from

> **Like Early Reading First, RTI focuses on the prevention of academic and behavior problems.**

RTI research examining the role of early intervention in reading development (Vellutino, Scanlon, & Zhang, 2007).

Anticipating Student Needs: Prevention on Multiple Levels

The prevention orientation in NCLB follows from work done in other disciplines regarding multiple stages in program supports so that the least intrusive methods necessary are applied to support effective outcomes for all students. In particular, a three-stage prevention model common in the field of public health has been integrated into NCLB (Brown & Brown, 2005; Caplan, 1964; Doll & Haack, 2005; McCardle & Chhabra, 2004; Pressley et al., 2004). This three-stage prevention model, with primary, secondary, and tertiary components, offers a new way for educators to think about how best to help all students to be successful. According to this prevention model, programs and services designed for all students are known as primary prevention. In public health and medicine, an example of primary prevention is mandatory immunization for certain diseases. Immunization policies were developed in the last half of the 20th century because of scientific data documenting how vaccinating entire populations was in the general public interest (Freeman, 1994; Institute of Medicine, 2004).

Secondary prevention involves intervention for those who do not respond to the primary prevention methods. In health care, this includes giving flu shots to those known to be at risk for influenza due to identifiable characteristics matched to population risk factors. Individuals who are 65 or older, who have certain medical conditions, or who care for those who are ill have been shown to be much more at risk for catching the flu. Given this risk, a standard preventive health protocol involves targeting flu shots to those in the overall population who are at a greater risk for getting a bad case of the flu. The importance and effects of differential prevention efforts were observable in the way that novel H1N1 influenza virus inoculations were targeted in 2009–2010 at children and youths rather than older persons. Early data on the occurrence and spread of H1N1 flu had revealed that it affected children and youths much more severely than adults, including those over age 65. For this reason the U.S. Centers for Disease Control and Prevention (CDC) recommended that children and youths have priority for vaccination against this flu strain (Centers for Disease Control, 2009).

Tertiary prevention includes methods and procedures for treating active cases of a disease or condition. Using the flu example, tertiary activities include the actual treatment of flu symptoms. Once a case of flu is verified, there is no sense in primary or secondary prevention, but minimizing the dangers and discomfort from the flu are in the individual's and community's best interest. In similar ways, NCLB incorporated data from numerous studies about effective instructional practices into national education policy. Specifically, NCLB required states to develop educational programs that were based on evidence from scientific studies. In the case of reading, NCLB specifically required sequenced elements in effective reading programs for the purpose of organizing and targeting instruction to specific students at specific moments in time. As noted, this policy is grounded in a prevention model because specific NCLB programs such as Early Reading First and Reading First required evidence-based reading instruction as the core curriculum for all students but also included the requirement of increasingly more explicit and intensive instruction for those students who do not respond to the core instruction program.

NCLB incorporated other examples of prevention as well. One example was the Even Start program. This program included funding for preschool education activities designed to boost the readiness of all students for kindergarten and higher-grade instruction. NCLB documentation noted that

> Even Start programs will achieve quality through new requirements to use scientifically based research evidence to design program activities, especially reading-readiness activities for preschool children. The new state indicators of program quality will allow states to make informed decisions about continuation funding for subgrantees based on whether or not they are showing sufficient progress. (U.S. Department of Education, 2002b, p. 32)

Of note, the Even Start guidelines require that states and programs document evidence of student progress. This feature of the guidelines is firmly rooted in a prevention model, because only by examining the results from primary prevention activities can one determine which individuals in a given population need secondary prevention programs. Monitoring student progress is a key element of RTI because it reveals which students are doing OK and which ones need more help.

NCLB included language related to other aspects of primary prevention as well. For example, NCLB included funding for before- and after-school programs for students whose parents work long hours. Such programming relates to primary prevention because other research has shown how students who are well supervised outside of school are more likely to achieve better school outcomes. By offering high-quality before- and after-school programs, students whose parents must work long hours to make ends meet are more likely to be as successful in school as those whose parents can take them to school and be with them as soon as school ends each day. The scientific nature of such programs must meet the same standards of evidence. For example:

> **There is room for creativity and innovation in RTI activities. Programs such as before- and after-school enrichment can be an important resource for students at risk.**

> A [before- or after-school] program must be based on an objective assessment of the need for before- and after-school programs (including summer school programs) and activities in schools and communities; an established set of performance measures aimed at ensuring quality academic enrichment opportunities; and, if appropriate, scientifically based research that provides evidence that the program will help students meet state and local academic achievement standards. (U.S. Department of Education, 2002b, p. 86)

Taken as a whole, the core provisions of NCLB incorporate evidence-based practices in systematic and data-driven ways that both match and complement our RTI model in numerous ways.

RTI COMPONENTS IN IDEA 2004

Additional efforts to integrate RTI with education policy were featured in the most recent reauthorization of the federal special education law, the Individuals with Disabilities Education Improvement Act (IDEA, 2004). Specifically, RTI language was explicitly incorporated into the legislation. Some of the impetus for including RTI language in special education policy came from the same research evidence that promoted its inclusion in NCLB. In addition to the scientific evidence for specific reading instruction methods, other data have shown a large increase in the number of students who are receiving special education services (National Center for Education Statistics, 2004). The disability for which students most commonly receive special education services is specific learning disability. Additional data further reveal that the majority of students who have been identified as learning disabled have reading problems (Swanson, Harris, & Graham, 2003). The evidence of increases in the number of students receiving special education services alongside the high number of those students having reading problems suggested that focused efforts to meet the needs of students with reading problems were required.

The specific language in IDEA (2004) included three elements that integrate evidence-based practices, including (1) a requirement for the use of scientifically based reading instruction, (2) evaluation of how well a student responds to intervention, and (3) emphasis on the role of data in decision making. In essence, these three requirements are the core components of RTI. IDEA 2004 also included language allowing school districts to make determinations about learning disabilities without using IQ scores. The IDEA 2004 language regarding how RTI data can be used for special education eligibility determination is discussed in Chapter 3.

Scientifically Based Instruction in All Areas

The IDEA 2004 requirement for evidence-based reading instruction practices came directly from the research literature about scientifically based methods (National Reading Panel, 2000). IDEA 2004 specified scientifically based instruction for reading only and did not include such a requirement for math, writing, or behavior instruction; this omission was attributed to the smaller amount of research on instruction in these areas. More recent evidence has shown that effective scientifically based instruction for math, writing, and behavior can be applied within an RTI model as well (Axtell, McCallum, Bell, & Poncy, 2009; Burns, Ganuza, & London, 2009; Fairbanks, Sugai, Guardino, & Lathrop, 2007; Gresham, 2004; Kroeger & Kouche, 2006).

The second RTI element found in IDEA 2004 related to data. The law stated that the procedures for determining whether a student has a disability need to take into consideration how a student responds to effective instruction. Recent evidence has shown that when RTI methods were implemented with fidelity student outcomes improved and fewer students ended up needing special education (Denton et al., 2006; Hardy, 2008; VanDer-Heyden, Snyder, Broussard, & Ramsdell, 2007).

The third element in IDEA 2004 specified that the decisions about a student's response to intervention have to be data-based. This requirement builds on the second element by requiring not only that data about student performance be collected but also that it be reviewed regularly. Taken together, the RTI language in IDEA 2004 captured many elements seen in NCLB about evidence-based practices but added an increased emphasis on using data to inform instruction. The main thrust behind the evidence and data-based language in IDEA 2004 came from the concern that too many students end up in special education. While special education is recognized as an important and crucial resource for students with disabilities, many educators, administrators, and policymakers have long been concerned that it is often perceived as the only mechanism by which a student can receive additional instruction and support. As noted in Chapter 1, RTI is fundamentally a general education initiative. Given that all students in a school participate in RTI at Tier 1, and that Tiers 2 and 3 are for general education students, it is *not* another form of special education. But, for students who are not successful at Tiers 1, 2, and 3, special education may be an essential resource to support their educational success. For these reasons, RTI provides a systematic way to offer all students a continuum of instruction based on their learning needs.

> **RTI is *not* about or for special education. It is a *general education* initiative that includes components for all students.**

ARRA OF 2009

Most recently, another federal law has offered states additional resources to support RTI. The RTI-related language in both NCLB and IDEA 2004 spelled out requirements for using scientifically based instruction and data-based decision making when utilizing the federal funds allocated in those laws. Neither offered much in the way of additional money to make RTI a reality in classrooms and schools. Although NCLB provided additional money to states and schools through Reading First, these funds primarily benefited only certain schools and students. Similarly, IDEA 2004 for the first time allowed school districts (i.e., local education agencies) to use up to 15% of their federal IDEA money for RTI activities for students not in special education. However, this 15% allowance is not really very much money, because the federal allotment for special education granted to states is much less than each district actually spends.

The ARRA of 2009 set up a more open pathway to grant states money to support RTI activities and initiatives. ARRA was passed by the U.S. Congress in response to the major economic downturn that affected the U.S. and world economies beginning in 2008. ARRA was a major spending law that provided money to all areas of the U.S. economy in an effort to restore consumer confidence, stabilize banks, and encourage spending at all levels of the economy. A specific section of ARRA applied to U.S. public schools. Division A, Title XIV of ARRA, known as the State Fiscal Stabilization Fund, was set up to be administered by the U.S. Department of Education. This fund included money that each state's governor could request for the purpose of improving and reforming education in each state. Importantly, the criteria established by the U.S. Department of Education for distributing the funds required that state applicants demonstrate how the funds would utilize current and future school-based data to improve educational outcomes for all students. For example, Section 14005 (State Applications), in subsections (c), 4–5, require that states

> (4) describe how the State would use its grant funding to improve student academic achievement in the State, including how it will allocate the funds to give priority to high-need local educational agencies; and (5) include a plan for evaluating the State's progress in closing achievement gaps. (American Recovery and Reinvestment Act, 2009)

Education money in ARRA 2009 created an important opportunity for states to review state and local educational outcomes to date and to seek additional resources to support responsive interventions for students who need them.

EMERGING STANDARDS IN EDUCATIONAL POLICY

Three major U.S. educational policies have reshaped key aspects of how student educational progress is understood. NCLB required that teachers use instructional practices validated in scientifically based studies. IDEA 2004 extended that requirement and stipulated that teachers collect their own data about student performance and utilize scientific methods to determine whether their own application of scientifically based practices improved outcomes for students. ARRA 2009 provided funding for states to extend and improve data-based instructional practices at the state and local levels. Notably, NCLB and ARRA resources apply to all students, while IDEA 2004 is activated only when a student encounters difficulties in the general education curriculum. Still, the requirement in IDEA 2004 that data about a student's performance in the general education curriculum be utilized in order to make a determination of learning disability means that certain IDEA policies will necessarily affect general education practices. In Chapter 3 we review and discuss the specific components in IDEA 2004 that have further expanded the application of evidence-based educational practices in both general and special education.

CHAPTER 3

RTI and Special Education
Prospects and Possibilities

RTI is a general education system for identifying and monitoring student learning needs. When we were writing the first edition of this book, the latest version of U.S. special education law, IDEA 2004, had just been passed by Congress and signed by the president, but the regulations for implementing the revised law had not yet been published. These regulations, published in August 2006, provide important guidance on how RTI works alongside special education procedures. Again, it must be emphasized that RTI is a general education system that supports all students. That being said, the data obtained as part of RTI also can be used as part of special education decision making. Specifically, RTI can be used as part of the assessment procedures to identify an SLD (see Box 3.1).

For a number of years researchers have called for a change in how students with an SLD are identified (Harry & Klingner, 2007; Holdnack & Weiss, 2006; Kavale, 2001). A number of reasons for changing the procedures and practices surrounding LD identification have

---

BOX 3.1. RTI and Special Education Eligibility

RTI is a general education system for supporting all students. RTI is about providing students with effective interventions and documenting student progress. In places where RTI has been used for a while, data show that it has resulted in fewer students receiving special education services (Burns & Gibbons, 2008; VanDerHeyden, Witt, & Gilbertson, 2007). As Martha Stewart might put it, "That's a good thing." Why? While special education has the goal of ensuring that all children in the United States have access to a *free appropriate public education* in the *least restrictive environment* (FAPE/LRE), it has not always achieved that goal (Kavale, 2001, 2002). RTI is about showing which interventions—whether in general education or special education—best advance the goal of improving student outcomes.

---

been identified, including the lack of evidence to support the current method, evidence that other methods work just as well or better, and a desire to do away with a practice whereby students must "wait to fail" (Elliott & Fuchs, 1997; Fletcher et al., 2004; Goodman & Webb, 2006; Reschly, 1997; Stanovich, 1991, 1993; Vellutino, Scanlon, & Lyon, 2000). This chapter addresses all three of these issues and presents information about how RTI procedures offer a better method for identifying students with learning disabilities.

PROBLEMS WITH IQ–ACHIEVEMENT DISCREPANCIES

When the initial special education law (i.e., Public Law 94-142) was passed in 1975, the IQ–achievement discrepancy formula method for identifying an SLD was adopted as a means of operationally defining the features associated with certain learning problems. Specifically, the presence of an average to above-average IQ along with lower-than-expected academic achievement provided a way of documenting that a student *could* learn but was *not* learning (Peterson & Shinn, 2002). Despite the apparent face validity and logic of the IQ–achievement model, many years' worth of data have shown that it does not reliably identify those students with learning disabilities (Fletcher, Morris, & Lyon, 2003; Fletcher, Francis, Morris, & Lyon, 2005; Glutting, McDermott, Watkins, Kush, & Konold, 1997; Shinn, 2007; Spear-Swerling & Sternberg, 1996; Stanovich, 2000; Stuebing, Barth, Molfese, Weiss, & Fletcher, 2009).

For example, many studies comparing different subtypes of reading difficulties have shown virtually no differences between those who were identified as having a specific reading disability and those with no disability (Shinn, 2007; Spear-Swerling & Sternberg, 1996; Stanovich, 2000). In these studies, students who were identified as having a reading disability (RD) were also documented to have a significant discrepancy between their intellectual capacity or quotient (IQ) and their academic achievement. The other students, referred to as "garden-variety" poor readers, had the same types of reading problems but no such discrepancy (Fuchs, Fuchs, Mathes, Lipsey, & Eaton, 2000; O'Malley, Francis, Foorman, Fletcher, & Swank, 2002; Stanovich, 1991, 2000; Vellutino et al., 2000, 2007). The studies comparing these groups have been quite consistent in finding that the presence of an IQ–achievement discrepancy neither establishes nor necessarily confirms the presence of a learning disability.

> **Despite many myths to the contrary, IQ does not accurately predict academic or behavior skills. Importantly, IQ is not necessarily a trustworthy indicator of an SLD.**

Far fewer studies have been done concerning the accuracy of IQ–achievement discrepancy scores for identifying other subtypes of learning disability, such as in math, writing, or behavior. Notably, a few studies have shown that the presence of a discrepancy does not automatically mean that a student is learning disabled (Graham & Harris, 1997). Barnett, VanDerHeyden, and Witt (2007) found that RTI procedures worked well to identify preschoolers with learning needs. Barnett et al. (2006) have suggested that RTI methods can also be used in identifying students with severe behavior problems in preschool and kindergarten. Gresham (2005) has suggested a very similar process for older students. Bryant, Bryant, and Hammill (2005) as well as Fuchs et al. (2007) have explored how RTI might help in resolving math difficulties. Ehren and Nelson (2005) noted that RTI might be a more accurate way of identifying students with speech and language impairments as well. Certainly speech and language pathologists play an important role in implementing RTI (Justice, 2006). Gilbertson and Ferre (2008) have noted that RTI can be a helpful model in supporting students who are deaf. All of these studies have in common the finding that the *nature of the interventions* provided to help students overcome school difficulties is more important than the etiology or symptoms (National Association of School Psychologists, 2002).

Why Is the IQ–Achievement Equation Problematic?

Many people are shocked to learn that the IQ score is not necessarily the best indicator of a student's ability. While there is evidence that IQs are modestly predictive of individual ability after the age of 10, they offer only limited guidance on students' abilities and potential before then (Salvia & Ysseldyke, 2009; Sattler, 2001). A number of research studies have shown that IQ is actually a very poor predictor of reading skill (Graham & Harris, 1997; Siegel & Himel, 1998; Stage, Abbott, Jenkins, & Berninger, 2003; Stanovich, 1991, 1993; Stuebing et al., 2002; Vellutino et al., 2000; Vellutino, Scanlon, Small, & Fanuele, 2006). What these studies have consistently shown is that IQ, as well as IQ–achievement score discrepancies, do not predict which students will have reading difficulties and which ones will benefit from additional intensive instruction (Lyon et al., 2004). If IQ scores do not help determine which students need additional instruction and which students have specific learning disabilities, there is no rationale to continue their use in that regard. Indeed, IQ scores of young children are so variable that they indicate very little about long-term abilities (Francis, 2003; Sattler, 2001). It is the lack of precision from IQ and IQ-achievement comparisons that has led many researchers and policy advocates to suggest alternative approaches to identifying students with an SLD.

Much of the recent research about students with an SLD has focused on what instructional methods and materials have been found to assist them. Importantly, many of the most critical skills taught in school need to be learned well before age 10 in order to have their optimal effects (Blachman et al., 2004; Schatschneider, Francis, Carlson, Fletcher, & Foorman, 2004). Research has shown that students who learn key reading subskills before grade 3 are very likely to be successful in school and life. Conversely, those students who do not learn to read by grade 3 are very likely to remain behind in reading for the rest of their school careers and are much more likely to drop out of school (Snow et al., 1998; Stanovich, 2000). Consider the paradox here. IQ data for students younger than 10 years is unreliable, but the early school experiences children have when they are 5–10 years old are the most important ones. Essentially, at the very time when it is most important to know which students are struggling in school IQ scores offer very little useful information. Importantly, tests of students' math and reading skills are more helpful in the early grades because they indicate the extent to which a student has mastered the specific skills and knowledge that predict later school success.

Interestingly, it is when achievement test scores are compared with IQ scores that predictors of student abilities are most likely to get confounded (National Association of School Psychologists, 2003). As noted, IQ scores are much less reliable for young children. While achievement test scores offer important information regarding student progress, when scores on tests of reading, math, and writing are compared with IQ scores, the effects of one on the other interfere. Specifically, when a student has struggled to learn certain core skills such as reading, basic arithmetic, and spelling, he or she has probably missed out on other elements of instruction, such as key content. This means that his or her general fund of knowledge and skills is likely to be lower than that of classmates who have mastered the basic academic skills (Kranzler, 1997). When tested, using an IQ–achievement discrepancy, it is possible (even likely) that difficulties with basic skills will interfere with obtaining accurate estimates of the student's IQ (Siegel, 2003). In such cases, the student's IQ and achievement scores are more likely to be similar and lacking a discrepancy. Students who have no discrepancy have not been eligible for extra instruction under past special education rules. Sadly, these students have had to get really far behind in their academic performance before they become eligible for special education services, that is, *they have had to "wait to fail."*

> **When IQ is used as a marker for learning potential, it forces students to "wait to fail" rather than immediately getting the instruction they need.**

Responding Instead of Waiting

The IDEA Improvement Act, passed by the U.S. Congress in November 2004, included language specifically incorporating RTI practices into special education procedures. A summary of the RTI language in the IDEA 2004 statutes is found in Table 3.1. Sections 602 and 614 of the statute include language specific to RTI. Section 602 of the law includes definitions of important terms in the law, including the definition of "specific learning disability." As shown in Table 3.1, the definition of SLD did not change from the definition found in the preceding versions of IDEA. Importantly, the definition still includes a reference to "basic psychological processes" as well as a variety of possible manifestations, including "the imperfect ability to listen, think, speak, read, write, spell, or do mathematical calculations." Again, as in prior versions, there are important rule-out criteria in the definition such that students cannot be identified as having a specific learning disability if the "learning problem . . . is primarily the result of visual, hearing, or motor disabilities, of mental retardation, of emotional disturbance, or of environmental, cultural, or economic disadvantage." Thus, the core definition of SLD in IDEA 2004 remains unchanged from its predecessors.

What is different in IDEA 2004 is the language found in section 614 of the law and in section 300.307 of the regulations. Section 614 covers the evaluation procedures allowable for special education eligibility. Items 5 and 6 of section 614 include language specifically related to RTI practices. Item 5 of this section provides additional clarification about the conditions under which a determination of SLD would be inappropriate due to lack of instruction. Here, the law specifies that "a child shall not be determined to be a child with a disability if the determinant factor for such determination is . . . lack of appropriate instruc-

TABLE 3.1. Sections of the IDEA 2004 Related to RTI Methods

Section	Excerpt
602	(30) SPECIFIC LEARNING DISABILITY.

(A) IN GENERAL. The term "specific learning disability" means a disorder in 1 or more of the basic psychological processes involved in understanding or in using language, spoken or written, which disorder may manifest itself in the imperfect ability to listen, think, speak, read, write, spell, or do mathematical calculations.

(B) DISORDERS INCLUDED.—Such term includes such conditions as perceptual disabilities, brain injury, minimal brain dysfunction, dyslexia, and developmental aphasia.

(C) DISORDERS NOT INCLUDED.—Such term does not include a learning problem that is primarily the result of visual, hearing, or motor disabilities, of mental retardation, of emotional disturbance, or of environmental, cultural, or economic disadvantage.

614   (5) SPECIAL RULE FOR ELIGIBILITY DETERMINATION. In making a determination of eligibility under paragraph (4)(A), a child shall not be determined to be a child with a disability if the determinant factor for such determination is:

(A) lack of appropriate instruction in reading, including in the essential components of reading instruction (as defined in section 1208(3) of the Elementary and Secondary Education Act of 1965);

(B) lack of instruction in math; or

(C) limited English proficiency.

(6) SPECIFIC LEARNING DISABILITIES.

(A) IN GENERAL. Notwithstanding section 607(b), when determining whether a child has a specific learning disability as defined in section 602, a local educational agency shall not be required to take into consideration whether a child has a severe discrepancy between achievement and intellectual ability in oral expression, listening comprehension, written expression, basic reading skill, reading comprehension, mathematical calculation, or mathematical reasoning.

(B) ADDITIONAL AUTHORITY.—In determining whether a child has a specific learning disability, a local educational agency may use a process that determines if the child responds to scientific, research-based intervention as a part of the evaluation procedures described in paragraphs (2) and (3).

tion in reading, including in the essential components of reading instruction (as defined in section 1208(3) of the Elementary and Secondary Education Act [ESEA] of 1965)." The text goes on to make a similar requirement for both math and writing instruction. Of note, IDEA 2004 requires the "essential components of reading instruction" only and not for math or writing. Here, it is important to know that the reference to the ESEA refers to the 2001 version of that act, which is NCLB. *What this means is that IDEA 2004 references NCLB in stating that students cannot be found eligible as students with specific learning disabilities if they have not received scientifically based instruction, which, in the case of reading, includes the five components of reading included in NCLB.*

The next portion of section 614 of IDEA 2004 includes language specifically related to evaluation for SLD. Item 6 (titled "Specific Learning Disabilities") removes the requirement that an IQ–achievement discrepancy must be used to identify SLD. Specifically, item 6(A) states that "a local educational agency shall not be required to take into consideration whether a child has a severe discrepancy between achievement and intellectual ability in oral expression, listening comprehension, written expression, basic reading skill, reading comprehension, mathematical calculation, or mathematical reasoning." This provision is a dramatic and important shift from earlier versions of IDEA, which focused on the use of the IQ–achievement discrepancy as the means for determining the presence of SLD.

Item 6(B) of section 614, also specifically related to SLD, adds more information about the procedures that may be used to identify learning disabilities. This next part integrates language from item 5 on scientifically based instruction with RTI procedures by stating that "in determining whether a child has a specific learning disability, a local educational agency may use a process that determines if the child *responds* to scientific, research-based *intervention* as a part of the evaluation procedures" (emphasis added). This statement is echoed in the implementing regulations for IDEA 2004 at §300.307(a)(2) (see Table 3.2). Here, the law allows for the use of RTI procedures as part of special education eligibility procedures. In combination, items 5 and 6 of section 614 of IDEA 2004 as well as §300.307(a)(2) of the implementing regulations create a new mechanism for determining how students with learning disabilities are identified. By requiring scientifically based instruction as a prerequisite for evaluation, and by including RTI methods as allowable assessment procedures, IDEA 2004 makes a significant commitment to utilizing data-driven decision making for all students (Lyon et al., 2001). This new language also includes a more specific bridge between general and special education by referencing NCLB requirements in the law. In doing so, lawmakers have made clear that all branches and components of public education, both general and specialized, should employ and report on data-based instructional practices.

EMPIRICAL SUPPORT FOR RTI IN SPECIAL EDUCATION PRACTICE

It is important to note that RTI data are not a perfect substitute for IQ–achievement discrepancies. A few studies have investigated the efficacy of RTI methods for determining eligibility for special education, and many researchers have pointed out the importance

TABLE 3.2. IDEA 2004 Regulations Related to Identification of an SLD

§300.307 Specific Learning Disabilities

Additional Procedures for Identifying Children with Specific Learning Disabilities

(a) *General.* A State must adopt, consistent with §300.309, criteria for determining whether a child has a specific learning disability as defined in §300.8(c)(10). In addition, the criteria adopted by the State—

 (1) Must not require the use of a severe discrepancy between intellectual ability and achievement for determining whether a child has a specific learning disability, as defined in §300.8(c)(10);

 (2) Must permit the use of a process based on the child's response to scientific, research-based intervention; and

 (3) May permit the use of other alternative research-based procedures for determining whether a child has a specific learning disability, as defined in §300.8(c)(10).

(b) *Consistency with State criteria.* A public agency must use the State criteria adopted pursuant to paragraph (a) of this section in determining whether a child has a specific learning disability.

Note. Authority: 20 U.S.C. 1221E–3; 1401(30); 1414(b)(6).

of continuing research to improve the data tools that can be used to document a lack of response to intervention (Ardoin, 2006; Ardoin, Roof, Klubnick, & Carfolite, 2008; Catts, Petscher, Schatscchneider, Bridges, & Mendoza, 2008; Davis, Lindo, & Compton, 2007; Jenkins, Hudson, & Johnson, 2007). Interestingly, a national survey of school psychologists found that 75% of respondents endorsed RTI as a better method for identifying a reading disability, but many of the same respondents reported they could also endorse the discrepancy method (Machek & Nelson, 2007). In a longitudinal study of RTI methods, Case, Speece, and Malloy (2003) found that RTI methods identified students as well as or better than discrepancy methods of identification. The student features used to distinguish which students had reading disabilities were consistent over the time that the students were in the study. A study by Fletcher et al. (2002) yielded similar results. Marston, Muyskens, Lau, and Canter (2003) reported similar robust findings from data collected longitudinally in the Minneapolis public schools. Newell and Kratochwill (2007) noted that RTI practices provide a way to address and reduce disproportionate numbers of linguistic, racial, and ethnic minority students in special education. Another application of RTI in relation to special education is in using tiered supports when it is time for students to leave special education (Powers, Hagans, & Miller, 2007).

The usefulness of RTI methods in identifying degrees of need among students and reducing the number of students receiving intensive services has been documented as well. O'Connor (2003) reported that RTI procedures are particularly helpful in identifying students with learning difficulties in the early primary grades. Such use of RTI enables teachers to determine which students need intensive services as early as first grade so that supports can be provided as quickly as possible. Many students whose learning difficulties were identified in first grade were able to be successful in third grade with much less intensive supports than expected. In similar research Tilly (2003) found that RTI practices are consistent with primary prevention activities as much as early intervention. By using RTI with preschoolers, teachers were able to prevent some special education placements altogether.

> **RTI practices not only boost favorable outcomes for students but also reduce the number of students requiring special education services.**

While much of the research on RTI has focused on very young children, some researchers have looked at the implications for older students. Torgeson (2003) reported that RTI methods hold promise for students in upper elementary school because these can provide high-quality instruction to students in a rapid and data-driven way. For example, Torgeson and his colleagues found that RTI procedures helped third-grade students improve their reading skills in significant ways. For those students still struggling at the end of the intervention, the data collected as part of RTI were useful in suggesting the next steps in the assessment process. It is noteworthy that the National Joint Committee on Learning Disabilities endorsed the RTI approach to LD identification as a better way to support students' learning needs (National Joint Committee on Learning Disabilities, 2002).

Since publication of the first edition of this book, a topic that has received a great deal of attention is whether RTI data are sufficient for identifying SLD or whether additional specialized testing with cognitive assessment is needed (Berninger, 2006; Feifer, 2008; Ofiesh, 2006; Reynolds & Shaywitz, 2009; Willis & Dumont, 2006; Wodrich, Spencer, & Daley, 2006). The debate over whether RTI data can fully replace cognitive assessments has two main aspects. One line of thinking focuses on how no single test or method can ever be used to identify a disability and that other testing is needed to verify the RTI results (Flanagan, Ortiz, Alfonso, & Dynda, 2006; Mastropieri & Scruggs, 2005). Some have referred to this as a cognitive hypothesis testing (CHT) method by which the RTI data help to create hypotheses about the cause of a student's problems while follow-up cognitive assessment test the hypotheses (Fiorello, Hale, & Snyder, 2006).

The second line of thinking in support of continued cognitive testing is that commonly used RTI assessments such as curriculum-based measures (CBM) are not precise enough to pinpoint the source of a student's learning problem (Hale, Kaufman, Naglieri, & Kavale, 2006). This line of thinking is supported by advocates for neuropsychological testing, who note that that approach attempts to provide a much more precise indication of the source of a student's learning problem (Mather & Kaufman, 2006; Semrud-Clikeman, 2005; Schmitt & Wodrich, 2008; Witsken, Stoeckel, & D'Amato, 2008). The debates over whether RTI data alone are sufficient to document SLD fully will likely continue for some time. Other recent findings in the literature about cognitive assessment have created significant shifts in how such tests are viewed (Witzken, Stoeckel, & D'Amato, 2008). For example, there is less focus on an overall IQ score and more consideration of a mutifactor theory of intelligence (Fiorello et al., 2007). There

> **RTI data can be used for SLD identification only if they are reliable and valid. Reliability and validity result from consistent implementation across classrooms.**

are even proposals for more complex "hybrid" models, such as in the work of Aaron, Joshi, Gooden, and Bentum (2008), who suggested a component model of reading diagnosis that includes cognitive, psychological, and ecological inputs.

Perhaps most important, whether or not RTI data are included in the process of determining whether a student has an SLD, the collection of such data and other assessments does not guarantee that the student will be eligible for special education (Fletcher, Francis, Morris, & Lyon, 2005). The referral and assessment process includes a comprehensive evaluation of the student's school history and current performance. The data collected during both Tiers 1 and 2 should be included in the comprehensive evaluation. These data document the implementation of scientifically based instruction, as required by NCLB and IDEA 2004. Depending on state and local district rules, additional testing also may need to be conducted (Zirkel, 2006; Zirkel & Krohn, 2008). Recall that IDEA 2004, and the regulations accompanying this law, bar states from requiring schools to use an IQ–achievement discrepancy as a criterion (Lichtenstein & Klotz, 2007). This provision is different from requiring the use of RTI data for SLD identification. Each state has its own special education regulations, and there are differences in how each state has interpreted the IDEA 2004 rules. Box 3.2 tells you how to learn about your own state's specific policies relating to RTI. As of 2010, four states—Colorado, Connecticut, Indiana, and Iowa—specifically require RTI data as the primary evidence of SLD. In general, the other states allow either RTI data or an IQ–achievement discrepancy approach (National Center on Response to Intervention, 2009).

It is important for teachers in all states to know when and how to use RTI data as part of special education decision making. Figure 3.1 provides a flowchart depicting the steps in such a decision. Box 3.3 describes each of the steps in the figure. An important aspect of such decision making relates to whether a state's special education system is categorical or

---

BOX 3.2. State Policies Regarding RTI

Each U.S. state has a responsibility to "translate" federal policies relating to special education into rules specific to that state since, under the U.S. Constitution, public education is the responsibility of the individual states and not the U.S. government. In practice, this arrangement means that there are over 50 separate statewide policies related to RTI, covering all the states plus the U.S. territories. Thanks to the Internet, however, up-to-date information about each state's RTI policy can be obtained relatively easily. The National Center on Response to Intervention (NCRTI) has a website dedicated to state RTI policies at *state.rti4success.org*.

If you are not sure what is your state's policy about RTI, this website will help you to learn. State RTI policies vary a great deal, ranging from Colorado (which requires RTI data as the only method for identifying SLD) to Alaska (where the state policy mimics federal policy verbatim). As RTI policies and practices are developed and implemented nationwide, states may decide to revise their initial policies. For this reason, it is a good idea to continually monitor your state's policies and to consider how best to use student data to inform both general and special education decision making.

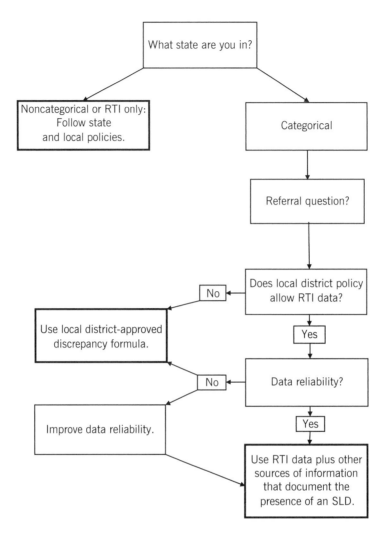

FIGURE 3.1. RTI and special education decision-making flowchart.

noncategorical. Categorical eligibility states require that 1 of the 14 allowed federal disability conditions be used to identify a student as eligible for special education. Noncategorical states do not require the use of these categories. In noncategorical states no disability label is needed, so the issue of what data are allowed is not pressing. In categorical states, the issue is very different and sets the stage for the rest of the process. In categorical states that require RTI data as the pathway, teachers must gather and use reliable RTI data and other indicators of student performance to decide whether a student is eligible to be designated as a student with an SLD. Importantly, teachers need to consider the referral question, namely: What are the features of the student's school problems? RTI data can be used as evidence for determination of SLD only and not for other disabilities.

When the referral question relates to SLD, the teachers must consult the local eligibility rules and criteria. The reliance on a local (e.g., district-level) policy for SLD determina-

BOX 3.3. How Do I Know When I Can Use RTI Data for Special Education Eligibility?

When can RTI data be used to determine a student's special education eligibility? Several factors must be considered in answering this question. (See the flowchart in Figure 3.1). Questions to consider are:

1. What state are you in?

   - All U.S. states have their own policies about whether RTI data can be used for SLD eligibility.
   - Four states—Colorado, Connecticut, Indiana, and Iowa—require the use of RTI data for SLD eligibility.
   - Other states allow the use of RTI data or IQ–achievement discrepancy data (see Box 3.2).

2. What is the referral question?

   - RTI data can be used as evidence to support eligibility for SLD only.
   - Other referral questions and learning needs must use the criteria specified in federal and state regulations.

3. What is your local school district's policy?

   - In states where RTI data are allowed, there must be a readily accessible district-level source that describes how such data are collected and analyzed.
   - Such policies are designed to ensure that decisions about SLD eligibility are consistent for all students in the district.

4. How reliable are your school's RTI data?

   - Before RTI data can be used as evidence of SLD, the districtwide data collection practices need to be highly consistent and reliable.
   - Usually, it takes a district 3–5 years of RTI practice to establish a reliable data system.

5. What other data need to be gathered?

   - As with all special education evaluations, other information must be gathered. No decision on special education eligibility can be based on only one type of evaluation.
   - In addition to the RTI data, there should be other evidence of SLD such as student performance samples, records of classroom observations, and additional assessment data (e.g., academic test scores, scores from tests of cognitive skills related to the learning difficulty).

tion is designed to ensure that all students in the same district are treated equally when such decisions are considered. In districts that allow use of RTI data, an additional step is to verify that the RTI data collection process is reliable and valid. This step is important because only accurate RTI data will really show whether a student has not responded to earlier interventions. When all of these requirements have been met, then RTI data can, and should, be used as evidence of an SLD. Importantly, such data are not the only source of evidence, and other information will be needed in the comprehensive evaluation as well. This requirement ensures that a decision about special education eligibility is not based solely on a single source of information.

Depending on the state rules and local policies, other assessments might be included in the comprehensive evaluation of a student referred to special education (Prasse, 2006). Additional assessments might provide information about cognitive processes and basic competencies not documented in the RTI data. For example, for a student with severe math difficulties, the additional assessment could include tests of memory skills to see whether the student has a basic difficulty in keeping numbers in memory while trying to add, subtract, multiply, or divide them (Fletcher, 2005). If the comprehensive evaluation findings show that the student has a persistent difficulty with both expected academic tasks (e.g., math computation) and one or more of the underlying cognitive processes that are needed to perform such tasks (e.g., working memory) then identification of a math learning disability is made.

RTI AS PART OF SPECIAL EDUCATION

As noted, the RTI language in IDEA 2004 was included for the purpose of helping to determine which students are eligible for special education. In addition the basic elements of RTI—scientifically based instruction, progress data, and data review—can be used after an eligibility determination is made. These practices can be incorporated into the IEP. For example, a student with an SLD in math would be provided with daily intensive math instruction by a special education teacher. Typically, IEP instruction would replace the general education instruction. In order to document this student's math progress, regular (at least weekly) data on the student's progress would be collected. Such data could include weekly 2-minute curriculum-based measures of the computation skills being taught. If the student did not show progress over a period of time, another (perhaps more intensive) math intervention could be tried, and the student's progress data would again be reviewed. Such data can be used as indicators of the IEP's success in meeting the student's needs.

Another question often raised about RTI and special education is whether special education is Tier 3 or, rather, another type of service delivery. Most RTI models include the three tiers described in Chapter 1. Some states have decided to have a four-tier RTI model, with special education as Tier 4; for example, Georgia uses a four-tier model. Other states, such as Maine, have special education embedded within each of three tiers, because most students who participate in special education also participate in varying levels of general education. Some RTI models include special education as Tier 3 (Fuchs & Fuchs, 2008). As noted in Box 3.2, each state's RTI policy is different, and exactly "where" special education services fit into RTI varies. Such variability fits with the connections between general and special education seen in NCLB and IDEA 2004.

SUMMARY

IDEA 2004 includes provisions specifically incorporating RTI policies and procedures. By including language that calls for scientifically based instruction in reading and math as a prerequisite for identification of a specific learning disability, IDEA 2004 includes an expectation that Tier 1 RTI procedures will be used. The special language in IDEA 2004 that allows RTI Tier 2 procedures to be used as part of the process by which a student is identified as having a learning disability supports schools in using systematic intervention procedures for addressing students' learning needs in a prompt manner. For example, as soon as a student is identified through screening data and/or a classroom teacher as having difficulty, Tier 2 instruction can begin. Tiers 1 and 2 of RTI serve as a critical bridge between general and special education. They also build on the language in NCLB that calls for high standards and outcomes for all students, including those with disabilities.

CHAPTER 4

Evidence-Based Interventions

Over the past decade the educational research literature has increasingly emphasized the importance of making sure that interventions being implemented with students in school settings are empirically based. For example, the journal *School Psychology Quarterly* devoted an entire issue (2002, Vol. 17, No. 4; 14 articles) to a thoroughgoing discussion of evidence-based interventions. The authors of the special *SPQ* issue reviewed and discussed the results obtained by the Task Force on Evidence-Based Interventions in School Psychology, which was founded in 1999 and supported by both the Division of School Psychology of the American Psychological Association and the Society for the Study of School Psychology (Gutkin, 2002). Additionally, in 2005 the U.S. Secretary of Education issued a priority statement that defines scientifically based evaluation methods. At the core of the *SPQ* articles is a belief that school psychologists and other school-based professionals have a professional responsibility for both promoting and implementing interventions that are evidence-based as well as objectively evaluating the effectiveness of these interventions. Box 4.1 lists and defines some includes frequently used research terms that are mentioned in this chapter.

Lest one think that this emerging emphasis on evidence-based practices is limited to national task forces and academic circles, one only needs to review professional standards and ethics manuals to find numerous references to evidence-based interventions. For example, a review of the National Association of School Psychologists' (NASP) *Professional Conduct Manual: Principles for Professional Ethics* and *Guidelines for the Provision of School Psychological Services* (2000) discloses several professional practice standards stating that school psychologists have an obligation to implement empirically based interventions, to use a data-based decision-making process to monitor and modify interventions, and to collect data to evaluate the efficacy of interventions. For example:

BOX 4.1. Frequently Used Assessment Terms

Adverse: acting against or in a contrary direction; harmful

Assessment: The results obtained from activities designed to determine the rate or amount of a student's learning

Dependent Variable: resulting condition or measure that constitutes the data and/or evidence used in research

Empirical: capable of being verified or disproved by observation or experiment

Evidence: an objective outward sign; something that furnishes proof

Experiment: an operation or procedure carried out under controlled conditions to discover an unknown effect or law, to test or establish a hypothesis, or to illustrate a known law

Hypothesis: a tentative assumption made in order to draw out and test logical or empirical consequences

Independent Variable: intervention condition that tests a specific hypothesis

Intervention: to come in or between by way of modification

Peer Review: a process by which something proposed (as for research or publication) is evaluated by a group of experts in the appropriate field

Reliability: the extent to which an experiment, test, or measuring procedure yields the same results on repeated trials; consistency of findings; accuracy of findings

Validity: the condition of being well grounded or justifiable; being at once relevant and meaningful; being logically correct

---

C. Assessment and Intervention

C4: School psychologists use assessment techniques, counseling and therapy procedures, consultation techniques, and other direct and indirect service methods that the profession considers to be responsible, *research-based* practice.

C6: School psychologists develop interventions that are appropriate to the presenting problems and are consistent with *data* collected. They modify or terminate the treatment plan when the *data* indicate the plan is not achieving desired goals. (NASP, 2000; emphasis added)

In addition some of the NASP practice guidelines specify that evidence-based practices are expected:

Practice Guideline 1

School psychologists use a decision-making process in collaboration with other team members to (a) identify academic and behavior problems, (b) collect and analyze information to understand the problems, (c) make decisions about service delivery, and (d) evaluate the outcomes of the service delivery.

School psychologists must (a) utilize current professional literature on various aspects of education and child development, (b) translate *research* into practice through the problem-solving process, and (c) use *research* design and statistics to conduct investigations to develop and facilitate effective services.

1.1 School psychologists define problems in ways that (a) identify desired goals (e.g., academic/behavioral), (b) are measurable, (c) are agreed upon by those involved, and (d) are linked appropriately to assessment strategies....

1.3 School psychologists develop and implement effective interventions that are based upon the *data* collected and related directly to the desired outcomes of those interventions.

1.4 School psychologists use appropriate assessment information to evaluate interventions to determine their effectiveness, their need for modification, or their need for redevelopment. Effectiveness is determined by the relationship between the actual outcome of the intervention and the desired goal articulated in the problem-solving process. (NASP, 2000, pp. 40–41; emphasis added)

NASP's Practice Guideline 1 makes it clear that school psychology professionals are expected to use research evidence in all aspects of decision making. Similarly, Practice Guideline 3 sets a clear expectation for setting goals for students and monitoring goal attainment:

Practice Guideline 3

School psychologists (in collaboration with others) develop challenging but achievable cognitive and academic goals for all students, provide information about ways in which students can achieve these goals, and monitor student progress toward these goals.

3.1 School psychologists apply current empirically based theory and knowledge of learning theory and cognitive processes to the development of *effective instructional strategies* to promote student learning and social and emotional development....

3.4 School psychologists assist in facilitating and implementing a variety of *research-based* instructional methods (e.g., cooperative learning, class-wide peer tutoring, cognitive strategy training) to enhance learning of students at the individual, group, and system level....

3.7 School psychologists are informed about advances in curriculum and instruction and share this knowledge with educators, parents, and the community at large to promote improvement in instruction, student achievement, and healthy lifestyles. (NASP, 2000, pp. 43–44; emphasis added)

Again, as in Guideline 1, research is specifically cited many times and sets a standard that all activities will revolve around evidence. Also present in Guideline 3 is the standard that instructional programs will be monitored while being implemented and student progress reviewed. These standards allow for a variety of theoretical and empirical perspectives, so long as they are scientifically based.

Practice Guideline 4

School psychologists make decisions based on multiple theoretical perspectives and translate current *scientific information* to develop effective behavioral, affective, or adaptive goals for all students, facilitate the implementation of programs/interventions to achieve these goals, and monitor progress toward these goals.

> 4.1 School psychologists use decision-making models (e.g., functional behavioral assessment) that consider the antecedents, consequences, functions, and potential causes of behavioral problems experienced by students with disabilities, which may impair learning or socialization. (NASP, 2000, p. 44; emphasis added)

School-based practitioners may find themselves in a quandary when these ethical principles and standards conflict with the practice of school psychology within educational settings.

Consider the following example. A school psychologist is a member of a student assistance team (SAT) that also includes the principal, regular education teacher, special education teacher, speech pathologist, social worker, and occupational therapist. The SAT meets on a weekly basis to review and discuss the needs of specific students (e.g., assessments, goals/objectives interventions, positive behavior support plans, etc.). During discussions of a student who has a long history of attention deficits and excess motor behaviors (e.g., fidgeting in seat, pencil tapping, rocking in seat, etc.), a team member recommended the possibility of using a procedure that she heard about during a professional conference. She described a procedure in which the student would be directed to listen to audiotapes featuring recordings of environmental sounds (e.g., ocean waves, bird calls, whale sounds, among others). She explained that the student's excess motor behavior was his way of seeking out environmental stimulation, stating that he was "environmentally starved." She hypothesized that audiotapes of environmental sounds would address his unmet needs, providing him with a "diet" of environmental input that would result in a *decrease* in excess motor behaviors and a concomitant *increase* in attending during instruction. She went on to report that this intervention had potential for increasing the reading skills of students with learning disabilities. She explained that the intervention would be particularly effective with students who have difficulties with reading comprehension because listening to the environmentally enriched audiotapes would provide them with sensory input that would stimulate a groundswell of contextual cues, resulting in a direct connection between words in print and environmentally laden visual imagery. She explained that, for the procedure to be effective, the student should (1) wear headphones to listen to the audiotapes, (2) be seated in a quiet and preferably isolated setting, and (3) listen to the audiotapes for 15 minutes at least three times each school day.

The reaction of team members was mixed, ranging from complete enthusiasm for this novel approach to outright skepticism. Given her solid grounding in NASP ethical principles and standards, the school psychologist stated that she was unfamiliar with this intervention and asked if there was a research base supporting its use in treatment of attention defi-cits and reading comprehension in elementary-level students. The colleague endorsing the intervention explained that she had learned about the intervention at a presentation at the conference from a "very credible professor" from _____, a well-known university on the West Coast. She explained that the presentation included videotapes of students listen-ing to the environmental audiotapes, and in each case the students were sitting quietly and were very attentive. She also explained that the presenter reported several cases of students who experienced gains in reading comprehension for as long as 3 years after exposure to the audiotapes. Several team members indicated that, given the current student's long history

> **Using evidence-based practices is the ethical thing to do.**

of attention deficits, this intervention might "be worth a try," adding that "we have nothing to lose." Several team members discussed trying this intervention with students who have reading disorders.

Faced with this dilemma, what should an educator do? Both professional ethics and standards as well as recent legislation mandate that interventions be evidence-based. How do we maintain our commitment to our professional ideals in situations when these ideals are compromised? Other questions to consider that are related to this quandary are:

- What is the rationale for requiring an evidence base for interventions?
- What constitutes evidence?
- Do anecdotal reports, subjective opinions, or testimonials constitute evidence?
- What do we do in those situations in which novel interventions are recommended but our review of the literature does not identify a solid research base?

Read on. The remainder of this chapter will answer these questions and provide the reader with a model for documenting the extent to which interventions are evidence-based.

WHAT IS THE RATIONALE FOR REQUIRING AN EVIDENCE BASE FOR INTERVENTIONS?

First of all, it's the right thing to do. Using interventions that have a proven track record *increases the probability* of positive outcomes for students. Notice that we did not use the term *guarantee*. We all know that in schools there are very few guarantees, and when it comes to interventions, *guaranteeing* their efficacy is foolhardy. Just because an interven-tion was shown to be effective with a group of students with learning disabilities in Port-land, Maine, and later found to be equally effective with a group of students with emotional disabilities in Waterloo, Iowa, there are no guarantees that the same intervention will be effective with the student population you are serving. However, when we select interven-tions that have a solid research base, provide the necessary resources to implement the intervention with precision, and collect meaningful data documenting student progress, we have greatly increased the chances of effecting positive student behavior change (Foorman, Breier, & Fletcher, 2003).

Second, interventions based only on theories, professional opinions, testimonials, and subjective evaluation, when subsequently evaluated empirically, have often been shown to be ineffective. Consider the case of facilitated communication (FC). FC is a procedure in which a facilitator (e.g., teacher, parent, educational technician) provides physical support that enables a person with one or more disabilities to type on a keyboard (or to point to a photocopied and laminated keyboard). Supporters of FC believed that this method increased the expressive communication skills of persons with disabilities. Based on theory and anecdotal reports, during the early 1990s its use was widely recommended by numerous academics and practitioners (e.g., school psychologists, speech pathologists, special educators, etc.). This intervention swept the country and was implemented within schools among students with a wide range of disabilities including cerebral palsy, Down syndrome, and autistic disorder, among others. When evaluated scientifically, however, this intervention was found not to have an empirical basis. In short, it was found to be an unreliable means of communicating for students with disabilities (see Box 4.2 on FC for additional information).

Third, continued implementation of ineffective interventions results in a lack of progress and delays the implementation of efficacious interventions. If an intervention does not result in positive outcomes for the student, then it is time to move on and employ interventions that are helpful. Students and their families have the right to expect that school practitioners will implement only those interventions that have a high probability of being beneficial. Moreover, students and their families have the right to expect that interventions will be implemented with precision (see Box 4.3) and that objective documentation will demonstrate student progress.

Students *have a right* to effective interventions.

DO ANECDOTAL REPORTS, SUBJECTIVE OPINIONS, OR TESTIMONIALS CONSTITUTE EVIDENCE?

Our media abound with instances of infomercials and advertisements proclaiming incredible treatment gains (or losses in the case of weight management products). While replete with testimonials espousing magnificent improvements, these interventions often do not have a solid research base objectively documenting their efficacy (see Box 4.4). Most of us can recall situations in which a family member, friend, or colleague reported the *personal* benefits of a particular intervention (e.g., diet, herbal treatment, exercise equipment, etc.). Testimonials are, in and of themselves, subjective and biased and therefore are not objective documentation of the effectiveness of the intervention. Likewise, a colleague may report perceived benefits of a particular intervention with a group of students. Without objective documentation, such opinions are not objective forms of evidence. Opinions are not proof. Testimonials are not objective. However, although not objective forms of evidence, these opinions are not valueless. Rather, from a scientist-practitioner perspective, these ideas can be considered to be hypotheses, ones that can be tested by using sound experimental procedures. When subjected to scientific examination and if supported by sound data, these hypotheses (ideas and opinions) may be found to be valid.

BOX 4.2. Facilitated Communication:
Placing the Intervention Cart before the Research Horse

During the early 1990s a new strategy for enabling persons with severe disabilities to communicate their needs swept the country. Facilitated communication (FC) was a method in which a "facilitator" (e.g., parent, teacher, therapist) provided physical assistance to support a person with a disability in his or her pointing to a keyboard (or laminated copy of a keyboard) and spelling out words and sentences. In its infancy of implementation within the United States, FC appeared to be a revolutionary procedure that would significantly enhance the communication skills and quality of life of thousands of persons with disabilities.

In our own experiences we witnessed numerous cases in which individuals identified with autism spectrum disorders, persons with cerebral palsy, and students with severe developmental disabilities who had significant expressive language delays were exposed to FC and were *reported* to demonstrate immediate and significant improvements in their ability to communicate. In some cases, individuals who were previously viewed as "untestable" were evaluated (by a facilitator, using FC procedures) and scored in the average to above-average ranges on measures of academic and cognitive performance. In short order, daylong workshops and training sessions began popping up across the country, and FC began to be more widely used in schools, homes, agencies, and institutions. Amazing success stories were reported. This new development appeared to be a life-altering intervention.

Next came objective research. Data from numerous studies began showing that persons with disabilities were not really directing their motions and that FC was not a consistent or reliable method of communication for persons with disabilities. Based on their reviews of this emerging *empirical* evidence, numerous professional organizations issued position statements that FC was invalid. For example, in 1993 the American Academy of Child and Adolescent Psychiatry (AACAP) stated that "studies have repeatedly demonstrated that FC is not a scientifically valid technique for individuals with autism or mental retardation" (AACAP, 1993). In 1994 the American Psychological Association, after reviewing numerous empirical studies, concluded their position statement by stating, "Therefore, be it resolved that APA adopts the position that facilitated communication is a controversial and unproved communicative procedure with no scientifically demonstrated support for its efficacy" (American Psychological Association, 1994). Comparable position statements followed from, successfully, the American Speech–Language–Hearing Association (1994), the Association for Behavior Analysis (1995), the American Academy of Pediatrics (1998), and the American Association on Mental Retardation (2005). Most recently, the National Autism Center published the results of its National Standards Project, in which facilitated communication was reviewed and ultimately judged to be ineffective (National Autism Center, 2010).

By the time a professional consensus emerged, however, countless numbers of persons with disabilities had been exposed to invalid interventions incorporating FC, and their families had been offered false hopes and promises. Thousands of taxpayer dollars and uncounted hours had been spent in using FC *instead of* safe, effective, and validated methods for teaching persons with developmental disabilities to communicate for themselves (Foxx, 1999). Clearly, in the case of FC the intervention cart had raced way ahead of the research horse.

BOX 4.3. Treatment Integrity

We can talk all day long about designing assessment-based, student-focused, and evidence-based interventions. However, if the intervention is *not* implemented correctly and consistently, then one can question whether an evidence-based intervention has actually been implemented and we have no idea of *how* it has been implemented. Lack of treatment integrity compromises (1) our assessment of student progress and (2) our ability to determine the efficacy of the interventions. *Treatment integrity* refers to the degree to which an intervention is implemented as designed. There are several ways of increasing treatment integrity. First, adopting a collaborative problem-solving approach to service delivery increases team members' acceptance and understanding of interventions. Second, providing all interventionists with training in the implementation of interventions and in data-recording procedures is also important. The use of direct instruction and performance feedback (e.g., coaching) represents a best-practices model of training. Third, providing ongoing feedback and support during the implementation phase cannot be neglected. This step involves conducting reliability checks in which a team member observes the interventionist's implementation of the intervention and (1) records the degree of accuracy of implementation of the components of the intervention and (2) simultaneously but independently records outcome data. This twofold observation permits one to analyze the extent to which the treatment is implemented precisely as intended but also interobserver agreement concerning the occurrence of target behaviors. More information about how to collect treatment integrity data is found in Chapter 7.

BOX 4.4. Pseudoscience, Nonscience, and Nonsense

School-based practitioners are bombarded with recommendations for interventions. Some are evidence-based, but many of these recommended interventions are *not* grounded in science or any form of objective analysis. For example, in our careers in school settings we have been confronted with recommended strategies to improve academic performance such as megavitamin therapy, sensory integration, optical training, auditory training, and guided reading without direct exposure to print, among others. We refer to those interventions that do not have a solid empirical basis as falling within the categories of pseudoscience, nonscience, and nonsense.

Pseudoscience

Pseudoscience refers to those interventions that do not have a scientific basis but are "dressed up" to superficially resemble science (Green, 1996). Pseudoscience often involves the use of scientific jargon (e.g., "statistically significant," "proven by years of research and study") or endorsements by persons with scientific credentials to promote the efficacy of the intervention. The pseudoscience phenomenon also applies to previously efficacious interventions that are generalized to the

(cont.)

BOX 4.4. *(cont.)*

treatment of behaviors for which there has been no documented efficacy (e.g., the use of psychostimulants to treat reading disorders). While psychostimulants have been found to be effective in increasing sustained attention, there is no objective evidence that these medications directly increase reading skills. These medications may contribute to an increase in reading performance (e.g., increased reading comprehension attributable to higher levels of on-task behavior during reading), but reading skills (e.g., decoding) are not enhanced by medications.

Nonscience

Nonscience is the category that includes those interventions that have no empirical basis whatsoever. These are the interventions that are based solely on testimonials, typically from persons who have no scientific background. Often based on personal experiences and subjective opinion, these interventions are on the same level of science as urban myths. You've heard the refrain "I have this cousin in Vancouver, and she found that providing her son with megadosages of vitamin C lead to a significant increases in reading skills . . . maybe we should try that with David" (the referred student with a history of reading disorders).

Nonsense

Nonsense refers to the category in which the intervention itself, while often highly creative, has no real face validity and when subjected to sound critical thinking is regarded as being benign at best, somewhat unorthodox, leaning toward the sublime and ridiculous, and in the worst-case scenario as being neglectful or dangerous. These interventions are typically paired with extraordinary claims espousing immediate and significant improvements in behavior. For example, we were presented with a case involving a preschool-age child who had a history of primary enuresis (i.e., she was not completely toilet-trained). A therapist had recommended, and the preschool team had subsequently implemented, a sensory integration intervention that was designed to result in independent toileting behavior. The intervention involved scheduled toileting (an evidence-based component in which children are prompted to use the bathroom at prespecified times or intervals) and a procedure in which preschool staff used wooden skewers with foam balls attached to drum (i.e., a drumroll . . . rat-a-tat-tat . . .) on the top of the head of the student as he or she sat on the potty chair. The procedure involved lightly drumming on the top of his or her head to "stimulate the need to urinate" and was delivered until the student urinated, at which point the drumming was immediately halted. The therapist reported that it was a very effective intervention, because each time it was used the student urinated. In this case, further assessment revealed that after 17 weeks of intervention the student had not once self-initiated the use of a toilet to urinate and continued to experience wetting accidents on a daily basis. When provided with an evidenced-based toilet-training intervention (e.g., Steege, 1997), the student became completely toilet-trained (i.e., self-initiated and no daytime accidents) within 3 days, with only occasional nocturnal enuresis.

WHAT CONSTITUTES EVIDENCE?

Interventions evaluated with sound experimental designs that result in socially significant behavior change constitute evidence. At the core of this process is the scientific method. The scientific method is a process of experimentation. The basic stages of the scientific method are as follows:

1. Formulate a research question.
2. Construct a hypothesis.
3. Design an experiment.
4. Conduct the study.
5. Collect data.
6. Analyze the data.
7. Confirm or disconfirm the hypothesis.

A sound experimental design includes the following characteristics:

1. Clearly defined independent variable(s) (i.e., specified input or intervention).
2. Clearly defined dependent variable(s) (i.e., resultant measurable data).
3. A set of procedures to consistently implement the independent variable (intervention).
4. Procedures for accurately measuring the dependent variable (resultant data).
5. A design that controls for threats to the internal validity of the study.

Based on a report from the American Psychological Association's Committee on Science and Practice (Weisz & Hawley, 1999), Kratochwill and Stoiber cochaired a task force on evidence-based interventions sponsored by Division 16 of the American Psychological Association and the Society for the Study of School Psychology (Kratochwill & Stoiber, 2002; Task Force on Evidence-Based Interventions in School Psychology, 2003). This task force offered a set of criteria for classifying interventions as being empirically supported, grouping school-based interventions into five intervention/prevention content focus areas: (1) school- and community-based intervention programs for social and behavioral problems, (2) academic intervention programs, (3) family and parent intervention programs, (4) schoolwide and classroom-based programs, and (5) comprehensive and coordinated school health services (Kratochwill & Stoiber, 2002; Task Force on Evidence-Based Interventions in School Psychology, 2003).

In order to identify the research evidence for selected interventions, the task force created coding criteria for reviewing studies. The coding criteria were organized into four research methodology types: (1) between-group research, (2) single-participant research, (3) qualitative research procedures, and (4) confirmatory program evaluation (Kratochwill & Stoiber, 2002; Task Force on Evidence-Based Interventions in School Psychology, 2003). A graphic representing the model used for coding studies is found in Figure 4.1. As a result of the task force's application of the model to specific studies and data, it was decided to incor-

Methodological focus	Intervention/prevention content focus				
	School- and community-based intervention program for social and behavioral problems	Academic intervention programs	Family and parent intervention programs	Schoolwide and classroom-based intervention programs	Comprehensive and coordinated school health services intervention programs
Between-group research					
Single-participant research					
Qualitative research procedures					
Confirmatory program evaluation					

The qualitative and confirmatory program criteria have been integrated into the group and single-participant manuals.

FIGURE 4.1. Organization of the Task Force *Procedural and Coding Manual* by content and methodological domains. Adapted from Kratochwill and Stoiber (2002, p. 350). Copyright 2002 by The Guilford Press. Adapted by permission.

porate the qualitative research procedures and confirmatory program evaluation methods into the between-group and single-participant research methods categories. After reviewing the coding model and using it on a trial basis with a number of studies, the task force created a coding manual for identifying whether a proposed intervention has sufficient empirical support to be called evidence-based. The full text of the task force's report and the *Procedural and Coding Manual for Review of Evidence-Based Interventions* are available at *www.eric.ed.gov* by typing in the report's title.

The manual includes specific coding criteria for studies that take into account the research design, participants, setting, outcomes, and internal/external validity criteria. Using a 4-point Likert-type scale, the task force identified nine key features of intervention studies to be coded. These nine features are (1) measurement, (2) comparison group, (3) primary/secondary outcomes significant, (4) educational/clinical significance, (5) durability of effects, (6) identifiable intervention components, (7) implementation fidelity, (8) replication, and (9) school- or field-based site (see Table 4.1). According to the *Manual*, for an intervention to qualify as being evidence-based, it must have been validated by one (or more) between-group or single-participant experimental design studies and meet certain minimum ratings on all nine of the enumerated features.

With *between-group experimental designs*, participants are randomly assigned to either an experimental or control group. The results of the study must show that the members of the experimental group outperformed the members of the control group based on an objective measurement of performance. The single-case experimental design (see Chapter 5 for a complete discussion and examples) may involve one subject (i.e., $n = 1$) or a small group of participants. In contrast to the situation in between-group designs, participants are not assigned to experimental or control groups. Rather, each participant experiences the intervention, with his or her behavior (dependent variables) measured before, during, and after implementation of the intervention. An intervention is found to be effective when favorable

TABLE 4.1. Criteria for Documenting the Efficacy of Interventions

Feature	Strong evidence/ support	Promising evidence/ support	Marginal or weak evidence/ support	No evidence/ support
1. Measurement	3	2	1	0
2. Comparison group	3	2	1	0
3. Primary/secondary outcomes significant	3	2	1	0
4. Educational/clinical significance	3	2	1	0
5. Durability of effects	3	2	1	0
6. Identifiable intervention components	3	2	1	0
7. Implementation fidelity	3	2	1	0
8. Replication	3	2	1	0
9. School- or field-based site	3	2	1	0

behavior change occurs during presentation of the intervention condition but remains stable during the baseline (no-treatment) condition(s).

In 2005 the U.S. Department of Education published definitions of scientifically based research (see *Federal Register*, Vol. 70, No. 15, January 25, 2005, Notices), as follows:

Definitions

As used in this notice—

Scientifically based research (section 9191(37) NCLB):

(A) Means research that involves the application of rigorous, systematic, and objective procedures to obtain reliable and valid knowledge relevant to education activities and programs; and

(B) Includes research that—

  (i) Employs systematic, empirical methods that draw on observation or experiment;

  (ii) Involves rigorous data analyses that are adequate to test the stated hypothesis and justify the general conclusions drawn;

  (iii) Relies on measurements or observational methods that provide reliable and valid data across evaluators and observers, across multiple measurements and observations, and across studies by the same or different investigators;

  (iv) Is evaluated using experimental or quasi-experimental designs in which individual entities, programs, or activities are assigned to different conditions and with appropriate controls to evaluate the effects of the condition of interest, with a preference for random-assignment experiments or other designs to the extent that those designs contain within-condition or across-condition controls;

  (v) Ensures that experimental studies are presented in sufficient detail and clarity to allow for replication or, at a minimum, offer the opportunity to build systematically on their findings; and

  (vi) Has been accepted by a peer-reviewed journal or approved by a panel of independent experts through a comparably rigorous, objective, and scientific review. (U.S. Department of Education, 2005)

The U.S. Department of Education now requires the use of evidence-based instructional practices.

The USDOE guidance specifies the following types of research designs as acceptable.

Random assignment or *experimental design* means random assignment of students, teachers, classrooms, or schools to participate in a project being evaluated (e.g., treatment group) or not participate in the project (e.g., control group). The effect of the project is imputed by considering the differences in outcomes between the treatment and control groups. *Quasi-experimental designs* include several designs that attempt to approximate a random assignment design. *Carefully matched comparison groups design* means a quasi-experimental design in which project participants are matched with nonparticipants on the basis of key characteristics that are thought to be related to the outcome.

Regression discontinuity design means a quasi-experimental design that closely approximates an experimental design in which participants are assigned to a treatment or control group based on a numerical rating or the score of a variable *unrelated* to the treatment. Eligible students, teachers, classrooms, or schools above a certain score ("cut score") are assigned to the treatment groups and those below the score are assigned to the control group. This design allows studies of schools that demonstrate the greatest need for improvement (Clements, Bolt, Hoyt, & Kratochwill, 2007).

Single-subject design means a design that relies on the comparison of treatment effects on a single subject or group of single subjects.

Treatment-reversal design means a single-subject design in which a pretreatment, or baseline, outcome measurement is compared with a posttreatment measure. Treatment would then be stopped for a period of time, and a second baseline measure of the outcome would be taken, followed by a second application of the treatment or a different treatment. For example, this design might be used to evaluate a behavior modification program for disabled students with behavior disorders.

Multiple-baseline design means a single-subject design to address concerns about the effects of normal development, timing of the treatment, and amount of the treatment with treatment-reversal designs by using a varying time schedule for introduction of the treatment and/or treatments of different lengths or intensity.

Interrupted time series design means a quasi-experimental design in which the outcome of interest is measured multiple times before and after the treatment for program participants only.

The importance of the specificity in the USDOE research design guidance is that it describes the basis of true scientific evidence for instructional practices in education. In the past, the research methodology used in examining instructional practices was not scrutinized. The USDOE has changed this practice and now uses the research criteria described here to determine whether a proposed practice is truly scientifically based. Specifically, the USDOE uses these criteria to review published studies and summarize the evidence for or against practices. Such reviews are then published as resources for educators on sites such as the What Works Clearinghouse and Doing What Works.

GETTING BY WITH A LITTLE HELP FROM OUR FRIENDS

Determining the evidence base for potential interventions is a daunting and often overwhelming enterprise. Indeed, the vast volumes of research pertaining to the multitude of interventions that have been developed to address the academic, social, behavioral, and mental health needs of students is seemingly endless. So, what to do ... what to do? While school-based practitioners could conduct intensive literature reviews, develop study groups, and critique research articles to determine the evidence base of intervention, we advocate a more practical approach wherein we search databases in which reviews/critiques have previously been conducted by expert teams. This approach is comparable to how many of us make decisions in our daily lives. For example, when choosing a restaurant, we often rely on the opinions of credible and discriminating friends or published restaurant reviews. Before purchasing a new car, we often read reviews published in auto trade magazines. So, similarly, when determining the evidence base for educational interventions, we often rely on the reviews of professional colleagues.

For example, the National Autism Center recently published the results of its National Standards Project. This comprehensive endeavor was conducted to (1) identify and evaluate the level of research support available for educational and behavioral interventions used with individuals (below 22 years of age) with autism spectrum disorders (ASD), (2) assist team members in selecting and designing evidence-based services, and (3) identify limitations of the existing research involving individuals with ASD (National Autism Center, 2009). The project began with the development of a model for evaluating the research involving treatment/interventions with persons with ASD. A team composed of highly qualified and experienced scholars, researchers, and clinicians representing diverse fields of study designed the Scientific Merit Rating Scale and evaluated hundreds of research studies, specifically addressing the following dimensions:

1. The experimental rigor of the research design.
2. The validity of the dependent variable.
3. Evidence of treatment fidelity.
4. The method of selecting participants.
5. The generalization data collected.

In addition, the team designed and used a Treatment Effects Rating Scale to evaluate each research study to determine whether the intervention effects were:

- Beneficial (i.e., when there was sufficient evidence that favorable outcomes resulted from the intervention);
- Unknown (i.e., when there was not enough evidence to determine intervention effects);
- Ineffective (i.e., when there was sufficient evidence that favorable outcomes *did not* result from the intervention); or
- Adverse (i.e., when there was sufficient evidence that the intervention was associated with harmful effects).

After all of the studies were evaluated, the research panel combined the results of the Scientific Merit Rating Scale and the Treatment Effects Rating Scale to identify the level of research support currently available for each of the 38 educational and behavioral interventions examined. The 38 interventions were next categorized according to the Strength of Evidence Classification system as follows:

- *Established:* Sufficient evidence is available; the interventions are established as effective.
- *Emerging:* One or more studies showed favorable outcomes, but additional high-quality studies are needed to consistently demonstrate effectiveness.

- *Unestablished:* Little or no evidence was available to draw firm conclusions about intervention effectiveness.
- *Ineffective/Harmful:* Sufficient evidence is available to determine that an intervention is ineffective or harmful.

The National Standards Report included 11 interventions as *established*, with the overwhelming majority of these interventions based on research found in behaviorally based journals (e.g., applied behavior analysis, behavioral psychology, positive behavior support). Twenty-two interventions were within the *emerging* classification, five were evaluated as *unestablished*, and none was classified as *ineffective/harmful* (National Autism Center, 2009).

In short, we "rely on a little help from our friends." See Table 4.2 for a listing of sources and their websites that include information on evidence-based interventions.

TABLE 4.2. Sources of Information about Research-Based Interventions

Source	Where to find it
What Works Clearinghouse	*www.whatworks.ed.gov*
Florida Center for Reading Research	*www.fcrr.org*
Oregon Reading First Center	*reading.uoregon.edu*
Social Programs That Work	*www.evidencebasedprograms.org*
Collaborative for Academic, Social, and Emotional Learning (CASEL)	*www.casel.org*
Promising Practices Network	*www.promisingpractices.net*
Center for the Study and Prevention of Violence, University of Colorado	*www.colorado.edu/cspv/blueprints*
Big Ideas in Beginning Reading	*reading.uoregon.edu/curricula*
California Learning Resource Network	*www.clrn.org*
Campbell Collaboration	*www.campbellcollaboration.org*
Florida Center for Reading Research	*fcrr.org/FCRRreports*
National Center for Learning Disabilities	*www.ncld.org*
National Institute for Literacy	*www.nifl.gov*
National Reading Panel	*www.nationalreadingpanel.org*
National Registry of Evidence-Based Programs and Practices/Substance Abuse and Mental Health Services Administration	*nrepp.samhsa.gov/index.asp*
Oregon Reading First	*orgeonreadingfirst.uoregon.edu*
Promising Practices Network	*www.promisingpractices.net/programs.asp*
Wing Institute	*winginstitute.org*

Note. Data from the following: Hunley and McNamara (2010) and Twyman and Sota (2009).

EMPIRICAL VALIDATION IN SCHOOL SETTINGS

In those situations in which novel interventions are recommended (i.e., where thorough review of the literature does not identify a research base documenting a given intervention's efficacy), school-based professionals face choices. Essentially one is left with two choices in those situations. One could simply decide that since there is not adequate empirical evidence to support the use of the intervention, then it should not be used with students—end of story. Or, alternatively, one could decide that the intervention likely has merit and hypothesize that it could have beneficial outcomes. In this case, we suggest that you go with the old adage that "extraordinary claims require extraordinary proof." In short, in the absence of a solid research base, one must create one. And, of course, that means conducting a research study. "Oh, no!" you say. "Are Rachel and Mark suggesting another thesis or dissertation?" Perhaps, but not necessarily. What we are suggesting is that if one is to go the route of implementing what constitutes an experimental trial, then one should use basic experimental methodologies to examine objectively the efficacy of the intervention. Most practitioners do not have the time or resources to conduct between-group studies with large groups of randomly assigned students. However, in our experience applications of novel interventions usually involve one student or a small group of students. In those cases, single-subject experimental design methodologies fit the bill quite nicely. We will discuss and provide examples of single-case designs in the next chapter.

A CAUTIONARY NOTE ABOUT EVIDENCE

Thus far we have discussed the importance of identifying a body of evidence that supports the efficacy of interventions. While an intervention may be sound empirically, it may not be applicable to all students. One of the responsibilities associated with identifying an evidence base involves knowing how to interpret the evidence. A series of solid studies consistently documenting the efficacy of a particular intervention may prove to be the base supporting an intervention with one group of students but not necessarily another. Thus, while a study may have sound *internal validity* (i.e., the study minimized errors and controlled for potential extraneous variables), it may have limited *external validity* (i.e., limited generalizability across populations of students).

When one considers external validity, one asks such questions as "What relevance do these findings have outside the confines of the experiment?" and "To what student populations and settings are these findings applicable?" As mentioned previously, just because the study was effective with a group of students with learning disabilities in Portland, Maine, does not mean that the identical intervention will be *applicable to* and *effective with* a group of students with learning disabilities in Waterloo, Iowa. Moreover, the results of a study using single-subject experimental methodology with three students with developmental disabilities may not be an adequate base of evidence on which to build an intervention with students with emotional disability.

An old research adage continues to apply today, namely, "A limitation of between-group designs is its generalizability to individual cases, and a limitation of single-subject design methodology is its limited generalizability to groups of individuals." Statistically significant findings from between-group research might tell us that, *on average*, the experimental group outperformed the control group. But that would not guarantee that all individuals did or will show benefit if the intervention is used with them. Similarly, a single-subject design might demonstrate treatment gains with the individual but would not guarantee that the intervention will be successful beyond the limited subject pool.

When it comes to identifying interventions for individuals or small groups of students, it is important to recognize that the selection of intervention(s) needs to consider the empirical base as well as the applicability of the intervention to the student(s). In many cases, interventions prove to be person-specific, based on the unique characteristics of the student, his or her learning history, and his or her response to previously implemented interventions. As school professionals operating within a problem-solving model of service delivery, our job is to conduct sound assessments, identify those unique characteristics of the student, and select interventions that are matched to the learning needs of the particular student involved.

SUMMARY

An intervention is said to be evidence-based when it has been found to be effective in cases of well-designed and robustly implemented experimental analysis. Practitioners need to be good consumers of published research. They need to read published studies with a critical eye to determine (1) whether the experimenters used sound research methodology and (2) whether the procedures employed are applicable to *your* population of students. In most cases we advocate a two-phase process of employing evidence-based interventions. Phase 1 involves conducting a literature review to identify relevant articles that support the intervention. At this point one reads the articles with a critical eye, examining both the internal and external validity of the study. Phase 2 involves the implementation and objective evaluation of the intervention, using single-subject experimental design methodology. Thus, our body of evidence consists of (1) previously conducted research that supports the intervention and (2) a current research base that documents the effectiveness of the intervention on a case-by-case basis. In the next chapter we outline the process of documenting the efficacy of interventions with specific students.

CHAPTER 5

Single-Subject Experimental Design

School-based practitioners have the dual responsibility of conducting meaningful assessments that lead to the design of effective interventions and objectively evaluating the effectiveness of those interventions. In this chapter we describe how single-subject experimental design methodology is used within a problem-solving approach to assess student behavior and to evaluate the efficacy of interventions. The terms *single-subject* and *single-case* are used to refer to this type of data collection and will be used interchangeably to describe this method.

Single-subject experimental design methodologies are critical components in both the assessment and intervention phases of RTI. These methods are based on a problem-solving model of addressing student difficulties at school (Berg, Wacker, & Steege, 1995; Brown-Chidsey et al., 2008; Polaha & Allen, 1999; Steege, Brown-Chidsey, & Mace, 2002; Steege & Wacker, 1995). Single-subject experimental design methodology is based on a hypothesis-testing approach in which specific designs are used to test specific hypotheses. For example, functional analysis procedures typically utilize either a reversal design or alternating-treatments design to compare the influence of such variables as contingent social attention, removal of instructional stimuli, and tangible reinforcers (e.g., candy or toys) on the occurrence of specific target behaviors. Alternating-treatment designs are also used to compare the relative effectiveness of two or more interventions, thus serving both an assessment and evaluation purpose. Case study (AB), reversal (ABA), or multiple-baseline designs are most often used during Tiers 1 and 2 to evaluate the efficacy of interventions.

Unlike between-group designs, which include experimental and control groups, single-subject experimental designs involve the evaluation of a single person or small group before, during, and following implementation of the intervention. Single-subject experimental designs control for threats to the internal validity of a study by:

1. Establishing a baseline measure (dependent variable) of student behavior or academic performance.
2. Introducing an intervention (independent variable).
3. Documenting the effects of the intervention through repeated measurement.
4. Either withdrawing and reintroducing the intervention and studying its effects or repeating the baseline and intervention phases.

When the implementation and withdrawal of the intervention result in behavior change, a functional relationship between the independent variable (intervention) and dependent variable (measures of behavior/performance) is demonstrated. When the student's behavior change is observed during the intervention phase only, one can be certain that the intervention is responsible for changes in student behavior. With single-case experimental designs, replication is demonstrated with the student across settings (e.g., math and science classes; home and school), behaviors (e.g., math worksheets and science homework), and personnel (e.g., special education teacher, mainstream teacher) (Steege et al., 2002).

Polaha and Allen (1999) and Steege et al. (2002) identified a number of reasons why single-case experimental designs are a best-practices method for evaluating the effectiveness of interventions, including:

1. Objective documentation of student progress is demonstrated.
2. Ongoing interventions allow the team to identify effective and ineffective components quickly and make necessary adjustments to the interventions (i.e., data-based decision making).
3. Practitioners have an ethical responsibility to evaluate the efficacy of interventions and single-subject experimental designs.
4. Federal, state, and agency regulations require documentation of intervention effectiveness.
5. Such interventions are applicable to and easy to use with individuals and small groups.

Additionally, single-subject experimental designs allow for comparison of the effectiveness of interventions, permitting the team to select the most efficacious intervention, thereby directly addressing the needs of the student(s) (Swanson & Sachse-Lee, 2000).

> **Single-case design provides the methodology for confidently answering such questions as "Is Johnny benefiting from [intervention] _____?" and "Did it work?"**

SINGLE-SUBJECT METHODS AS PART OF RTI

Within the RTI model, single-case experimental design methodology is typically used (1) to compare the relative effectiveness of an intervention, (2) to "test drive" an intervention to determine its treatment potential, and (3) to document student performance. Before discussing each of these uses, a review of the basic components of single-subject experimental design is offered.

Basic Components of Single-Subject Experimental Designs

Data Recording Procedures

It all boils down to collecting accurate and meaningful data. We can design and precisely implement a comprehensive student-centered and empirically based intervention, but if we fail to measure accurately the effect of the intervention (i.e., recording the dependent variable) or record irrelevant variables (i.e., the error of misplaced precision), then we are unable to determine with any degree of objectivity whether the student has benefited from the intervention. There are a number of procedures that have been used to measure a wide range of academic, social, and interfering behaviors. Both Steege et al. (2002) and Watson and Steege (2003) offer descriptions and examples of the following types of recording procedures:

- Frequency recording (the number of times a behavior occurs).
- Duration recording (how long a behavior lasts).
- Intensity (the relative magnitude of a behavior).
- Whole-interval recording (percentage of intervals in which behavior occurs for an entire interval of time).
- Partial-interval recording (percentage of intervals in which behavior occurs for part of the interval).
- Performance-based recording (Likert ratings estimating the relative occurrence of behaviors).
- Permanent products recording (tangible outcomes such as number of words spelled correctly).
- Recording steps completed without assistance when performing a behavior chain.

Daly, Chafouleas, and Skinner (2005) described a procedure for specifically recording reading behaviors. For example, students are prompted to read aloud a graded reading passage, and the observer records the number of words read correctly in 1 minute (i.e., oral reading fluency) and the following reading errors:

- Mispronunciations
- Substitutions
- Omissions
- Latency (more than 3 second delay)

In order to make certain that the recording methods match the overall objective of the intervention, certain questions should be considered when selecting a behavior recording procedure. Suggested questions are as follows:

- Is the behavior being measured an expected outcome of the intervention?
- Is the behavior recording procedure sensitive enough to measure the expected behavior changes?
- Will the behavior recording procedure capture the magnitude of the behavior? For example, while a frequency recording procedure could be used to measure the occurrences of tantrum behavior, if the duration of tantrums is highly variable (e.g., lasting from 15 seconds to 15 minutes), then a frequency recording procedure may not be a valid measure of the tantrum behavior. (Note: a 15-second tantrum is very different from a 15-minute tantrum.)
- Are there adequate resources (e.g., time, staff, materials) to collect the data accurately? For example, a 6-second whole-interval recording procedure may be the "gold standard" for measuring on-task behavior. However, there may not be adequate resources to use a whole-interval procedure, and instead a performance-based procedure is selected (see Steege, Davin, & Hathaway, 2001, for an examination of the reliability and accuracy of performance-based recording procedures).

Figure 5.1 shows the stages of single-subject data graphed by phase. In the first intervention, the level of the student's skills went up by a few points but then stayed at that level. For this reason a second intervention was put into place, and then both the level and slope (rate of progress) improved dramatically.

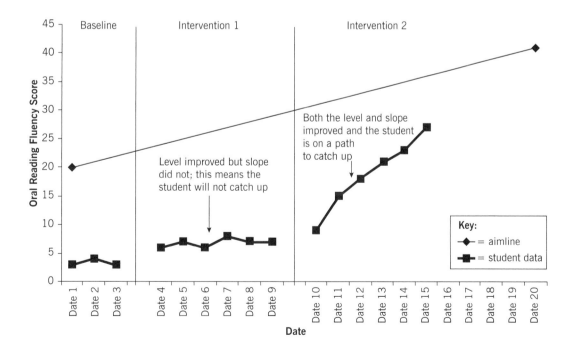

FIGURE 5.1. Understanding level and slope.

Indirect Measurement: An Error of Misplaced Precision

Sometimes practitioners attempt to measure student behavior but inadvertently end up recording *their own* behavior. For example, in a recent consultation we discovered that the team implementing an IEP was measuring the effectiveness of a behavioral intervention by keeping track of how often the procedure was used as opposed to how often the target behavior occurred. In this case, the team had decided to use a brief (2-minute) time-out from the reinforcement procedure to reduce the socially reinforced disruptive behaviors of a 4-year-old student within a preschool program serving students with mild developmental delays. The team designed a data recording procedure in which the teacher was trained to record the number of time-outs that were utilized while the external observer recorded the instances of misbehavior. Presumably the decreased use of time-out would reflect a reduction in disruptive behaviors—but *only if* each occurrence of the disruptive behavior resulted in the use of a time-out. In the first of four 2-hour observations we noted that the student displayed disruptive behavior six times. Time-outs were used, but the data form showed only four such occurrences. The next day disruptive behavior was observed as occurring six times, and yet the time-out procedure was used and recorded only three times. The third day's observations revealed that disruptive behavior occurred eight times and that the time-outs were employed only twice. During the fourth day's observations the target behavior was observed seven times, and time-out, were taken just twice.

The graph in Figure 5.2 reflects both sets of data (i.e., the data recorded by the teacher and those recorded by the external observer). If the team only considered the teacher's data, it might at first glance appear that the intervention "worked" (i.e., the number of time-outs taken decreased over time). If the team considered the external observer's data, however, it would conclude that these data showed that disruptive behavior actually *increased* over time. In this case, obviously, the use of an *indirect assessment method* (i.e., recording time-outs) would have resulted in underestimating true occurrences of misbehavior since the implementation protocol was not observed. See Box 5.1 for a brief note about direct observation versus self-monitoring in recording behavior.

Baseline Phase

Accurate measurement begins with the baseline. The baseline phase provides information about the preintervention level of occurrence of the target behavior (i.e., the dependent variable). The baseline data also serve as the basis by which intervention effects are subsequently assessed (see Box 5.2). The baseline data serve two critical functions:

1. The baseline describes the current state of the student's performance level or behaviors, defining the extent of the student's "problems" objectively.
2. The baseline provides a basis for predicting likely behavior or performance if no intervention is implemented (Shernoff, Kratochwill, & Stoiber, 2002).

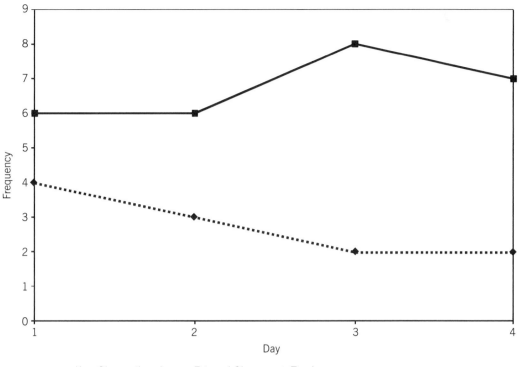

FIGURE 5.2. Comparison of teacher-based and external observer data.

BOX 5.1. Direct Observation versus Self-Monitoring

This chapter has focused on direct observation and recording of behaviors. Direct measurement of behavior typically involves an external agent (e.g., parent, teacher, school psychologist) observing and recording the behavior of the student. Self-monitoring is a form of direct recording in which the student acts as his or her own "agent" and monitors and records either overt (observable) or covert (e.g., thoughts, feelings) behaviors.

BOX 5.2. How Do I Obtain Baseline?

If you have already conducted benchmark assessments, you have established a starting point. These data may constitute a baseline, or you may need to conduct additional assessments (i.e., survey-level assessments). Consider the case of a student with reading difficulties. If the student scored "0" on the fall benchmark, additional information about the student's performance is needed, which might include measures of letter-naming fluency, phonemic segmentation, and nonsense-word fluency, for example. Conducting *three separate assessments of each skill* generally meets the minimum requirement for establishing baseline levels of performance. Once stability in a baseline has been attained, one is able to implement the intervention.

Hayes, Barlow, and Nelson-Grey (1999) suggest that the following five guidelines must be adhered to when establishing baseline levels of behavior or performance:

1. *Length of the baseline.* At least three data points are needed to establish a baseline level of behavior or performance.

2. *Stability of the baseline. Stability* refers to fluctuations or variability in a student's behavior over time. A baseline is considered to be unstable when great variability or erratic trends in behavior obscure the detection of treatment effects.

3. *Overlap of baseline and intervention data.* When there is considerable overlap between baseline and intervention data (i.e., extreme scores in the baseline are equivalent to or exceed intervention data), the determination that the intervention resulted in the treatment gains is weakened.

4. *Level of the data.* The level of baseline behavior must be serious enough to warrant intervention and be likely to show marked treatment gains.

5. *Trends in the data.* Trends during the baseline period should not be in the desired direction (i.e., an increasing trend when one expects to increase a skill). Figure 5.3 illustrates stable and unstable trends during a baseline period.

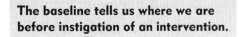

The baseline tells us where we are before instigation of an intervention.

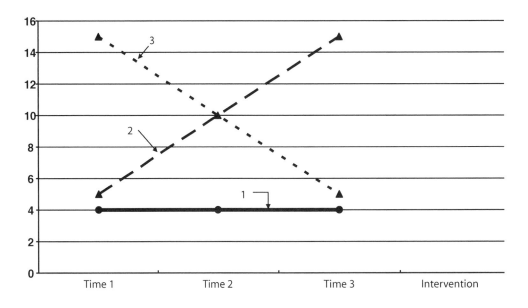

FIGURE 5.3. Baseline descriptions. 1 = Stable baseline. 2 = Stable baseline for behavior that is expected to decrease during intervention; unstable baseline for behavior that is expected to increase during baseline. 3 = Stable baseline for behavior that is expected to increase during intervention; unstable baseline for behavior that is expected to decrease during intervention.

Intervention Phase

Once a stable baseline has been identified, the intervention can begin. This process involves implementing the specific procedures related to the intervention. During this phase, the student's behaviors are recorded, using the same outcome indicator (dependent variable) that was measured during the baseline phase. During this stage it is critical that

1. The intervention be implemented consistently and with precision.
2. If an intervention package (i.e., an intervention that has multiple components) has been selected, the entire package be implemented.
3. The procedures for recording behavior during the baseline phase be the same procedures used to record the same behaviors during the intervention phase (we want to make sure that we are comparing apples to apples).
4. A phase change line be included to separate the baseline and intervention phases (see Figure 5.4).

Comparing Interventions

Throughout our careers in schools we have encountered numerous situations in which members of the student assistance team identified two or more competing interventions to try. Most of you are familiar with this scenario: screening assessments have been conducted, results have been reviewed, several recommended interventions have been discussed, and now team members are trying to select the one method of choice to use with this student.

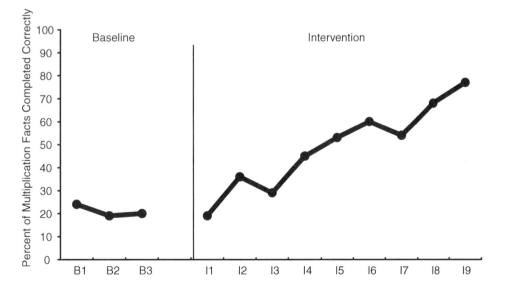

FIGURE 5.4. Case study (AB) design.

Or, consider the situation in which an intervention has been recommended as a replacement for an ongoing intervention. The SAT is divided, and members of the team may spend an inordinate amount of time discussing the pros and cons, the merits and disadvantages, of each intervention. When teams fail to use a data-based decision-making process, they often become paralyzed with indecision and end up doing nothing. Or they become frustrated and someone makes an "administrative decision" and impulsively selects a specific intervention. Often the selection of intervention is based on insufficient evidence or a subjective factor such as:

1. Research to support the intervention ("A study was recently published that demonstrated the effectiveness of the intervention with a group of students with LD in a classroom in Kalamazoo, Michigan").
2. Anecdotal evidence ("It worked with Johnny—maybe it will work with Jill").
3. Familiarity ("I've used this strategy with students for years").
4. Intuitive appeal ("This *ought* to work").

When team members are divided about what intervention to use, single-subject experimental design methodology is a valuable tool for objectively comparing the proposed interventions (see Box 5.3 for an example of how two interventions were compared).

BOX 5.3. Test Driving Hypothesis: Laptop Computer versus Pencil and Paper

Steege et al. (2002) described an example in which a student with both cerebral palsy and learning disabilities in the areas of reading comprehension and written language was expected to complete all written assignments by using pencil and paper. The school psychologist and special education teacher recommended that the student be provided with and taught to use a laptop computer to complete written assignments. They hypothesized that, once she was able to use a laptop computer, the student would demonstrate discernible increase in the efficiency, quantity, and quality of her written work. Because previous requests for a laptop computer for students with disabilities had been denied by the school's administration, they decided to test drive their hypothesis by undertaking a single-subject experiment. Using an alternating-treatments design, the school psychologist and special educator compared the relative effectiveness of the laptop versus pencil-and-paper methods in improving her writing performance.

The results of the assessment clearly demonstrated that, when directly compared with handwriting, the laptop computer strategy consistently resulted in higher levels of written language performance (Steege et al., 2002). This finding resulted in the school district's reversing its previous policy and authorizing the purchase of a laptop computer for this student as well as others. In this case, the "data did the talking" and allowed the team to make a data-based decision about a course of action that supported the student.

Test Driving the Intervention

Let's say you've made the decision to buy a new car. Being a prudent car buyer, you begin the process by first conducting a screening of available makes and models. Based on this initial screening, you narrow your choice to three manufacturers and five different car models. You next begin the assessment phase. You go to dealerships, check out the cars, and request brochures. You go home, study the brochures, comparing the vehicles across a host of dimensions and variables. Next, you turn to the literature (e.g., car magazines, auto reviews online), where you locate several articles in which these cars have been subjected to a variety of performance tests and have been rated for features such as handling, comfort level, dependability, safety, etc. Now comes the really fun part—the test drive. This is where you really get a feel for the vehicle, where the rubber literally meets the road.

Typically, it's the test drive that determines whether or not this car meets your needs and expectations. How many people walk into a showroom without ever test driving a vehicle and simply say "That's the car for me" and purchase the car on the spot? Not many. However, in school settings, how many times are we asked or do we ask others to try an intervention without conducting a thorough needs assessment, without reviewing the relevant literature, or without taking a "test drive"? In our experience, all too often this happens—remember facilitated communication (or perhaps you'd just rather forget it)? Within a collaborative problem-solving model, we typically recommend that, following the comprehensive assessment and design of intervention, we conduct a brief "test drive" to "get a feel for the intervention." Specifically, we conduct the test drive of the intervention to answer the following questions:

1. Is the intervention effective (i.e., does it result in the expected behavior change or performance)?
2. Is the intervention doable, and do we have adequate resources (e.g., time, materials, etc.) to implement the intervention as designed?
3. Are staff members implementing the intervention correctly (i.e., observing treatment integrity), and, if not, what types of and how much training are needed?
4. Are the data recording procedures valid (i.e., matched to the dimensions of the behavior and recording meaningful behavior change)?
5. Are staff members able to collect the data accurately?
6. Are there aspects of the interventions that need to be modified?

A clear advantage of taking a "test-drive" approach is that, if the answer to any of the preceding questions is "maybe" or "no," then the necessary modifications to increase the effectiveness of the intervention, its implementation, and the recording of data can be made before too much time passes and the student's school success is at risk.

Documenting Student Performance over Time

Having completed a successful test drive, we are now ready to implement the intervention. Essentially this involves implementing the intervention and continuing to record and analyze the student's response to the intervention over time. Ongoing data collection serves three important purposes. First, continued recording of behavioral outcomes allows for objective documentation of student progress on specific goals and objectives. Second, analysis of data enables team members to make data-based decisions about whether or not to modify the intervention. Third, continued measurement allows for objective determination of the degree of effectiveness of the intervention.

> **Data recording tells us how well and how fast we are achieving success.**

CASE EXAMPLES

> **Specific single-subject designs enable us to conclude with confidence that the measured behavior changes result from the intervention, not other variables.**

The following case examples illustrate the application of single-subject experimental design methods within a problem-solving model of school-based practice.

Case Study (AB Design)

In the following case study, the design (two phases: baseline followed by intervention) was used to document the effects of the intervention during the "test-drive" phase of a math intervention. Noreen is a fourth-grade student who has not yet learned her multiplication facts. Her teacher was concerned about this and decided to conduct an individualized session with Noreen to work on this material. In order to determine Noreen's baseline multiplication fact skills, her teacher gave her multiplication fact probes with 25 problems on each page (see Table 5.1 for operational definitions of the math intervention variables). Noreen was given 2 minutes to complete each page, and the percentage of correct answers was recorded on a graph. Data from the baseline and intervention phases of this case study are shown in Figure 5.3. During the baseline phase, Noreen got between 20 and 25% of the problems correct. After implementation of the individualized sessions with her teacher, Noreen's multiplication fact accuracy increased to 80%.

TABLE 5.1. Operational Definitions of Noreen's Math Intervention Variables

Target behavior(s)	Recording procedure(s)	Dependent variable
Accurate completion of randomly selected multiplication facts in vertical number format	Student completes multiplication problems while being timed for 2 minutes	Percentage of multiplication facts completed correctly

Interpretation

This intervention was determined to be successful, because the data revealed that it resulted in the desired outcome of improving Noreen's multiplication fact skills.

The drawback to the case study single-subject design is that it does not include review of data collected over a long period of time or when the target skill is used in another setting. In Noreen's case, the obtained data provided a good "test drive" in that they documented that the sessions with her teacher resulted in improved skills. Still, Noreen's newly gained multiplication skills are of limited value if they are only used during individual sessions with her teacher. To learn whether these skills generalize, at least one additional intervention phase would be needed to evaluate Noreen's accuracy in multiplying numbers in another setting, such as while doing independent work in class or on a test. The following examples show how application of multiple single-subject design phases produces better and more educationally relevant data.

Multiple-Baseline-across-Behaviors Design with Generalization Probes

In this example, Teddy is a third-grade student who has struggled on his weekly spelling tests. Baseline data about Teddy's spelling accuracy revealed a consistent 25% spelling accuracy rate on three tests (see Figure 5.5). Teddy's teacher implemented a new spelling intervention designed to improve his spelling accuracy. Table 5.2 includes operational definitions of spelling intervention variables. This intervention involved direct instruction of the sounds in words to help Teddy learn the correct spelling of specific words. In order to learn whether Teddy generalized the spelling skills to other words not specifically taught, his teacher evaluated his progress with two sets of words, (1) words taught and (2) words not taught. Teddy's progress in spelling was monitored by having him take a weekly spelling test that included an equal number of both sets of words. In order to evaluate the efficacy of the program on Teddy's spelling of both word sets, his accuracy rate on each set of words was graphed separately. As shown in Figure 5.4, Teddy's spelling accuracy improved, and he was able to spell about 65% of both word sets correctly at the end of 13 weeks of instruction.

Interpretation

These data support the hypothesis that direct instruction of letter–sound correspondence resulted in increases in spelling accuracy on word set 1. Skills acquired during intervention with word set 1 generalized to word set 2. Thus, direct instruction with additional word samples was not indicated.

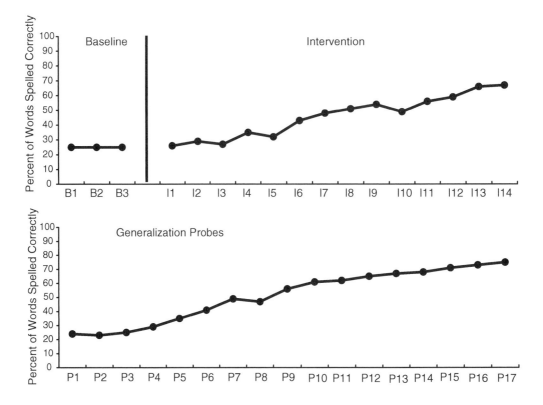

FIGURE 5.5. Multiple-baseline-across-behaviors design with generalization probes.

Multiple-Baseline-across-Behaviors Design without Generalization Probes

The next example is very similar to the preceding one (Teddy). It shows how the use of a multiple-baseline-across-behaviors-design can be used to assess the generalizability of skills from two word sets, but with staggered implementation of intervention and with two maintenance probes at a later date. In this case, Max, one of Teddy's classmates, began the same spelling intervention, but slightly different recording procedures were used. In Max's case, he did not appear to generalize the correct spelling of the words not taught. This finding is seen in Figure 5.6, where the top portion of the graph depicts performance on taught words and the bottom portion depicts performance on words not taught. Because Max continued to spell the untaught words with only about 20% accuracy, 2 weeks after the spelling inter-

TABLE 5.2. Operational Definitions of Spelling Intervention Variables

Target behavior(s)	Recording procedure(s)	Dependent variable
Accurate spelling of words on weekly spelling tests	Student writes spelling words dictated by teacher	Percentage of words spelled correctly

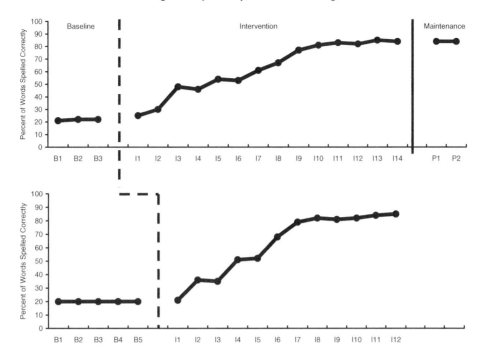

FIGURE 5.6. Multiple-baseline-across-behaviors design without generalization probes.

vention began his teacher started teaching him both sets of words, using the same explicit procedures. Within 2 weeks of the explicit spelling instruction Max's spelling performance improved to about 40%. After 10 sessions he spelled all the words with about 80% accuracy. Because of Max's lack of generalization of the untaught words at the beginning of the intervention, his teacher decided to do some follow-up skill maintenance probes with him. A number of weeks after the intervention ended, she gave Max two spelling tests 1 week apart. Max correctly spelled about 80% of the words on the maintenance phase spelling tests, indicating that he maintained the spelling skills learned during the intervention.

Interpretation

These data support the hypothesis that direct and systematic instruction of spelling words from word set 1 resulted in increases in accurate spelling of the words on weekly tests. Generalization of acquired skills to word list 2 did not occur. Implementation of the intervention with word set 2 resulted in the acquisition of the relevant knowledge. Thus, only when the intervention was implemented did improvements in student behavior occur.

Alternating Interventions

In the next example an alternating-treatments design was used to compare the relative effectiveness of two different interventions for Megan, a fifth-grade student. Megan's accuracy on spelling tests at the beginning of the school year was very poor. She got less than 20% of words correct over 3 weeks. Her teacher was very worried because spelling is one of the subtests on the state's fifth-grade achievement test. Those students who fail two or more sections of the test must repeat the fifth grade. Megan's teacher discussed her concern about Megan's spelling with the literacy coach. The consultant suggested the use of a phonics-based spelling program. Megan's teacher was all set to use this method when she overheard another teacher in the faculty room saying that the copy–cover–say spelling instruction method was best. The teacher asked her colleague why she felt that method was best and was told it had worked "for years and years." Megan's teacher felt uncertain which spelling instruction method was best, so she decided to try them both and see how Megan responded to the two interventions.

Megan's teacher used a counterbalanced implementation of the two interventions so that the effects of the two different instructional methods could be compared. First, 100 phonetically regular words were split into two sets of 50 words each. Each set of 50 words was matched to one of two spelling instruction methods, (1) systematic phonics and (2) copy–cover–say. In the systematic phonics spelling instruction the teacher taught the students to spell the phonetically regular words by having them match the sounds in the words to the letters or letter combinations (orthographic units) that match the sounds. For example, students learned to spell the word *hat* by identifying each of the sounds in the word—/h/a/t/—and writing each letter corresponding to its sound. The copy–cover–say spelling instruction method involved giving the students 10 new phonetically regular words each week and having them copy each word five times. Once they had written each word five times, they folded their papers in half to cover the words and they repeated the spellings aloud. The two lesson types were counterbalanced by alternating each type every other school day.

Student progress in each of these methods was monitored by giving a 20-word spelling test at the end of each week, with half of the words from the phonics lessons and the other half from the copy–cover–say method. Megan's results are shown in Figure 5.7. The per-

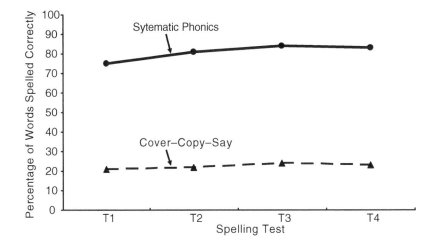

FIGURE 5.7. Alternating interventions.

centage of words that Megan spelled correctly is shown along the *Y* axis. The solid line on the graph shows the percentage of phonics lesson words she spelled correctly; the dashed line shows the number of copy–cover–say words she spelled correctly. The graph indicates that Megan learned to spell words from the phonics lessons with about 80% accuracy but spelled the copy–cover–say words with only about 20% accuracy.

Interpretation

These data support the hypothesis that intervention 1 (i.e., systematic phonics-based spelling) was more effective in increasing Megan's rate of correctly spelled words than intervention 2 (i.e., copy–cover–say).

Comparing Performance across Multiple Dependent Variables

The preceding case study example was used to document the effectiveness of reading fluency instruction in increasing performance on three separate dependent variables (e.g., sight words, fluency, and comprehension). This method was used to learn whether a specific reading fluency intervention would lead to improvements in sight word reading and comprehension as well as increased reading fluency. The design was employed with Gavin, a seventh-grade student with reading difficulties. Gavin began his seventh-grade year by telling his language arts teacher that he "hates reading." The teacher asked Gavin why he hated to read, and Gavin replied, "It takes too long. Asking someone is faster." Gavin's teacher decided it would be good to learn more about Gavin's reading skills; so, he had Gavin complete three curriculum-based measurement silent-reading fluency (SRF) passages. CBM–SRF passages are also known as maze reading passages and are reading-level-controlled texts from which every seventh word has been replaced with three words from which the reader selects while reading. Only one of the three word choices is the correct word. Students are timed while they read the passages; in this case, Gavin's teacher gave the passages to all of the students in Gavin class, and they had 3 minutes to complete each passage.

Gavin obtained scores of 1, 1, and 0 on the three passages. The average score for the class was 15 correct selections on each passage. Due to Gavin's very low score as compared to other students, his teacher decided to measure his reading with two other assessments. First, she had Gavin read three CBM oral reading fluency (ORF) passages. On these passages Gavin read aloud for 1 minute while his teacher recorded his errors on her own copy of the passage. Gavin obtained scores of 21 on all three ORF passages. The national fall ORF benchmark for seventh-grade students was 110 words in 1 minute. The teacher then had Gavin read isolated sight words on 3″ × 5″ index cards. The words were selected from a list of the 500 most common words in English. From a bank of 20 words, Gavin was able to read 18 correctly. Based on the three reading data sets collected, Gavin's teacher concluded that he could read (decode) most words but that he read very slowly. The lack of fluency in Gavin's reading appeared to interfere with his reading comprehension.

Gavin's teacher decided to try a reading fluency intervention to improve his reading skills. The intervention involved having Gavin practice reading both sight words and connected text every day for 20 minutes. The operational definitions for each activity in the intervention are found in Table 5.3. First he took a set of 20 sight words and read them aloud to the teacher. She recorded his accuracy. Next, Gavin read a controlled-level text silently to himself five times. Finally, he wrote a summary of the short story to show what he learned from it. At the end of each week Gavin completed three assessments of his reading improvement. First he read a random selection of 20 of the 500 common sight words while his teacher recorded his accuracy. Next, he completed a CBM–ORF passage and recorded his progress. Finally, Gavin completed a CBM–SRF (maze) passage and recorded the number of correct word choices on a graph. These data are summarized in Figure 5.8. The data show that Gavin improved his sight word reading a small amount, going from 90–95% accuracy (i.e., 18–19 correct answers out of 20) to 100% (20 of 20) accuracy. His ORF score went from 21 words read correctly during baseline to 77 words at the end of 12 weeks. Gavin's SRF score improved from 1 correct word selection to 18 correct selections.

Interpretation

These data support the hypothesis that the reading fluency (speed) intervention was effective in increasing all three reading skills. In this example, daily practice in reading sight words as well as short stories resulted in not only an increase in sight word accuracy but also concomitant increases in reading fluency and comprehension.

SUMMARY

This chapter has provided information about how single-subject research design methods can be used as a component in RTI procedures to promote positive academic outcomes for students. Additional information about how to interpret progress data can be found in the book *RTI in the Classroom* (Brown-Chidsey, Bronaugh, & McGraw, 2009). Starting with a basic case study design to "test drive" an intervention and following up with generalization and maintenance, or instructional methods comparisons, were shown to lead to better skills for students across several learning areas. Next we will describe the key features of effective instruction that need to be used as part of RTI.

TABLE 5.3. Operational Definitions of Reading Intervention Variables

Target behavior(s)	Recording procedure(s)	Dependent variable
Sight word reading	Teacher holds up 3″ × 5″ cards with taught words on them; student reads words and teacher records if correct or incorrect.	Number of correctly read isolated sight words
Reading fluency	Student orally reads a reading-level-controlled short story for 1 minute; teacher records all misread words while the student reads.	Number of words read correctly in 1 minute
Reading comprehension	Student silently reads a reading-level-controlled short story for 3 minutes; the story has been adapted so that every seventh word is replaced with a blank line under which are three words. While reading the student circles one of the three words to fill in the blanks in the story.	Number of correct word selections made in 3 minutes

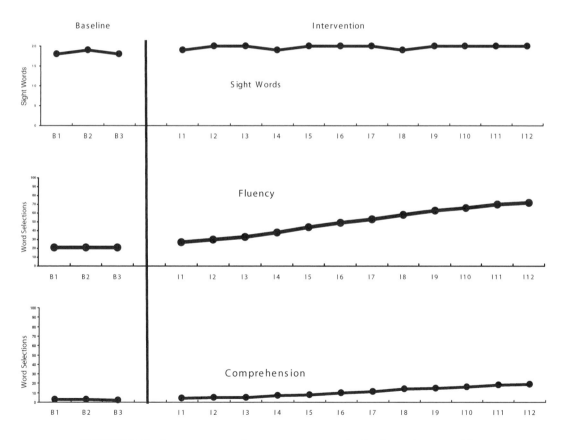

FIGURE 5.8. Comparing performance across multiple dependent variables.

CHAPTER 6

How to Teach
So That Students Will Learn

*Key Components of Effective Instruction
and Assessment*

RTI PUTS INSTRUCTION FIRST

The preceding two chapters have provided information about the importance of scientifically based instruction methods and case study data collection methods. This chapter includes a discussion of how scientifically based instruction can be combined with case study data collection to yield effective responsive intervention practices. The instructional and data collection methods we cover reflect the emerging legal standards found in federal and state policies. As noted in Chapters 2 and 3, these educational policies seek to bring together general and special education practices such that effective instruction is provided to *all* students from the very beginning of their educational careers. This chapter begins with a discussion of the features of effective instruction, followed by connections to effective data collection and analysis procedures. Together, these are the cornerstones of RTI.

EFFECTIVE INSTRUCTION

Chapter 4 provided a definition and discussion of scientifically based instruction. Scientifically based instruction is the essence of *effective* instruction. In order for any instructional practice, program, or intervention to be considered *effective* for future use, it must have data showing that it worked in the past. Effective instruction also can be thought of as scientifically based instruction because it is the scientifically based data that document how it is effective. Scientifically based and effective instruction includes only those practices that have been validated in numerous research studies. Such practices have been identified for instruction in many skill areas, including both academics and behavior (Fuchs et al., 2005; Gresham, 2004). To make sense of the voluminous information about effective instructional practices, we have synthesized the findings into a core set of effective instructional features and practices. Following the lead of Kame'enui and Carnine (1998), our list will focus on the "big ideas" about effective instruction. Table 6.1 summarizes the key components of scientifically-based effective instructional practices. There are 5 core components and 11 practices that define *effective* instruction. The five core features are (1) content, (2) delivery, (3) pace, (4) responses, and (5) assessment. The practices related to these are the teaching methods associated with positive educational outcomes for learners (Foorman, 2003).

> **While there is an extensive literature on effective instructional practices, the underlying core principles have rarely been included in published instructional materials.**

TABLE 6.1. Key Components and Practices of Scientifically Based Instruction

Component	Practices
Content	1. Matched to that which students are expected to learn or need to know in order to progress in the curriculum and school program. 2. Fits in between the knowledge and/or skills that students have previously learned or will learn in subsequent instruction.
Delivery	1. Explicit description of knowledge and/or skills to be learned is given by the teacher. 2. Students are given many and frequent opportunities to rehearse the new knowledge and/or skills. 3. All students are actively engaged with the knowledge and/or skills to be learned throughout the lesson.
Pace	1. Intensive "massed" practice of new material is provided during the early stages of learning. 2. Judicious review of previously learned knowledge and skills is incorporated at regular intervals.
Responses	1. Correct student responses are reinforced by the teacher with verbal praise or specific reinforcers. 2. Incorrect student responses are addressed immediately during the lesson and followed with student rehearsal of the correct response.
Assessment	1. Students are assessed continuously during the lesson; daily student performance data are recorded. 2. Summative data about student progress is reviewed at least weekly to determine whether instructional changes are needed.

Content

The first key component of effective instruction is appropriate content, referring to the substance of what is to be learned. For example, in a language arts class it could be the eight parts of speech or the difference between active and passive sentence construction. There are two main teaching practices associated with scientifically based and effective content selection. The first is matching the content to the larger curriculum or program of study. A number of studies have shown that when teaching content matches with and complements an overall program of study, specific lessons and activities are more effective (Carnine, 1981, 1989; Carnine & Jitendra, 1997). Specifically, when a lesson is matched to the larger set of knowledge and skills that students are expected to learn or need to know to progress in the curriculum and school program, the individual learning content is more likely to be mastered by students (Axtell et al., 2009; Gibb & Wilder, 2002; Fuchs et al., 2006).

A second important practice related to subject matter content is sequencing individual lessons in an order that allows new information to build on prior learning (Bransford, Brown, & Cocking, 2000; Cognition and Technology Group at Vanderbilt, 1997; Daly, Martens, Barnett, Witt, & Olson, 2007). Studies by experts in numerous fields have shown that when instruction follows a logical "order of operations" mastering the content is facilitated. Another term for an instructional sequence is an instructional hierarchy. In the case of school-age students, teachers need to have some idea of what students have learned previously as well as what will be taught in subsequent grades. For example, in the case of elementary school mathematics instruction, it is important that teachers know that children generally should learn addition before subtraction and multiplication before division. When teachers work within the context of an identified skill sequence, they are better able to provide instruction that fits in between the knowledge and/or skills that students have previously learned and what they will learn in subsequent instruction (Bransford, 1979).

> **Using an instructional hierarchy to organize teaching helps to make the content accessible to all students.**

Delivery

The second major component of effective instruction is the delivery method, referring to method(s) that teachers use to present information and solicit student learning. Delivery methods include lectures, discussions, inquiry activities, and assigned readings. There are three teaching delivery practices most associated with positive outcomes for students (Williams & Carnine, 1981). First, a direct and explicit description of the knowledge and/or skills to be learned is given by the teacher to the students (Burns et al., 2009). Examples of direct and explicit instruction include telling students the general topic to be covered as well as the precise details, rules, and operating procedures necessary to carry out the learning correctly (Carnine, Kame'enui, & Maggs, 1982; Engelmann, 1999; Gersten & Carnine, 1986; Stein, Carnine, & Dixon, 1989). The second delivery method most associated with positive learning outcomes is giving students many and frequent opportunities to rehearse the new knowledge and/or skills (see Box 6.1). For example, when students need to learn their mul-

---

BOX 6.1. Practice, Practice, Practice

Anyone who has ever tried to learn a new skill knows the importance of practice. This is true whether the skill is playing the piano or throwing a baseball. Those who put time into practicing achieve better results and more "perfect" performance than those who do not. Even the top musicians and athletes practice many hours every day to improve their skills. When a famous violin player wants to learn a new piece of music, he or she must start by looking at the individual notes, play them in the correct order, and then practice the piece countless times to get it right. If a competitive diver wants to learn a new dive, he must practice each part and then put the moves together into one smooth action that makes it look easy. But it's not. Perfect—or near perfect—performance comes from practice, practice, and yet more practice.

The same is true of academic skills such as reading, writing, and mathematics. Those who learn the subcomponents, put them together, and then practice by using the skills regularly are better readers, writers, and math users than those who look briefly at a word or number but never practice using it. The importance of practice in everyday classroom instruction has been demonstrated in many research studies (Axtell et al., 2009; Carnine, 1989); it needs to be integrated into all levels of RTI activities for students to make the progress we expect and desire.

---

tiplication facts, learners of all ability levels are more likely to do this if they are provided with many opportunities to rehearse (i.e., practice, practice, practice) each fact many times (Carnine, 1997b; Kroeger & Kouche, 2006). The third important delivery practice is to provide students with continuous exposure to the content, meaning that the learning materials need to be physically present and accessible to the students while they engage in learning activities. In the case of learning multiplication facts, each student needs to have his or her own set of multiplication fact cards to review, practice, and review again. High levels of learner engagement with content have consistently been associated with positive learning outcomes for all students (Carnine, 1989).

Pace

The third major component of effective instruction is pace (see Box 6.2). High-quality lessons that promote student learning attain a pace that follows the "Goldilocks" principle, that is, neither too fast nor too slow, but "just right." The right pace for a lesson is related to the content to be taught and the place in the curriculum where the material falls. Knowledge and skills in the early part of a program of study will need to be covered more slowly, but information contained in later sections of the program can generally be taught at a faster pace (Bransford et al., 2000; Carnine & Granzin, 2001). Two instructional practices that inform and shape the pace are massed practice and judicious review (Kame'enui & Carnine, 1998). *Massed practice* refers to a lesson time when all of the activities relate to one area of learning. These lessons have a clear and single focus and revolve around students learning some-

> **Instructional pacing needs to follow the "Goldilocks" principle: neither too fast nor too slow, but just right.**

BOX 6.2. Slow Learner or Fast Teacher?

Some students who struggle in school are able to be successful if the pace of instruction is matched to how quickly they can handle the material. For example, many students who have been identified as having a learning disability are allowed extra time to complete tasks, including exams. Another way of looking at the needs of such students would be to ask "Is the teaching too fast?" This question radically changes the way we look at the difficulties students have in schools. Instead of automatically assuming that a student is doing poorly because the student has limitations—is a slow learner—we can usefully examine the pace of instruction. By conducting a comprehensive assessment of student and instructional variables, we may find a mismatch between the "slow" learner and the "fast" teacher.

It is important to monitor the pace of instruction since instruction that is too fast may result in errors and the compromised acquisition of skills. This issue has important implications for RTI practices because one of the ways to test a hypothesis about a student's school performance is to assess and change environmental variables. The teaching approach is an environmental variable that can be adjusted. In fact, when teachers are empowered to make changes in instructional methods and materials, students' knowledge and skills are thereby maximized. Given that there is ample evidence showing that the pace of instruction influences learning outcomes, teachers need to be given the autonomy and resources to adjust the pace of classroom activities as part of the intervention process. RTI methods provide the team with data-based recommendations for making student-centered changes that can result in more meaningful and enduring outcomes.

thing specific. An example of massed practice is having students learn, repeat, and review the names of the presidents of the United States until they can say them with a high degree of accuracy. The other important instructional pacing practice is judicious review, which refers to having students recall to mind and use previously learned information on a regular basis so that it remains in their permanent store of knowledge or skill sets over a protracted period of time. An example of judicious review would be to include study and recall of certain presidents on a regular basis so that students fully internalize this information.

Responses

The fourth key component of effective instruction relates to student–teacher interactions during lessons. Specifically, it is the responses that the students and teachers make to each other that characterize effective instructional responses. Teachers need to verify and praise correct student responses so that students know when they are correct. Providing validation and reinforcement to students as they learn increases the likelihood that they will use those same responses again in the future (Fairbanks et al., 2007). Of course, when students give incorrect answers or performances, teachers need to provide immediate corrective feedback. This step is important because it prevents students from learning incorrect information. Teachers need to address students' incorrect responses immediately during the lesson and follow up with students' practicing the correct response. Regardless of the student's answer, teachers need to provide immediate feedback to the student in order to maximize correct learning.

Assessment

The last key component of effective instruction is assessment. There are two assessment activities critical to effective instruction, which can be summarized as formative and summative assessments (Kaminski & Good, 1998). Effective instruction includes formative assessments as part of the instructional design. Formative assessments are those that happen at regular intervals along the way toward a specific learning goal. These assessments allow both the student and the teacher to determine whether the student is making progress toward the instructional goals. Specifically, in effective formative assessment practices students are assessed continuously during the lesson, and daily student performance data are recorded to track student progress. This approach supports effective instruction because, if the data show that a student is not making progress, the teacher can immediately reteach certain lessons before moving on to more difficult material. Importantly, if a student needs more intensive or lengthy instruction on a regular basis, the obtained formative data can be used to help determine whether a student needs specialized instructional support. If, alternatively, all or most of the students in a class do poorly on an assessment, most likely the instruction was not effective, and other teaching methods are needed.

The final effective teaching practice is the use of summative assessment. Although formative data are a cornerstone of effective instruction, summative data also are important because they allow the student and teacher to reflect on whether the student achieved the goals set forth in the overall instructional program. For example, just as formative data about medical students' knowledge of anatomy, physiology, and chemistry are important indicators of their mastery of key health-related details, summative information about how well they can synthesize discrete facts well enough to treat live patients is essential. School-age children benefit from summative assessment as well because it offers a way of determining how well they have learned the core skills necessary to move on to more advanced learning. When formative and summative assessment data are combined, they offer comprehensive and powerful indicators of students' learning progress. They are essential for effective instruction because they indicate whether the various instructional practices utilized by teachers are achieving the requisite goals related to student success.

> **Assessment is vital to RTI because it shows whether instruction is working. Various types of assessments are included at all RTI tiers.**

In addition to the key components of effective instruction described above, another way to boost student success is to start early. Numerous studies have shown that responsive intervention that begins in kindergarten or first grade is far more effective and less costly than instruction provided at higher grades (Chard et al., 2008; Koutsoftas, Harmon, & Gray, 2009; Menzies, Mahdavi, & Lewis, 2008; Mesmer & Mesmer, 2008). Importantly, students who received the types of instruction described above in early grades (e.g., K–1; Kame'enui & Simmons, 2002) had the best outcomes (Simmons et al., 2008). Students can benefit from instruction provided in later grades, but findings have shown that the instruction needs to be more intensive to be as effective (Eber et al., 2008; McComas et al., 2009). All of these data support the use of research-based instruction from the first day of school as the best way to meet the educational need of all students.

CORE COMPONENTS OF DATA COLLECTION AND ANALYSIS

As outlined in Chapter 1, data-based decision making is the linchpin of RTI. In order for the data underlying RTI decisions to be fully useful, it needs to be reliable and valid. As pointed out in Chapter 5, there are a number of research-backed and time-tested ways to use data to document the efficacy of specific instructional procedures. Whether one uses group-based or single-subject research designs to learn about the effectiveness of an instructional program, certain requirements of effective data collection and analysis must be adhered to so that the obtained data will be meaningful (see Table 6.2). There are four key components of effective data collection and analysis that enhance the likelihood that RTI procedures will yield positive outcomes for students. These are (1) defining the target skill or behavior, (2) specifying the setting(s) where data will be collected, (3) using an accurate data recording format, and (4) conducting careful data analysis and interpretation.

TABLE 6.2. Key Components and Practices of Data Collection and Analysis

Components	Practices
Target skill or behavior	1. The desired skill or behavior is operationally defined in clear language that includes topography, frequency, duration, and intensity. 2. Code(s) for the specific skill(s) or behavior(s) are developed to be used during data collection.
Setting(s)	1. The location(s) where the skills or behaviors will be observed and recorded are described. 2. If more than one setting is identified, codes for the specific settings are developed.

Data recording format	1. Data recording procedures and materials are developed that specify:
	  a. Who will collect data.
	  b. Where data will be recorded.
	  c. When data will be recorded.
	  d. How data will be recorded.
	2. If needed, the materials necessary for recording data are collected and stored in an accessible location.

Analysis and interpretation	1. Once a specified amount of data are collected, the obtained information is reviewed to determine whether the intervention method produced the desired outcomes. 2. Data are used to revise, increase, decrease, or discontinue the intervention.

Target Skill or Behavior

The first step in collecting accurate data for RTI decision making is to define the target skill or behavior that needs to be evaluated. By having a clear and precise conception of the skill or behavior that is to be taught, the data collected about that behavior are more likely to be relevant and therefore useful (Steege et al., 2002; Steege & Watson, 2009). Importantly, the desired skill or behavior needs to be operationally defined in clear language that includes topography, frequency, duration, and intensity. *Topography* refers to the surface characteristics, or "look," of the behavior. *Frequency* refers to how often the behavior occurs. In some cases the *duration* of the behavior is a critical part of the definition, because it is only while the behavior is happening that interference with the student's learning is a concern. Finally, the *intensity* of the behavior refers to the extent to which the behavior is problematic and extreme. For example, certain self-injurious behaviors are very "intense" because they are life-threatening. These behaviors (e.g., head banging) need to be addressed much more immediately than others because they may entail serious irreversible consequences (Steege & Watson, 2009).

A second practice related to the target skill or behavior is to create code(s) by which the behavior(s) can be identified during data collection so that data recording can be fast and accurate. For example, in the case of on-task classroom behavior, the operational definition could be:

> *Student is looking at the stimulus materials related to the assigned task and performing visual, motor, or verbal tasks accompanying the assignment.*

The codes associated with this definition would need to be dichotomous and document that the student was either on-task, as defined above, or off-task. In other words, the student can be coded as either on-task or off-task—but not both at the same time. Since the definition includes visual, verbal, or motor behaviors accompanying the assigned task, it might be helpful to include in the codes identifiers for the target behavior (OT) as well as codes for when the student is off-task visually (OVi), off-task verbally (OVe), and off-task motorically (OM). Together, these codes provide a way to document what the student does during each of the intervals when the student was observed. Importantly, all those who will be observing the target behavior(s) need to practice using them in training sessions so that everyone applies them in consistent ways.

Settings

In addition to detailing descriptions of the behaviors and codes to be used with them, it is important to determine in advance the settings where the observations will be conducted. Specifically, the environmental conditions and antecedents related to the target behaviors(s) need to be described. This description is important because the environment may contribute to the obtained data in important ways. If the same or different observers collect observations but do not note or explain the setting(s) in which the data were collected, the nature of the obtained information may vary in important ways. Importantly, in the case of RTI, data should be collected in specified settings so that the effects and interactions between and among the variables can be investigated. If data need to be collected in more than one setting, then codes for each setting need to be developed as well.

Data Recording Procedures

A third and critical component of effective data collection and analysis is to develop data recording procedures and materials that specify who will collect data, where data will be recorded, when data will be recorded, and how data will be recorded. A number of pre-packaged data recording forms are available; so, it may not be necessary for individual teachers and others to create new forms for each situation. Several such forms are found in Steege and Watson (2009) and Shapiro (2005). Additional tools for creating materials may be found at the website *www.interventioncentral.org* (Intervention Central, 2010). An associated practice that is important for promoting effective data collection materials is to collect and organize them in locations where data collectors can access them quickly when needed.

Analysis and Interpretation

The final key component of data-based decision making is data analysis and interpretation. There are two practices that underlie this component. First, once a specified amount of data are collected, the obtained information is reviewed to determine whether the intervention method produced the desired outcomes. This review involves comparing an individual student's obtained scores with those that were set as goals for that student. Two major aspects of the data should be considered, namely, level and slope. *Level* refers to the score value obtained by the student on a given measure. For example, a student's raw score on a math test would provide an indicator of the student's math level. A level score can be used to identify how an individual student's math performance compares to other students. The second way to review student data is to look at slope. *Slope* is the rate of progress that a student is making. For example, the number of new words that a student can read correctly each week reflects the student's rate of progress. Slope data reveal how rapidly a student is moving toward a preset goal and can be used to predict whether the student will meet the goal in the requisite period of time.

> **Having a plan for data collection and analysis is very important because only when data are readily available for review can they be used effectively.**

Both level and slope data are important. If only level data are used, a student may be seen as making progress, but it cannot be determined whether the rate of progress will be sufficient to meet learning goals. Similarly, if only slope data are used, a student may be observed to make good progress, but the relative standing of that student's skill as compared to his or her peers will not be known. Thus, the first step in data analysis is to review the level and slope data to identify a student's current standing and progress. The first practice leads directly to the second, in which the collective data are used to revise, increase, decrease, or discontinue the intervention. Decisions about how to proceed with a student's instructional program are made on the basis of whether the student's level and slope data indicate progress toward a specific goal. Helpful ways of interpreting student data are provided in the case studies described in Chapter 5.

SUMMARY

When scientifically based instruction is used along with regular data collection, RTI methods are the natural result. While it is possible to collect data from nonscientifically based instruction, such practices are not as likely to assure that all students will make measurable educational progress. However, when scientifically based instruction practices are used, the data collected during instruction enable teachers to shape and reshape instruction to optimize outcomes for all students. In order to illustrate how RTI promotes positive outcomes for students, the next chapter features a step-by-step discussion of RTI procedures.

CHAPTER 7

RTI Procedures

10 Steps to Address Learning and Behavior Difficulties

USING RTI TO MEET STUDENTS' NEEDS

As outlined in Chapter 1, RTI is a general education system of support for all students. Specific activities at each tier provide increasingly intense supports for students with learning and behavior difficulties. This chapter presents examples of what RTI "looks like" when used on a school- and districtwide basis, including the phases focusing on all students, some students, and individual students. To assist in describing the steps necessary to implement RTI procedures, we developed a 10-item RTI implementation checklist (see Form 7.1 at the end of the chapter). This checklist provides an overview of the major steps needed to implement RTI. Some of these steps include a number of other activities; so, we have also included worksheets for specific RTI steps to assist with planning and implementation of each part of the process (see Forms 7.2–7.11 at the end of the chapter). Interspersed with descriptions of the 10 RTI steps we present case examples of specific steps.

Step 1: Implement Scientifically Based General Education Core Instruction

The first step in using RTI procedures is to select and implement scientifically based general education practices. This requirement means that all teachers at every grade level need to have scientifically based instructional materials that they use systematically with all their students. As noted in Chapter 2, the Reading First grants referred to the general education reading curriculum as a "core" program, the term *core* often being used to describe Tier 1 RTI instructional materials and methods. Research has shown that scientifically validated instructional materials and methods can make a difference in student learning (Carnine & Carnine, 2004; Stanovich & Stanovich, 2003). Many teachers, as well as the general public, may believe that all published educational materials and methods have been verified in scientific research. Sadly, this is not true. There is no "Surgeon General's warning" or Food and Drug Administration approval process for teaching materials (Stein, Stuen, Carnine, & Long, 2001). While the standards relating to scientifically based instruction found in Reading First and NCLB provisions have created more awareness of scientific evidence for teaching practices, at the present time school personnel have the responsibility for choosing teaching materials and methods that will yield optimal student outcomes. This responsibility means that teachers, principals, and curriculum coordinators need to know how to identify and verify the evidence base for instructional materials and methods.

Selecting Effective Teaching Tools

There are a number of activities that can help educators choose high-quality scientifically based instructional tools. These activities fall into three categories: (1) professional development, (2) field research, and (3) expert consultation. Professional development activities include both preservice and inservice learning. At the preservice level, all teaching, administrator, and specialist students need to take at least one class in effective teaching practices (e.g., educational psychology) and at least one class in research methods. A grounding in educational psychology provides educators with a broad knowledge of what specific instructional methods are most effective for the largest number of students. Knowledge of research methods provides educators with the skills to evaluate the strength of the evidence for any given teaching tool. Courses in research methods should include basic statistics, research designs, reliability, validity, and the importance of using research methods matched to the characteristics and features of the target population for which the product has been developed (Carnine & Gersten, 2000).

Once educators have knowledge and skills in implementing effective teaching methods and research principles, they can go on to engage in their own field research activities. Such research includes learning about and critically evaluating teaching materials (e.g., "core" curricula) that they are considering for adoption (U.S. Department of Education, 2004). Field research includes a number of stages, such as locating possible curricula in publishers' catalogs and websites, reviewing the research results from applications of the curriculum, visiting schools where the curriculum is being used, and connecting the proposed curriculum to local instructional goals (Stein et al., 2001).

In many cases, educators may be doing some or all of these "research" activities but may not be doing them systematically across the district or for every subject area. An effective core program can make a significant difference in RTI success. Recall the RTI triangle (Figure 1.1) from Chapter 1. RTI starts with the core program for all students. Some 80% of students should be suc-

> **Tier 1 is the most important part of RTI. Tier 1 includes "core" instruction in each curriculum area. Tier 1 instruction should be effective for about 80% of students. When fewer than 80% of students are successful with Tier 1 alone, core instruction needs to be improved.**

cessful with Tier 1 instruction alone, but the extent to which this aim is met depends largely on the quality of the Tier 1 materials and methods used.

To promote more systematic use of curriculum field research, Form 7.2 provides a reproducible worksheet that can be used to accompany curriculum research. A completed version of the worksheet is found in Figure 7.1. In this example, three specific general education primary grade reading curricula were reviewed. The data revealed that two of the three were evaluated scientifically. Both Open Court and Read Well have data indicating they are effective in teaching reading. In order for a school district to decide which one to select, personnel would need to decide which curriculum best matches the local instructional goals.

Intervention Integrity

After a specific general education curriculum has been chosen, it needs to be implemented in all classrooms with a high degree of consistency (Telzrow, McNamara, & Hollinger, 2000). If instructional materials and methods are not used as designed, they are not likely to be effective (Dykeman, 2006). In an ideal world, all curricula would not only be scientifically based but also come with implementation checklists. Such checklists are stepwise lists of all the steps necessary to use a set of materials and methods with a high degree of accuracy and consistency. The process of checking the implementation of a procedure is known as treatment fidelity and has been shown to have a significant role in achieving the desired outcomes (Sanetti & Kratochwill, 2005). If an implementation checklist is not provided for a curriculum, one can be created by analyzing the essential elements needed to implement the instruction. A blank intervention integrity checklist is found in Form 7.3 at the end of the chapter. This checklist can be used by both classroom teachers for self-evaluation of intervention integrity or by observers who record whether all steps in completing a lesson are done correctly.

An example of a completed intervention integrity checklist is found in Figure 7.2. In this example Ms. Jones completed a self-evaluation of her correct implementation of a specific reading lesson when she introduced the letter *B*. She wrote in the date, time, and topic of the lesson and then checked "yes" or "no" to indicate whether she had completed each step. For those steps that she did not complete, Ms. Jones wrote a note indicating what happened that prevented the correct implementation of those steps. Checklists such as this one can be used to monitor and review the extent of consistency and accuracy of implementation of instruction at all RTI tiers. Intervention integrity checklists provide a way to ensure that all teachers who are using a specific curriculum use it in the same way so that students have the benefit of highly consistent instructional procedures.

Step 2: Conduct Triannual Universal Screening of All Students' Performance

Once a scientifically based instructional program has been implemented, the next step in RTI is to collect data on every student to learn which students are making effective progress

Program	Publisher (Date)	Research Evidence	Connections to Local Goals	Observations
Open Court	*SRA (2005)*	*Foorman, B., Francis, D., Fletcher, J., Schatschneider, C., & Mehta, P. (1998). The role of instruction in learning to read: Preventing reading failure in at-risk children. Journal of Educational Psychology, 90, 37–55. This study of 285 first- and second-grade students compared three types of classroom reading programs: (1) direct instruction in sound–spelling correspondences (Open Court Reading); (2) less direct instruction in sound–spelling correspondences; and (3) implicit instructions in the alphabetic code as part of reading connected text. Results showed better outcomes for children in the Open Court group.*	*Our local goals include direct, systematic teaching of phonics in general education classrooms.*	*We observed an Open Court lesson at Wedgewood Elementary, and the students were highly engaged and learning.*
Read Well	*Sopris West (2002)*	*Jitendra, A. K., Edwards, L. L., Starosta, K., Sacks, G., Jacobson, L. A., & Choutka, C. M. (2004). Journal of Learning Disabilities, 37, 421–440. Differences in student characteristics and in the amount of Read Well instruction received (2–7 weeks) seemed to account for differences in performance. Overall, the findings from Year 1 and 2 studies indicate the benefits of Read Well's instructional intensity and duration for children who struggle with emerging reading skills.*	*Read Well puts a heavy focus on repeated practice of phonics skills, an area of emphasis in our local goals.*	*Observation of students in a Read Well classroom showed that each had his or her own materials and were practicing independently.*
Houghton Mifflin Reading	*Houghton Mifflin (2005)*	*No research found.*	*This new program is advertised as integrating phonics with graded literature-based texts.*	*Observation of students in a grade 1 classroom showed that students were eager to use the software but not as engaged with their workbooks.*

FIGURE 7.1. Example of a completed Instructional Materials Review Worksheet.

Teacher's Name: _Mary Jones_   Date: _10/12/09_   Time: _9:15–10:00_

Subject/Lesson: _Reading: Letter "B"_   Evaluator: _X_   Self   Other: _____

Directions: The individual implementing this intervention is to complete this form at the end of every day regarding how he or she implemented the intervention during _that_ day.

Intervention implemented by: _X_   Classroom teacher   _____ Other: _____

Intervention Component	Completed Yes	No	Comments
1. Handed out student materials.	X		
2. All students read all review words.		X	Peg was late to class and missed word review portion.
3. Immediate feedback given to students.	X		
4. Introduced new letter and sound, using script in teacher's manual.	X		
5. All students repeated new sound.		X	Alex was called to the office before practicing new sound.
6. Immediate feedback given to students.	X		
7. All students read story out loud.	X		
8. Each student correctly answered one question about story.		X	I forgot to call on Mark and Lynn.
9. All students produced three legible copies of letter of the day.	X		
10. Immediate feedback given to students.		X	Visitor came into classroom as I was giving feedback to students, and I skipped row 3 students.

FIGURE 7.2. Example of a completed Treatment Integrity Checklist.

and which ones need additional support. Suggested time frames for collecting screening data have been developed:

- Fall (September 15–October 15)
- Winter (January 1–31)
- Spring (May 1–31)

A number of specific planning activities are necessary to ensure that universal screening data are accurate and valid. To assist with such planning, blank universal screening worksheets are found in Forms 7.4 and 7.5. Figures 7.3 and 7.4 depict completed worksheets used to plan and carry out the details of a screening process. These details include selecting and obtaining materials, training personnel and organizing materials for those who will conduct the screenings, conducting the screenings on stated days (including make-up days for absent students), managing the student database, and identifying which students need additional instruction (Burns, 2002; Burns & Gibbons, 2008).

Screening Materials

A growing number of published tools are available for screening. Summaries of academic and behavior screening assessments are presented in Tables 7.1 and 7.2. Universal screening assessments need to be standardized for use with all students, and these need to be reliable and valid (Jenkins, Zumeta, Dupree, & Johnson, 2005). An excellent resource for detailed information about available screening tools can be found at the National Center for Response to Intervention (NCRTI) website at *www.rti4success.org* in the Tools/Interventions section. In the case of academic skills, CBM, including the Dynamic Indicators of Basic Early Literacy Skills (DIBELS), are research-based ways to document students' academic skills (Glover & Albers, 2006; Good & Kaminski, 2002; Shinn, 2005). During the early days of CBM all materials were created directly from the local curriculum. Since then, a large number of research studies have shown that generic CBM materials work just as well as locally created items (Fuchs & Deno, 1994).

The largest published set of screening materials is known as AIMSweb and is published by Pearson Education (2008). AIMSweb screening materials include reading, spelling, writing, and math probes for grades 1–8. In addition, AIMSweb has preschool and kindergarten materials for early literacy and numeracy. AIMSweb materials are available online, and purchasers download and print what they need. The AIMSweb system includes online data management services as well. AIMSweb has both oral and silent-reading measures. Deno et al. (2009) showed that silent-reading passages known as the maze task are reliable universal screening tools for upper elementary grade students. Another type of premade CBM materials for early literacy and reading are the DIBELS. DIBELS for specific prereading skills are available for preschool through grade 1. DIBELS measures of oral reading are available for grades 1–6. DIBELS can be obtained in two different ways. These materials are available for free downloading at the DIBELS website (*dibels.uoregon.edu*). In addition, the

(text continues on page 93)

School/District: _Riverview Elementary/Sunnyside District_ Year: _2009–2010_ Benchmark: (F) W S

Task	Person(s) Responsible	Deadline	Costs	Completed	Initials
Select materials for benchmarks	_Assessment Committee_	March 2	none	Feb. 27	KPR
Obtain/copy needed materials	_Karen and Maria_	June 1	$500	May 22	MRS
Make student name labels (if needed)	_Not needed—teachers do_	—	—	—	—
Train those collecting data	_Sept. 1_	$150	Sept. 1	DSS	
Organize/distribute materials	_Maria and Peggy_	Sept. 15	none	Sept. 14	MRS
Collect benchmarks on stated dates	_K–2 teachers and students_	Oct. 15	none	Oct. 9	MRS
Collect make-up benchmarks from absent students	_Maria and Peggy_	Oct. 12	none	Oct. 12	MRS
Enter student scores into computer	_Peggy_	Oct. 20	none	Oct 19	PHD
Create and distribute data summaries	_Maria and Peggy_	Oct. 26	none	Oct 23	PHD
Identify students of concern	_Teachers and principals_	Nov. 2	none	Oct 30	PHD
	IMPLEMENT NEXT RTI STEP: TIER 2 INSTRUCTION				

Notes: _Need more clipboards for Winter benchmarks._

FIGURE 7.3. Example of a completed Benchmark Planning Worksheet.

What	When	Who	Where	Materials Needed	Data Ready by
Fall Benchmarks	Oct. 5, 6, 7 9:10–11:30	All K–2 teachers and students; Title I staff and paraprofessionals	Kindergarten in Library Grade 1 in Gym Grade 2 in Cafeteria	CBM packet for each student Clipboards Stopwatches	October 26
Winter Benchmarks	Jan. 11, 12, 13 9:10–11:30	All K–2 teachers and students; Title I staff and paraprofessionals	Kindergarten in Library Grade 1 in Gym Grade 2 in Cafeteria	CBM packet for each student Clipboards Stopwatches	February 1
Spring Benchmarks	May 5, 6, 7 9:10–11:30	All K–2 teachers and students; Title I staff and paraprofessionals	Kindergarten in Library Grade 1 in Gym Grade 2 in Cafeteria	CBM packet for each student Clipboards Stopwatches	May 26

FIGURE 7.4. Example of a completed Benchmark Implementation Worksheet.

TABLE 7.1. Summary of Published Curriculum-Based Measurement Materials

Publisher	Web address	Materials	Grades
DIBELS[a]	dibels.uoregon.edu	Early Literacy	Preschool–1
		Reading: Oral	1–6
Intervention Central[a]	www.interventioncentral.org	Reading software: Oral and silent	1–12
		Math software	1–6
Pearson	www.pearsonassessments.com	Early Literacy	Preschool–1
		Reading: Oral	1–8
		Silent (maze)	1–8
		Spelling	1–8
		Early Numeracy	Preschool–1
		Math	1–8
Pro-Ed	www.pro-ed.com	Measuring Basic Skills Program (Macintosh computer program) for:	
		Reading	1–6
		Math	1–6
Sopris West[b]	www.sopriswest.com	Early Literacy	Preschool–1
		Reading: Oral	1–6

[a]All materials at this site can be downloaded and used for free.
[b]Sopris West has the exclusive rights to sell packaged versions of all the DIBELS materials.

TABLE 7.2. Summary of Published Behavior Screening Tools

Screening tool	Web address	Materials	Ages
Conners' Rating Scales—Revised	psychcorp.pearsonassessments.com	Parent, Teacher, and Adolescent Self-Reports	3–17
Drummond's Student Risk Screening Scale	sch-psych.net/word-notes/SRSS.doc	Parent/Teacher Survey	5–18
Eyberg Child Behavior Inventory	www3.parinc.com	Parent/Teacher Survey	2–17
Revised Behavior Problem Checklist	www3.parinc.com	Parent/Teacher Survey	5–18
School-Wide Information System	www.swis.org	Web-based data tool for office referral data	5–18
Systematic Screening for Behavior Disorders	store.cambiumlearning.com	Parent/Teacher Survey, audio- and videotapes	5–12

same DIBELS items can be purchased in packaged sets from Sopris West. The two forms are very similar and measure the same skills.

Also included in the list of CBM materials in Table 7.1 are Internet sites where the materials can be downloaded for free, used online, or created by using free online software. For those schools that require more customized CBM items, there is a website—*www. interventioncentral.org*—where they can create their own materials for free. The site is a service of the Syracuse (New York) public schools. At the site there are a number of CBM tools, including software applications for creating both reading and math CBM items. The reading probe generator creates oral reading fluency probes from text that is entered by the user. Probes can be created from literature or expository texts. The reading software also calculates the readability level of each probe generated. Intervention Central also includes a math probe generator. This software allows users to create math computation probes for addition, subtraction, multiplication, and division. Users can choose how many problems will be on each page, what type of skill the problems will measure (e.g., adding sums to 18), and how large the font size will be. Both the reading software and math software generate a student copy and a teacher copy for every probe created. The Intervention Central site includes links to a number of other CBM tools, including free literature-based silent reading probes for grades 4–6, CBM manuals for teachers, and graphing tools.

The website *EasyCBM.com* is a newer resource for CBM tools. The site offers free CBM items in reading and math. Some of the assessments must be printed to use, and others can be used in print or online form. EasyCBM also offers a free data management tool that shows student progress. Pro-Ed Publishing sells Macintosh computer CBM software for reading and math. This software is for computer-based testing only; so, students must be at an individual computer station to use it. The software covers math and reading skills for grades 1–6, providing immediate corrective feedback to the student that includes graphs of student progress over time. The students' scores are summarized in teacher reports that show which students made progress and which ones did not.

For social skills and behaviors, several screening tools exist (see Table 7.2), including the Systematic Screening for Behavior Disorders. The Conners' Rating Scales—Revised (CRS-R) have been used for many years to identify specific behaviors students have in different settings. The short form of the CRS-R can be used as a screening tool to learn which students exhibit such behaviors at the start of each school year. Drummond's Student Risk Screening Scale is a free measure (see website) that can be used to identify specific behaviors of concern in students in grades K–12. There are no norms for this measure, so the data are used as an initial informal screening only. The Eyberg Child Behavior Inventory provides a quick and easy way to complete a format for identifying students of concern, ranging from preschool through high school. The Revised Behavior Problem Checklist is a somewhat more detailed screening survey for school-age students.

The School-Wide Information System (SWIS) is an online data collection tool that permits easy recording of office discipline referrals (ODRs) and other behavior incidents in a school. SWIS allows teachers and administrators to see where in a school building the majority of behavior problems occur as well as to identify readily which students end up in the office most often for behavior problems. Such data help identify which building locations need more adult supervision and which students might benefit from Tier 2 social skills intervention. Finally, the Systematic Screening for Behavior Disorders (SSBD) is a multiple gating method for identifying students at risk for behavior problems. It starts with very brief teacher assessment and then involves collecting more data about the students identified by teachers (Severson, Walker, Hope-Doolittle, Kratochwill, & Gresham, 2007). Additional screening measures are in development that may offer enhanced tools for screening all students. One screening tool that combines academic and other indicators is the Brief Academic Competence Evaluation Scales (BACESS; Elliott, Huai, & Roach, 2007).

Data Management

Another important aspect of the screening process is data management. To be maximally useful, data collected from the benchmarks need to be organized and shared in systematic ways. At a minimum, the students' scores need to be entered into some type of database. The simplest form of such a database is paper-based. Student data can be summarized by simply rank ordering the students according to their scores. Most schools utilizing RTI methods have a system of entering screening scores into some kind of computer database. There are a variety of hardware and software tools available for schools to use to manage RTI data. Although there are many manufacturers of these products, they can be grouped into two types, standalone and network-based.

STANDALONE DATA MANAGEMENT

RTI data can be entered into one standalone computer workstation. The chosen computer could run any type of operating system, including Apple (Macintosh), Windows, UNIX, or others. The critical requirement for the computer is that data management software be installed on it. Examples of such software include Microsoft Excel, Open Office, and others. If the school has specialized data management software for other student information such as attendance, grades, and assessment, the benchmark data can probably be entered into that data set instead of a separate file. It is ideal to have all student data in one common place so that information about students is centralized and important related data can be simultaneously retrieved and reviewed. If the benchmark data are housed on one computer, it is *essential* that the data file(s) be backed up on disk on a regular basis. The downside to using only one computer workstation to store the data is that, were the computer or file to be damaged, the data might be lost. For this reason, it might be better to store and manage the data on a computer network, if available.

NETWORK DATA MANAGEMENT

An alternative to using one computer to store RTI data is to use a computer network in which the data are stored on a central server but can be accessed by many people through computers on the network. There are a number of benefits to managing RTI data on a computer network. First, the way that computer networks are set up and managed includes regular data backups and multiple storage locations, which means that the data are less vulnerable to permanent loss if the computer is damaged. Second, when data can be accessed from a number of locations, many people who need access to the data can obtain it quickly and easily for instructional decision making. Finally, the type of network used may enhance the nature of the screening reports and offer multiple ways to display the data. For example, data can be displayed for an entire grade or class or for an individual student.

There are several Internet-based RTI data services that offer flexible ways to manage student information. All of these data services must be purchased by the school or district, and the rates are set and vary by service provider. There is a data service that accompanies the DIBELS that is set up to provide group and individual score reports specifically for all DIBELS measures. This service can be used only with DIBELS data but is fast and less expensive than that of most other service providers. AIMSweb has a data management service system that allows for data from all AIMSWeb measures as well as DIBELS to be entered and stored. In addition, AIMSWeb also has an RTI-specific data management tool for managing students' scores as they move between different stages of RTI. The most crucial feature of the data management system used to support RTI activities is that it be sustainable over time for the types of data needed. EasyCBM includes online data management as well. In situations where no pre-made computer data tool is available, Box 7.1 offers instructions for how to create student data graphs.

Step 3: Identify Students at Risk

Once screening data are organized, they can be used to review and identify which students are not meeting grade-level learning goals. It is important to realize that some students will have skill deficits in multiple areas (Fletcher, 2005). A two-part process for reviewing student data is recommended. The first part includes comparing the scores obtained by all students with external performance standards. Two main types of performance standards exist: criterion-based and normative. *Criterion standards* refer to a specific performance goal that has been shown to predict later school success. For example, a score of 40 or higher on first-grade spring DIBELS Oral

> **Universal screening data indicate which students need additional instruction. Screening data are not diagnostic but they can provide information about the starting point for additional instruction.**

Reading Fluency is highly predictive of reading success in later grades. Therefore, all students who score 40 or higher at the end of first grade are considered to be at low risk for later reading problems, but those who score below 40 are at some level of risk.

The other basis for comparison of screening data is normative. Normative data might include the scores of a large number of students in the same grade who completed the same assessment. For example, third-grade oral reading fluency norms show the typical reading performance of third graders. Two types of norms can be used: local or national. Local norms consist of the scores of all students who attend the same school or are in the same district. National norms include samples of students from around the U.S. National norms are not necessarily available for all skills; however, when available, they are an important basis

BOX 7.1. Creating Cool Graphs of Student Data

All of the graphs of student data in this book were created by using Microsoft Graph, which is a part of the Microsoft Office software suite. To create graphs like ours do the following:

1. Open Microsoft (MS) Word.
2. Click on the "Insert" menu item.
3. Highlight and click on "Object … "
4. A dialogue box will appear in which you can select what to insert.
5. Scroll down the right side of the box and locate "Microsoft Graph Chart."
6. Click on "Microsoft Graph Chart," then click on "OK."
7. A set of new windows will appear on your screen. One will be the graph, and another is the datasheet into which the graph values are entered. Both will appear with preentered sample data.
8. Click on the first column of the datasheet and change the value to reflect your data. If you have more than one dependent variable to graph, change the next row of data, and so forth, until all desired values are entered.
9. Click the upper-right "go away" box on the datasheet.
10. Click once in the white area of the graph, then right-click your mouse to open a command box. In this box highlight and click on "Chart Type … "
11. A new dialogue box will open. In the left side of the box click on the preferred chart type (probably "line").
12. After selecting the chart type, choose the chart subtype from the box on the right-hand side of the dialogue box. We use the first type in the middle row, described as a "line with markers displayed at each data value."
13. Click "OK" to select this chart type. Note that you can set this format as your default chart type by clicking this box before closing the dialogue box.
14. The chart should appear with your data. You can change the size of the chart in your document by clicking and dragging the corner/side arrows.
15. You can edit every part of the chart by right-clicking on any part of the chart and entering new values in the dialogue box for that feature.

of comparison, because they can shed light on whether a school's performance levels are in line with national trends. Both the DIBELS and AIMSweb websites have continuously updated national norms for their measures. Table 7.3 shows the national norms for second graders' scores on oral reading fluency. Compare these scores with those shown in Table 7.4 for a few second-grade students. Those students with low scores should be considered to be at risk for reading problems.

When normative data are used for comparing individual student performance with the average performance of all the students in the same grade, a decision must be made about what students are at risk. This process is made easier if the students' scores are organized

TABLE 7.3. Oral Reading Fluency National Norms for Second-Grade Students

Percentile	Fall	Winter	Spring
90	110	136	152
75	85	111	128
50	60	85	102
25	31	61	76
10	15	32	53

Note. From Pearson Education, Inc. (2008). Reprinted by permission.

according to percentiles so that those students scoring at or below a specific percentile rank are reviewed in detail. Researchers have looked at various "cutoff points," or specific percentile ranks, as starting points for reviewing individual student scores when an external performance criterion is not available. The specific percentile ranks that usually serve as starting points for reviewing students' scores are the 16th to 25th percentile. The 25th percentile roughly approximates the low end of the average range of scores and offers an inclusive starting point for reviewing data. The 16th percentile represents the bottom end of one standard deviation from the overall average score. It is not so important what particular percentile rank is chosen as the starting point; rather, it is the certainty of systematically reviewing the data for all students below a specific rank that is critical.

The process of reviewing those students who score at and below a certain level allows teachers to consider each student's overall skill development in each area of concern. This process can be facilitated through use of an Instruction Planning Worksheet. A blank worksheet is provided as Form 7.6 and a sample completed one is shown in Figure 7.5. This worksheet provides spaces for entering the name of each student at risk as well as the specific nature of the current instructional need. This is important because not all at-risk students will have the same needs. For example, in the area of reading, some students may need to learn sound–symbol correspondence, while others may need to work on reading more fluently. By listing each student at risk, the teacher can consider what the exact instructional needs are and create customized instructional interventions that match the student's needs.

TABLE 7.4. Fall Oral Reading Fluency Scores and Percentile Ranks for Second-Grade Students

Student	ORF score	Nearest percentile rank
Brown, Ben	84	75
Martin, Steve	12	8
Reynolds, Gail	51	40
Wilson, Martha	16	11

Student	Describe Instructional Need	Instructional Method to Be Tried	Progress Monitoring Measure	Program Start Date	Progress Review Date	Person Responsible
Smith, Mary	Segment words orally	Early Reading Intervention (ERI)	PSF	Nov. 3	Nov. 30	PHD
Gray, Billy	Blend words while reading	Project Read	NWF	Oct. 29	Nov. 30	MRS
Cohen, Nick	Read more rapidly	Great Leaps	ORF	Nov. 5	Nov. 30	MRS
White, Polly	Segment words orally	Early Reading Intervention (ERI)	PSF	Nov. 4	Nov. 30	PHD
O'Reilly, Mark	Match sounds to letters	Sound Partners	NWF	Nov. 5	Nov. 30	PHD
Webber, Karl	Match sounds to letters	Sound Partners	NWF	Nov. 3	Nov. 30	PHD
Gage, Robin	Number identification	Touch Math	CBM-M-100	Nov. 4	Dec. 1	KPT
Plummer, Max	Number identification	Touch math	CBM-M-100	Oct. 30	Dec. 1	KPT
Silver, Duane	Adding single digits, no regrouping	Incremental Rehearsal	CBM-M	Nov. 2	Dec. 1	EBC
Black, Melissa	Adding digits with regrouping	Incremental Rehearsal	CBM-M	Nov. 5	Dec. 1	EBC
Boxer, Fred	Adding single digits, no regrouping	Incremental Rehearsal	CBM-M	Nov. 4	Dec. 1	EBC

FIGURE 7.5. Example of a completed Tier 2 Instruction Planning Worksheet.

Occasionally a student's instructional needs will not be clear from the screening data alone. Teachers need to consider any other data they may have about the student's performance along with the benchmark scores. If required, additional brief testing with other CBM measures may shed further light on the student's current needs (Shinn, 1989, 1998).

In cases where a student's current instructional need is not made clear by either the screening data *or* classroom performance, an additional type of analysis may be used. Error analysis is a way of examining a student's pattern of errors to see what skills the student needs to learn. For example, a student experiencing math difficulties might get all instances of a certain type of problem correct but also get all of another type wrong. If there is a consistent pattern in the errors that a student makes on a screening assessment or in classroom work, then that information can be very helpful in planning corrective instruction. Figure 7.6 shows a completed error analysis for a third-grade student with a large number of errors during oral reading. A blank version of this worksheet is included as Form 7.7. Doing the error analysis involves recording the number of items the student got right (31), the number of errors (11), and finally the specifics of the actual errors made. Usually, by describing the specific types of errors that the student made, teachers can much more readily identify what additional instruction the student needs.

In a few cases, a careful review of a student's error profile may still not reveal the type of instruction needed. Two additional steps that can be helpful in such cases include conducting a brief experimental analysis (BEA) and determining whether the student has a skill or performance deficit (Daly, Persampieri, McCurdy, & Gortmaker, 2000). BEA is a stepwise method for identifying what type of instruction a student needs. It is accomplished by using several instructional methods with the student in quick succession while collecting data to see which one works best (Martens & Gertz, 2009). Usually all the teaching exercises are conducted during the same session, and it's normally clear which instruction approach worked best for the student. This method has been used to identify reading, math, and behavioral interventions (Jones, Wickstrom, Noltemeyer, & Brown, 2009; Wilber & Cushman, 2006). A method related to the BEA is a skills versus performance analysis. Also known as a "can't do/won't do" assessment, this method involves asking the student to demonstrate the target skill under specified conditions (VanDerHeyden & Witt, 2008)—including doing the task when asked and doing it for a particular reward (i.e., a reward contingency). If the student does the task only when the reward is offered, that alternative suggests that the student can *do* the task but "won't" under certain conditions. In contrast, if the student does not complete the task under either condition, then it's probable that the student truly "can't" do the task and needs further instruction to learn how. See Box 7.2 for more information about skill deficits versus performance deficits.

Step 4: Provide Scientifically Based Small-Group Instruction

After identifying which students need additional instruction, teachers then provide those students with Tier 2 interventions involving RTI procedures. As earlier noted, this instruction is typically provided in small groups of four to six students at a time. For example, in the area of math, those students not meeting a grade 1 winter goal of correctly adding two

Student's Name: _John Smith_   Grade: _3_

Universal Screening Data Analyzed:

Reading: Math:

____ Initial Sound Fluency (ISF)   ____ Oral Counting (OC)

____ Letter Naming Fluency (LNF)   ____ Number Identification (NI)

____ Letter Sound Fluency (LSF)   ____ Quantity Discrimination (QD)

____ Phoneme Segmentation Fluency (PSF)   ____ Missing Number (MN)

____ Nonsense Word Fluency (NWF)   ____ Single Skill Type: _____

_X_ Oral Reading Fluency (ORF)   ____ Mixed Skill Types: _____

____ Maze   ____ Math Concepts and Applications (MCAP)

____ Other: _____   ____ Other: _____

Writing: Behavior (lists behaviors of concern):

____ Correct Letter Sequences (CLS)   ____ Systematic Screening for Behavior Disorders

____ Total Words Written (TWW)   ____ Social Skills Improvement System

____ Correct Word Sequences (CWS)   ____ Other: _____

____ Other: _____   ____ Other: _____

Based on the screening data collected, answer the following questions:

1. How many items did the student get correct? _31_

2. How many errors did the student make? _11_

3. List the actual errors here: _on, part, at, said, last, made, from, today, with, keep, dawn_

   _____

   _____

   _____

   _____

   _____

4. What is the primary type of error made? _Skipped many words and said only the first letter_
   of many words.

   _____

   _____

   _____

5. Other notes about student's work: _____

   _____

   _____

   _____

FIGURE 7.6. Example of a completed Error Analysis Worksheet.

BOX 7.2. Skill Deficit versus Performance Deficit

Throughout our careers in school psychology we have encountered countless case examples when IEP teams have struggled to determine whether a student's lack of educational performance was attributable to a motivational issue or, rather, truly reflected a deficit in skills. We've all experienced this skill deficit versus performance deficit dilemma. It usually begins with the team discussing a student's academic or social delays and then shifts to a debate as to whether the student lacks (1) the necessary skills or (2) sufficient motivation to perform the required task (e.g., reading fluency, reading comprehension, math computations, writing assignments). This discussion may become heated, often with two camps emerging (e.g., "She can't do it" vs. "She won't do it"). With battle lines drawn and emphatic arguments pro and con persuading no one differently, team members steadfastly retreat into their respective camps and wearily agree to "agree to disagree" as the meeting dissolves with no resolution of the problem.

An especially troubling aspect of these discussions is the idea that performance deficits are rooted in such internal variables as "low motivation," "low aspirations," "inadequate drive," and/or "self-fulfilling prophecies of failure." Paired with these hypotheses is the tidy but unacceptable assumption that until the student changes (i.e., energizes his or her motivational state) educational interventions are futile, thereby absolving team members of any responsibility for action.

We advocate a direct assessment approach that tests the hypotheses underlying the skill deficit versus performance deficit debate. An excellent example of this direct assessment approach is the "can't do/won't do" assessment procedure described by VanDerHeyden and Witt (2008). Briefly, their method includes first identifying highly reinforcing tangible activity reinforcers (e.g., through stickers, art supplies, edibles for younger students; homework-free cards, in-school privileges, and lunch line passes for older students). Next, instructional materials and an assessment procedure is identified (e.g., math worksheets, percentage of correct answers). Following a baseline phase, students are told that rewards will be earned if subsequent performance improves (e.g., "We are going to do a math worksheet today. The last time you did this you completed 55% of the problems correctly. Today, if you beat your personal score by 5% you will earn one of the rewards."). This second phase is referred to as the "incentive condition." Within this model, if a student's performance improves during the incentive condition, then the student has "responded to the reinforcement intervention," thus confirming the hypothesis that poor performance was influenced by low motivation. On the other hand, if during the incentive condition the student's performance does not improve, then the skill deficit hypothesis is supported. *Note:* Chapter 10 includes case examples illustrating the "can't do/won't do" assessment model.

---

single-digit numbers should be given additional instruction in adding single digits up to a sum of 10. A review of available materials is needed to know what small-group (Tier 2) instructional methods or programs are likely to help these students. As with Tier 1 interventions, evidence for the efficacy of Tier 2 interventions needs to be examined. A blank worksheet for summarizing evidence supporting the effectiveness of possible Tier 2 interventions is presented as Form 7.8, and Figure 7.7 presents a completed Tier 2 Instructional Materials Review Worksheet. This worksheet allows comparison of specific programs and the research validating their efficacy. In the case of math, far fewer research studies have documented which programs work better than others. The two empirically validated programs listed are Touch Math, which has been found to help some students in developing

Program (publisher and date)	Knowledge and Skills Covered in Program	Program Age/Grade	Research Evidence Supporting Program	How Is Student Progress in Program Monitored?	Costs (with training)
Touch Math (Innovative Learning Concepts, 2004)	Number Identification, Quantity, Basic Operations	K–2	Scott, K. S. (1993). Multisensory mathematics for children with mild disabilities. *Exceptionality, 4*(2), 97–111. Showed greater gains for students in Touch Math group.	Not specified	$719.00 (for first-grade kit)
Incremental Rehearsal	Computation Fluency	K–4	Burns, M. K. (2005). Using incremental rehearsal to increase fluency of single-digit multiplication facts with children identified as learning disabled in mathematics computation. *Education and Treatment of Children, 28,* 237–249.	Weekly CBM math probes	Free
Schoolhouse Mathematics Laboratory (SRA, 2000)	Number Identification, Computation Fluency, Applied Problems	1–3	No research found.	Built-in skill checks	$849.95

FIGURE 7.7. Example of a completed Tier 2 Instructional Materials Review Worksheet.

basic math skills, and incremental rehearsal, shown to aid children identified as learning disabled in mathematics computation.

In some situations there may not be a packaged "program" that addresses a student's learning needs—particularly so for math interventions. But there are many excellent math improvement methods that teachers can use, often with materials they already have in their classrooms. The incremental rehearsal intervention listed in Figure 7.7 requires only math flash cards but uses a specific sequence of teaching steps.

A preplanned intervention for a small group of students, is called a standard protocol. Standard protocols are interventions that can be used with many students at the same time. Box 7.3 includes additional resources for locating both Tier 2 *and* Tier 3 interventions. Once a program of instruction has been selected, it should be used until one of two outcomes occurs: either the student reaches and maintains the instructional goal and no longer needs additional assistance, or the small-group sessions yield data indicating that the intervention is not working, in which case another intervention is immediately undertaken.

Step 5: Monitor Student Progress toward Learning Goals

In Chapter 5 we noted key principles to use when reviewing student data. The length of time a Tier 2 intervention needs to be maintained varies from one student to another. Tier 2 instruction should be continued until at least three data points have been collected, since that is the minimum necessary before data can be reviewed (Brown-Chidsey et al., 2008; Riley-Tillman & Burns, 2008; Steege et al., 2002). However, many Tier 2 interventions will last much longer than the time needed to collect three data points (Vaughn et al., 2009; Wanzek & Vaughn, 2008). Something that must be kept in mind is that the frequency of progress monitoring will determine how quickly three more data points are gathered. At Tier 2, it is recommended that progress checks be done at least monthly—and every 2 weeks if possible. Given the variability in daily routines in most school settings, it is likely that there will be some days when the intervention does not happen or when students are out sick. It is important that any intervention be tried long enough for changes in student performance to be possible (Walker, Carta, Greenwood, & Buzhardt, 2008). Detailed information about

---

BOX 7.3. Tiers 2 and 3 Instructional Resources

The following websites list and describe interventions for Tiers 2 and 3.

Intervention Central	*www.interventioncentral.org*
Florida Center for Reading Research	*www.fcrr.org*
Free Reading	*www.free-reading.net*
What Works Clearinghouse	*ies.ed.gov/ncee/wwc*
Doing What Works	*dww.ed.gov*

how best to conduct progress monitoring is available elsewhere (Brown-Chidsey, Bronaugh, & McGraw, 2009).

> **Progress monitoring is essential for RTI to work. Even if the most effective interventions in the world are put in place, without progress data, no one will know if they are working.**

One of the best ways to ensure that progress monitoring occurs systematically is to pick the progress measure at the same time that an intervention is undertaken. As noted earlier in this chapter, there are a number of different measures available, as publishers of screening measures also often publish progress measures. Recent research has provided verification of the importance of progress monitoring in RTI (Stecker, Fuchs, & Fuchs, 2008). Research has also identified a wider choice of progress measures as well as more detail about their measurement properties (Christ & Silberglitt, 2007; Compton, Fuchs, Fuchs, & Bryant, 2006; Griffiths, VanDerHeyden, Skocut, & Lilles, 2009). Progress measures for behavior are important too, and tools such as the Daily Behavior Report Card (DBRC) can provide the information needed to know whether Tier 2 behavior interventions are working properly (Riley-Tillman, Chafouleas, & Briesch, 2007).

Data Review

Figure 7.8 shows data for a student, Nick, after 3 weeks of general education instruction (9/17–9/30 plottings) and 6 weeks of Tier 2 intervention with the scientifically based small-group program Sounds Sense. This graph shows that Nick made relatively little progress in decoding nonsense words as measured by weekly DIBELS measures. Nick's score increased by 3 points at week 4 but then dropped slightly during the 2 subsequent weeks. There is little in these data to suggest that Nick's skills will improve substantially enough if this intervention is continued. There is a limit to how long an intervention should be used if the data suggest it is not really working. In cases like Nick's, when the daily or weekly assessment data suggest that a student is not making progress, the Tier 2 activities should be changed or replaced with another type of intervention. The new intervention should be used until at least three more data points have been collected, and then the data should be reviewed to see if the new intervention is working.

Knowing exactly how long to use an intervention and how to interpret the data constitutes one of the key requirements underlying RTI. Riley-Tillman and Burns (2008), in their book on the subject, supply excellent insights on how to interpret progress data. Here a brief summary of ways to examine data productively is given. In general progress data may indicate either (1) no response, (2) a small response, or (3) an adequate response. As Barth et al. (2008) note, educators should determine in advance how the data will be reviewed and what the criterion for an adequate response will be. Exciting research in medical settings has shown that actual neural activation can be observed with functional magnetic resonance imaging (fMRI; Odegard, Ring, Smith, Biggan, & Black, 2008). Since public schools do not have ready access to fMRI equipment, we must rely on other methods. Thankfully, such other measures as CBM have been shown to be reliable and accurate indicators of students'

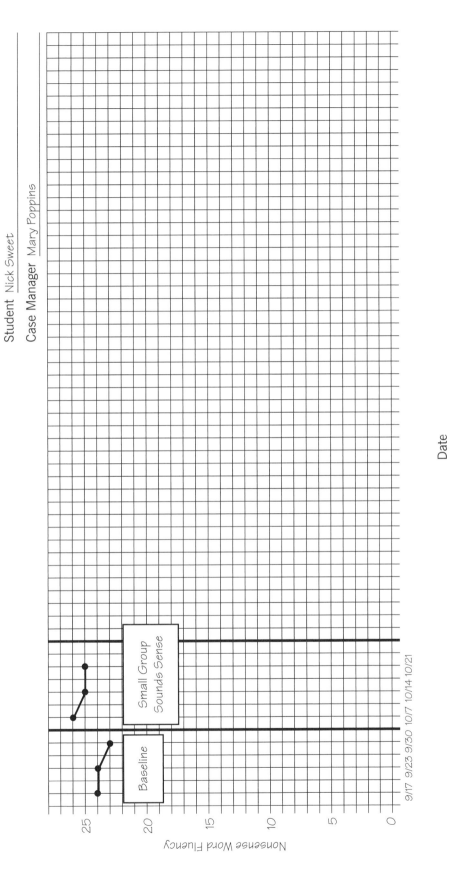

Student _Nick Sweet_

Case Manager _Mary Poppins_

Nonsense Word Fluency

25 · 20 · 15 · 10 · 5 · 0

Baseline

Small Group
Sounds Sense

9/17 9/23 9/30 10/7 10/14 10/21

Date

FIGURE 7.8. Example of a completed Progress Monitoring Graph.

academic and behavioral progress (Silberglitt & Hintze, 2007; VanDerHeyden & Burns, 2009; Van DerHeyden et al., 2007; Walker, Carta, Greenwood, & Buzhardt, 2008).

To assist teachers and teams in making sense of progress data, we have included a Student Progress Review Worksheet. A blank version is reproduced as Form 7.9, and Figure 7.9 shows a completed sample. This worksheet allows the teacher to review specific questions about a student's progress and make decisions based on the data. Data review sessions have been identified as essential for effective RTI practices (Duhon, Mesmer, Gregerson, & Witt, 2009). In this case, over the 6 weeks of instruction Nick's progress data showed little improvement, with all the test data varying only 3 points. Based on these data, his teacher decided to change his program. Starting on October 26, she switched him to a smaller group of two students. Nick's progress in the new grouping will be reviewed later in this chapter. Importantly, his teacher set a specific date to review his program again to see if the new group size helps Nick.

As seen in the examples for Nick, student progress data are at the center of RTI practices. Importantly, students who participate in Tier 2 instruction need to be assessed regularly for two reasons. First, frequent feedback on performance has been shown to enhance student progress. Second, only by collecting regular data will the student and teacher know whether the additional instruction is yielding the requisite progress in improving the student's skills. As noted, the nature of the progress data to be collected should be decided at the time the intervention is developed. In some cases, intervention programs come with progress assessment tools. For example, Great Leaps for reading and math includes daily assessment as part of the sessions, and progress monitoring charts are included in the kits. In cases where an intervention does not come with a progress measure, published ones can be used. Progress monitoring assessment items have been developed for basic reading, spelling, and math skills. The DIBELS system has progress monitoring forms for all DIBELS tasks, including oral reading fluency, in English and Spanish (Good & Kaminski, 2002). EasyCBM has progress measures in reading and math. The AIMSweb CBM measures include progress monitoring items for reading, spelling, writing, and math for purchase (Pearson Education, 2008). In situations where there is no appropriate progress measure set for the intervention being used, teachers can develop them by using the software at *www.interventioncentral.org*. There are two critical features that need to be integrated into progress monitoring assessments. First, they need to involve performance of exactly the same skills as those being taught in the intervention. Second, there need to be at least 20 forms of the items so that different forms can be used (so students will not memorize the answers).

In addition to the progress monitoring items themselves, teachers will want to have a way to graph student progress data. A reproducible graph for such purposes is found in Form 7.10. This graph has equal intervals across both the X and Y axes, and the student or teacher can fill in the numbers for the Y axis and dates on the X axis. Sample completed graphs are shown in Figures 7.8 and 7.10. Ideally, students should fill in their own data because it saves time for the teacher and helps students be in closer touch with their own skill performance. Progress monitoring data should be collected at least monthly at Tier 2. Many teachers chose to gather weekly data for students in Tier 2 interventions. If the

Student: Nick Sweet   Grade: 1   Teacher: Mary Poppins

Name of Tier 2 instruction program: Sounds Sense

Who is the teacher? Mary Poppins

How many students (total) are in the instruction group? 4

How often are the instructional sessions held? Daily

How long is each session? 30 minutes

How many sessions has this student attended? 27 out of 30

Based on the progress monitoring data, how many data points indicate that the student's skills are improving? 1

Based on the progress monitoring data, how many data points indicate that the student's skills are not improving? 4

How do the student's current skills compare to typically achieving peers? Nick's current score of 25 is below the minimum benchmark of 30 for midyear grade 1 students

Based on the obtained data, what modifications to the current instructional program will be made? Nick has not made sufficient progress in Sounds Sense during the past 2 weeks. I will begin 2:1 daily sessions with Nick and another student to see if a smaller group helps improve his reading.

When will the modifications go into effect? Monday, October 26

When will the student's progress be reviewed again? Friday, November 13

ALL PROGRESS-MONITORING DATA AND GRAPHS REFERENCED ABOVE MUST BE ATTACHED

Person completing this form: Mary Poppins, MEd   Date: October 21, 2009

FIGURE 7.9. Example of a completed Student Progress Review Worksheet.

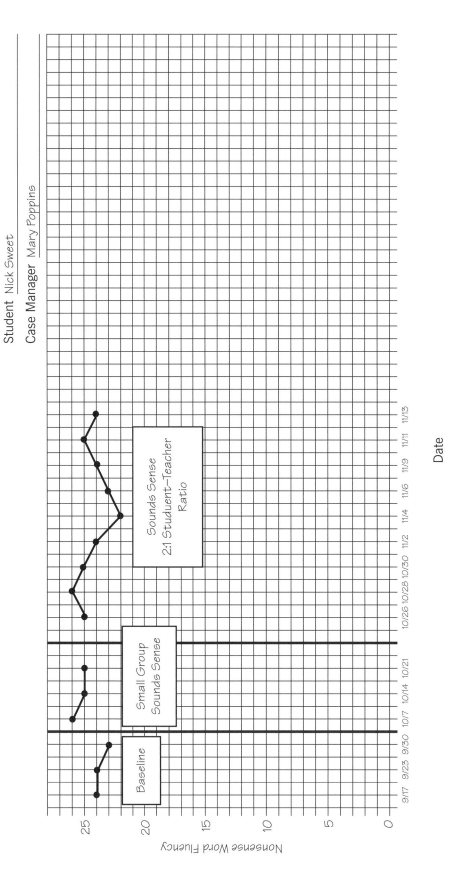

Student _Nick Sweet_

Case Manager _Mary Poppins_

Nonsense Word Fluency

Baseline

Small Group
Sounds Sense

Sounds Sense
2:1 Student–Teacher
Ratio

25   20   15   10   5   0

9/17 9/23 9/30 10/7 10/14 10/21 10/26 10/28 10/30 11/2 11/4 11/6 11/9 11/11 11/13

Date

FIGURE 7.10. Example of a completed Progress Monitoring Graph with additional intervention data.

progress data indicate that the student is making only very slow progress, an error analysis (like the one described earlier) can help identify where the student is encountering specific difficulties.

Step 6: Use Data-Based Instructional Decision Making

Once at least three data points are collected to show a student's progress, the graph can be reviewed to determine what the next step should be. As discussed in Chapter 5, the easiest way to conduct such a review is to use single-subject research methods. Specific criteria for reviewing the data are found in Chapter 5 on p. 62. The first step in such a process is to compare the student's performance from the preintervention stage (baseline) to the intervention stage. If none of the data points collected during each phase (baseline vs. intervention) overlap, then meaningful interpretations of the data can be made. If the intervention data share more than 20% of overlapping data points, then there is a concern that the intervention data are not meaningfully different from the baseline data. When data overlap too much, it is important to consider whether the intervention is working. In cases when the data points do not overlap more often than 20% of the time, if at all, intervention trends should be reviewed. Data showing an improvement in the student's skill suggests that the intervention is working. In these situations, the teacher needs to determine how soon the student is likely to reach the target performance level. If the data trend suggests that the learning goal will be reached in the expected time, the intervention should be continued until the student meets or exceeds the goal for at least 6 weeks (Powers et al., 2007).

Even when a student is making progress in the desired skills, the teacher needs to monitor the data continually to determine when the intervention can be reduced or discontinued. When a student has obtained six or more data points indicating grade-level performance of the skill, an intervention can be reduced or discontinued. Usually an intervention should be reduced gradually before being discontinued altogether. For example, a student who was receiving daily sessions could get two or three sessions a week with progress monitoring showing maintenance of the skill before the Tier 2 lessons are discontinued. In all cases, the data obtained from regular assessment of student progress totally determine the next course of action. For students who are successful as a result of Tier 2 interventions, additional RTI steps will not be needed. For those not successful yet, the remaining steps provide a way to continue student support.

Step 7: Increase the Intensity, Duration, and/or Frequency of Instruction

In cases where the data suggest that the student's skills are not improving sufficiently well, the current intervention needs to be changed or replaced. In some cases, intervention changes could include increasing the amount of time for intervention sessions, reducing the number of students participating in the sessions, or increasing the number of times the student practices the target skill during the intervention. If the teacher believes that such changes in the intervention are not likely to improve the student's skills sufficiently, then a new intervention should be undertaken. Importantly, many students who do not respond well to a first intervention will respond better to a second one. Often the intervention change that a student needs relates to *intensity*, that is, providing the student with more of the effective instructional practices described in Chapter 6 (Barnett, Daly, Jones, &

> **Teachers must know how to interpret progress data to make RTI work. When teachers adjust instruction in response to student learning needs, truly "responsive" instruction is provided.**

Lentz, 2004; Bryant, Bryant, Gersten, Scammacca, & Chavez, 2008; Clements, Bolt, Hoyt, & Kratochwill, 2007); Daly, Johnson, & LeClair, 2009). In Nick's case, his teacher decided to try teaching sessions with fewer students to see if the opportunity for Nick to respond more often in each session would help his reading skills. The progress data for this new intervention are shown in Figure 7.10.

As soon as the new intervention is implemented, the change in the instructional format needs to be noted on the progress monitoring graph. This can be done by drawing a vertical line at the point in the graph when the intervention changed (see Figure 7.10). So long as the same progress measure is being used with the new intervention, the new progress monitoring data can be recorded on the same graph as the old data. By recording the new scores on the same graph, comparisons between the interventions can more readily be made. *Any* changes in the intervention need to be noted on the graph with a vertical line. Even slight changes such as the length of sessions must be recorded so that the methodological differences between the interventions can be easily monitored.

Step 8: Review, Revise, or Discontinue Small-Group Instruction

As shown in Figure 7.10, Nick did not make any gains when the sessions included just two students. His scores on nonsense word fluency did not improve under the new conditions. As a result of these data, the problem-solving team decided to refer Nick for evaluation for special education. In our model of RTI, Tier 3 includes the special education referral and evaluation process *but not* special education itself (i.e., services provided through an IEP). All the data collected during the Tier 2 phases of the RTI process need to be used as part of the evaluation process and should accompany the special education referral form. Form 7.11 is a blank referral form, and Figure 7.11 shows a sample completed one. Importantly, this form provides information about the type, duration, frequency, and intensity of instruction used to help the student. A summary of the differences between Tiers 2 and 3 is found in Box 7.4.

As noted in Chapter 3, IDEA 2004 allows RTI data to be used as part of the evaluation procedures for determining whether a student has an SLD. Students who participate in Tier 3 are those for whom a group-based standard protocol intervention has not worked. For this reason, Tier 3 involves a different approach to helping students that relies on individual problem solving. Individual problem solving takes more time and energy than a standard protocol, but it is highly appropriate for students who do not respond adequately at Tier 2. The special education referral and evaluation process can take a long time. There are specific rules about what types of assessments to conduct, when team meetings will be

Student: Nick Sweet	Grade: 1	Teacher: Mary Poppins

Describe how student's instructional need was initially identified: Nick scored in the at-risk range on the kindergarten DIBELS at every benchmark period last year.

Tier 2 instructional methods that were used to improve student's knowledge/skills: 3 weeks of small-group Sounds Sense lessons with 4–5 students in the group followed by 3 weeks of Sounds Sense Lessons with 2 students in the group. Lessons covered sound–symbol mapping, practicing learned sounds in real and nonsense words, and reading short stories composed of learned words.

Who provided the Tier 2 instructional program?
Mary Poppins, Certified Highly Qualified Special Education Teacher

Progress monitoring measure used to record student's progress during Tier 2 instruction:
Nonsense word fluency of DIBELS

Tier 2 program start date: October 7	Tier 2 program review date(s): October 21, November 11

Describe the student's current instructional need(s): Nick needs to learn sound–symbol correspondence and master the alphabetic principle. He can decode a few words using this principle but has not mastered all letter sounds.

What, if any, additional instruction or supports is this student currently receiving?
Nick is receiving 30 minutes per day of Sounds Sense 2:1 instruction until a comprehensive evaluation can be completed.

ALL PROGRESS MONITORING DATA AND GRAPHS REFERENCED ABOVE MUST BE ATTACHED

Person completing this form: Mary Poppins, MEd	Date: November 11, 2009

FIGURE 7.11. Example of a completed Tier 3 Referral for Special Education Worksheet.

BOX 7.4. What's the Difference between Tier 2 and Tier 3?

In terms of the materials and methods, there is really no difference between the interventions used at Tier 2 and Tier 3. What distinguishes tier 2 and 3 interventions is the intensity applied. At Tier 2, less intensive instruction is provided, and at Tier 3 more intensive work is done. For example, at Tier 2, the intervention time is likely to be about 30 minutes 2-4 times a week. Usually there are 4-6 students in the Tier 2 intervention group. At Tier 3, longer sessions are held daily and there are usually fewer students in the group. Tier 2 interventions never replace the core instruction in the classroom; Tier 3 interventions sometimes replace certain core instruction. Below is a chart that lists key features of Tier 2 and 3 interventions in terms of type, group size, frequency, and other details. Notice that both Tier 2 and 3 interventions are always accompanied by regular progress monitoring.

Feature	Tier 2	Tier 3
Type	Scientifically based	Scientifically based
Group size	4–6 students	1–3 students
Frequency	2–4 times per week	5 times per week
Duration	20–30 minutes	30–90 minutes
Can replace core?	No	Yes
Uses progress monitoring?	Yes	Yes

held, and who will attend. While the referral process unfolds, the student will still need assistance. During Tier 3, students continue to participate in intensive intervention. Exactly what Tier 3 interventions to use depends on the student's needs. The interventions used at Tier 3 can be thought of as "diagnostic teaching." Specifically, this approach entails trying out very intensive instruction with the student, often one-on-one, to see if it helps. As with Tier 2, progress data must also be collected at Tier 3 (Stecker, 2007). Normally these data are collected frequently, such as weekly or even daily. These progress data are used as part of the evaluation process and document whether the student responds well to highly intensive instruction. An excellent resource or how to conduct Tier 3 interventions and assessments is the book *Tier 3 of the RTI Model* by Hunley and McNamara (2010). This book provides a step-by-step guide to selecting, identifying, and analyzing data from Tier 3 interventions.

Step 9: Comprehensive Evaluation

What about situations in which the student does not make progress despite use of several evidence-based interventions? When the best interventions known to help students succeed in school do not produce the requisite gains, and the student is still not making overall progress, the student should be referred for a comprehensive evaluation for special education eligibility. As noted in Chapter 2, RTI methods are included in both NCLB and IDEA 2004.

In other words, schools need to try to meet a student's learning needs before referring him or her to special education. Those students who are not successful in school despite the use of scientifically based instruction at Tiers 1 and 2 of the RTI model may have significant and chronic needs that are best met with more specialized educational services. Not all comprehensive evaluations are the same. As outlined in IDEA 2004, the evaluation procedures need to take into account the specific presenting needs of the student as well as the data collected as part of RTI procedures. The goal of the evaluation process is to identify and define the specific nature of the student's difficulties in school (Flanagan & Harrison, 2005). Even if the evaluation must be done very quickly, such as when a student is facing suspension or expulsion, RTI data are very important data to include (Clopton & Etscheidt, 2009).

> **When a student is still struggling despite carefully designed multi-tier interventions, additional information and resources are needed. The comprehensive evaluation is conducted to help provide more detailed information about the student's school difficulties. This information is used to generate alternative possible educational solutions.**

Step 10: Special Education Eligibility

If, as a result of comprehensive evaluation, the special education team determines that a student is eligible for special education services, the team will then need to develop an IEP that includes scientifically based instruction to meet the student's needs. Only a special education team has the legal right to determine whether a student is eligible for special education. A few students may be eligible for special education and receive all instruction through special education, whereas many others may participate in both general and special education programs. In all cases, student progress needs to be monitored frequently so that the effectiveness of the instruction is documented and changes to programs based on data can be provided. The progress monitoring steps used in Tiers 2 and 3 of RTI can also be used to monitor student progress in his or her IEP.

SUMMARY

This chapter has provided a comprehensive discussion of the steps included in RTI practices. There are 10 possible steps that educators need to consider when implementing RTI procedures in schools. Not all students will need all 10 steps. The worksheet forms included in the chapter offer educators tools to develop their own skills in utilizing RTI methods. Teachers may choose to customize the worksheets and procedures described here. So long as the instructional methods are scientifically based and accurate data about student progress are collected frequently, local adaptations of RTI are likely to yield beneficial results, on balance, for all students.

RTI Implementation Checklist

Check	RTI steps
_____	1. Implement scientifically based general education instructional methods. _____ Verify accuracy of instructional procedures with integrity assessment.
_____	2. Collect benchmarks of all students' performance at least three times during the school year.
_____	3. Identify which students scored below the benchmark target(s).
_____	4. Provide daily scientifically based small-group instruction to students with scores below benchmark target(s) for at least 3 weeks. _____ Verify fidelity of instructional procedures through an integrity assessment.
_____	5. Monitor student progress toward the benchmark(s), using daily assessments and data graphing for 3 weeks.
_____	6. Review, revise, and/or discontinue small-group instruction, based on student performance and progress toward the benchmark at the end of 3 weeks.
_____	7. For students not yet showing evidence of progress toward meeting the benchmark(s) by the end of the first 3 weeks, increase the intensity, duration, and/or frequency of instruction and continue to monitor progress for up to another 3 weeks.
_____	8. Review, revise, and/or discontinue small-group instruction based on student performance and attainment of the benchmark at the end of the second 3 weeks.
_____	9. For any student not showing evidence of meeting the benchmark(s) by the end of the school year, initiate a comprehensive evaluation to determine whether the student has a disability and is eligible for special education services.
_____	10. IEP team determines whether the student has a disability and meets the criteria for special education services; if the student is eligible for special education, an IEP is developed and becomes the student's new instructional program.

Instructional Materials Review Worksheet

Program	Publisher (Date)	Research Evidence	Connections to Local Goals	Observations

Treatment Integrity Checklist

Teacher's Name: _____   Date: _____   Time: _____

Subject/Lesson: _____   Evaluator: _____ Self Other: _____

Directions: The individual implementing this intervention is to complete this form at the end of every day regarding how he or she implemented the intervention during that day.

Intervention implemented by: _____ Classroom teacher _____ Other: _____

Intervention Component	Completed		Comments
	Yes	No	

Benchmark Planning Worksheet

School/District: _____ Year: _____ Benchmark: F   W   S

Task	Person(s) Responsible	Deadline	Costs	Completed	Initials
Select materials for benchmarks					
Obtain/copy needed materials					
Make student name labels (if needed)					
Train those collecting data					
Organize/distribute materials					
Collect benchmarks on stated dates					
Collect make-up benchmarks from absent students					
Enter student scores into computer					
Create and distribute data summaries					
Identify students of concern					
IMPLEMENT NEXT RTI STEP: TIER 2 INSTRUCTION					

Notes:

Benchmark Implementation Worksheet

What	When	Who	Where	Materials Needed	Data Ready by
Fall Benchmarks					
Winter Benchmarks					
Spring Benchmarks					

FORM 7.6

Tier 2 Instruction Planning Worksheet

Student	Describe Instructional Need	Instructional Method to Be Tried	Progress Monitoring Measure	Program Start Date	Progress Review Date	Person Responsible

Error Analysis Worksheet

Student's Name: _____   Grade: _____

Universal Screening Data Analyzed:

Reading:

_____ Initial Sound Fluency (ISF)

_____ Letter Naming Fluency (LNF)

_____ Letter Sound Fluency (LSF)

_____ Phoneme Segmentation Fluency (PSF)

_____ Nonsense Word Fluency (NWF)

_____ Oral Reading Fluency (ORF)

_____ Maze

_____ Other: _____

Math:

_____ Oral Counting (OC)

_____ Number Identification (NI)

_____ Quantity Discrimination (QD)

_____ Missing Number (MN)

_____ Single Skill Type: _____

_____ Mixed Skill Types: _____

_____ Math Concepts and Applications (MCAP)

_____ Other: _____

Writing:

_____ Correct Letter Sequences (CLS)

_____ Total Words Written (TWW)

_____ Correct Word Sequences (CWS)

_____ Other: _____

Behavior (lists behaviors of concern):

_____ Systematic Screening for Behavior Disorders

_____ Social Skills Improvement System

_____ Other: _____

_____ Other: _____

Based on the screening data collected, answer the following questions:

1. How many items did the student get correct? _____

2. How many errors did the student make? _____

3. List the actual errors here: _____

_____

_____

_____

_____

4. What is the primary type of error made? _____

_____

_____

_____

_____

5. Other notes about student's work: _____

_____

_____

_____

_____

Tier 2 Instructional Materials Review Worksheet

Program (publisher and date)	Knowledge and Skills Covered in Program	Program Age/Grade	Research Evidence Supporting Program	How Is Student Progress in Program Monitored?	Costs (with training)

FORM 7.9

Student Progress Review Worksheet

Student:	Grade:	Teacher:
Name of Tier 2 instruction program:	
Who is the teacher?	
How many students (total) are in the instruction group?	
How often are the instructional sessions held?	
How long is each session?	
How many sessions has this student attended?	
Based on the progress monitoring data, how many data points indicate that the student's skills are improving?	
Based on the progress monitoring data, how many data points indicate that the student's skills are not improving?	
How do the student's current skills compare to typically achieving peers?	
Based on the obtained data, what modifications to the current instructional program will be made?	
When will the modifications go into effect?	
When will the student's progress be reviewed again?	
ALL PROGRESS MONITORING DATA AND GRAPHS REFERENCED ABOVE MUST BE ATTACHED	
Person completing this form:	Date:

Progress Monitoring Graph

Student _____

Case Manager _____

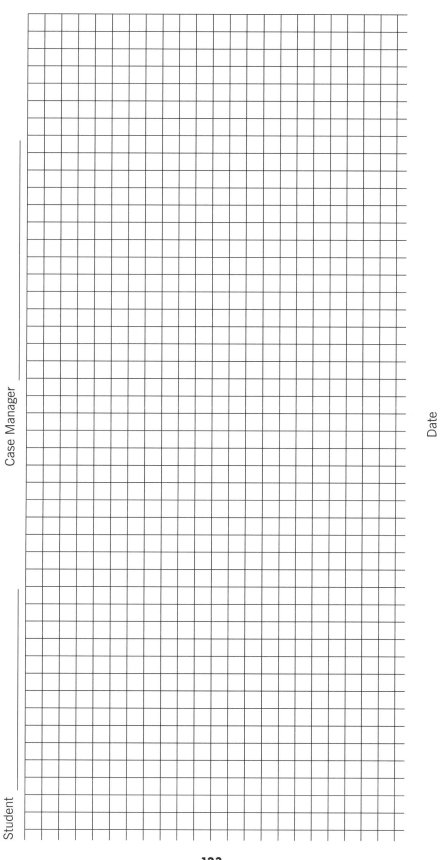

Date _____

Tier 3 Referral for Special Education Worksheet

Student:	Grade:	Teacher:
Describe how student's instructional need was initially identified:		
Tier 2 instructional methods that were used to improve student's knowledge/skills:		
Who provided the Tier 2 instructional program?		
Progress monitoring measure used to record student's progress during Tier 2 instruction:		
Tier 2 program start date:	Tier 2 program review date(s):	
Describe the student's current instructional need(s):		
What, if any, additional instruction or supports is this student currently receiving?		
ALL PROGRESS MONITORING DATA AND GRAPHS REFERENCED ABOVE MUST BE ATTACHED		
Person completing this form:	Date:	

CHAPTER 8

Using RTI Procedures with Students from Diverse Backgrounds

Considering Ability, Culture, Language, Race, and Religion

DIVERSE STUDENT BACKGROUNDS AND NEEDS

Students in U.S. schools come from a wide variety of backgrounds (National Center for Education Statistics, 2004). In some areas of the United States, the majority of students speak Spanish (or another language). Many students have distinct racial, cultural, and linguistic ability, and religious identities that are different from dominant U.S. traditions. As a result of these unique backgrounds, some students may enter school with expectations and beliefs substantially different from those held by their teachers. Indeed, although the population of school students is becoming increasingly diverse, the demographic profile of U.S. teachers remains primarily English-speaking and Caucasian (Jones, 2009; National Center for Education Statistics, 2004). One of the possible outcomes from such differences in student and teacher backgrounds is that students may feel misunderstood by their teachers (Cartledge, 1996). While RTI procedures have been shown to be effective with students from a wide variety of backgrounds and experiences, educators also need to take into account the unique qualities of their students when using RTI methods (Brown & Doolittle, 2008; Haager, 2007). Sadly, in the past, students from diverse backgrounds have been too frequently identified as having disabilities (Rinaldi & Samson, 2008). This chapter provides a discussion and explanation of how RTI steps can be used effectively with students who are possessed of both a wide variety of abilities and, equally, a wide diversity of cultural, linguistic, racial, and religious identities.

The remarkable range of backgrounds represented among U.S. families means that not all students share the same expectations regarding their school experiences (Boscardin,

Brown-Chidsey, & Gonzalez-Martinez, 2002a; Delpit & Kohl, 2006). For example, a student whose parents immigrated to the United States for the purpose of providing their children with a better education may start school with a totally different mindset than one whose parents had limited and only negative school encounters during their own childhood. While each family will have certain characteristics that are truly unique, certain features that can

> Don't be "color-blind"; diversity is about more than simply ethnicity, race, and languages. Diversity of ability, religion, and socioeconomic status is also an important aspect of how students differ.

be used to understand the typical school expectations of students and their families (Xu & Drame, 2008). Below we discuss five key features of students' backgrounds that are likely to influence their school expectations and experiences, namely, ability, culture, language, race, and religion.

Ability

Ability is a somewhat imprecise generic term that we have chosen to describe certain aspects of an individual student's early childhood competencies that relate to all domains of human development. The opposite of ability is *dis*ability. The term *disability* is widely used to refer to developmental proclivities that affect all aspects of a person's life. Still, the term *disability* has a distinctly negative connotation; thus, we prefer to use the term *ability* instead. By ability, we mean the person-specific characteristics and features that influence school experiences and performance. For example, a student with cerebral palsy may or may not have muscular or orthopedic difficulties that could affect school activities. Similarly, a student with autism could have person-specific behaviors that affect interpersonal communications. By using the term *ability*, we want to focus on what the student *can* do, not what he or she cannot do. By the time a student enters school, specific ability-related experiences are likely to have shaped his or her learning history, and these experiences are bound to have effects on the student and his or her family's expectations about school.

In the case of such conditions as hearing impairment, blindness, autism, and genetic abnormalities, a student's unique abilities and specific limitations will have been well identified long before his or her entry into school (Brown & Brown, 2005). Indeed, there is a huge benefit to early identification and intervention for many such conditions (Bagnato & Neisworth, 1991). For example, in the case of hearing impairment or deafness, it is likely that a student's family will have already made certain key decisions about the communication instruction desired for the student. This instruction could include using American Sign Language (ASL), Signed Exact English (SEE), oral language training, hearing aids, or a combination of all these approaches. For students with hearing loss, the choice of communication instruction begins well before kindergarten but will have a lasting impact of

> Diversity begins at home. "We are each an experiment of one.... We are all unique, never-to-be-repeated events" (Sheehan, 2009).

all subsequent schooling. Similarly, for students with conditions identified at birth and during early childhood, their history of past interventions must be taken into account when they initially enter school. The student's early childhood interventions and his or her experiences with them inevitably influence personal expectations and goals for subsequent school performance.

Other students may have ability characteristics that have not been specifically identified until the time of formal school entry. This is one of the reasons for *child find* requirements and activities. Child find is a provision of IDEA that requires all public schools, as well as preschool intervention programs for students ages 3–5, to locate and assist any and all students with developmental needs prior to kindergarten. The goal of child find is to identify and provide interventions for students who would benefit from early intervention services. Kindergarten screening procedures are part of child find activities because they offer a way to review the ability profiles of all students when they enter formal schooling at age 5. In some cases, students with developmental ability needs are not identified until the kindergarten screening—or even later. Again, the point in time when a student's specific ability profile is formally described is likely to meaningfully shape both the student's and family's expectations about his or her prospective performance in school.

For example, if a student is identified at the kindergarten screening as needing language intervention services, that occasion might be the first time that the student and his family had been informed about possible differences in that student's learning and developmental patterns as compared to other children of the same age. If the family went to the screening believing that the student was completely ready for kindergarten and with no obvious ability differences, then this news might well be shocking. How school personnel share such information about students' ability profiles is extremely important. If a family's first encounter with the school system includes information about how a child's abilities are lacking in some major way, that experience may well negatively influence how family members think about and react to later encounters with school officials. In order to optimize the family–school relationship, school personnel must take into account the family's beliefs, perceptions, and experiences about the student's abilities prior to school entry (Boscardin, Brown-Chidsey, & Gonzalez-Martinez, 2002b).

Culture

A second important background feature for school personnel to take into account is the student's culture. The term *culture* is also generic; however, we have chosen to include it because it offers a way of understanding important aspects of students' life experiences outside of school. Students' cultural backgrounds can overlap with all the other experiences we discuss. However, cultural patterns and beliefs are specific enough to warrant their own description. For example, students with hearing impairment or deafness have ability characteristics that must be taken into account by school personnel. They are likely also to have cultural experiences that overlap with their ability profiles. In the United States there is an identifiable "deaf culture" that must be understood by educators. Within deaf culture, hearing is considered unnecessary and visual communication with ASL or SEE is the norm. Understanding the presence of deaf culture is critical for those who work with students who are deaf or hard-of-hearing.

There are numerous other cultures that educators also must understand. It would be impossible to list all of the cultural variations likely to influence school expectations. However, we will discuss some cultural patterns that may influence a student's school experiences. One important cultural pattern is expectations relating to family–school communications and interaction. In some cultural groups, only very limited family–school communications are expected. In such cases, family members—as well as the student—expect that family events and school activities are entirely different and will not overlap. Similarly, some cultural traditions include specific ways of communicating with and referring to school personnel. For some cultures, very formal interactions are the norm. For example, the school principal, teacher(s), and other school personnel should always be referred to by their formal title, such as Dr., Ms., or Mr. In some cultures this expectation is reciprocal, and the parents and other family members expect to be called by their formal names too. If a teacher were to misunderstand this cultural expectation and refer to a parent or other family member by a first name, a significant miscommunication could occur (Boscardin et al., 2002b). In other cultures, the use of first names, even between children and parents or teachers, is readily accepted. All school personnel need to be aware of such cultural variations (Jones, 2009; Ortiz & Flanagan, 2002).

Language

As seen in the preceding examples, language is closely related to culture. Language and culture are interconnected and have a huge impact on students' school experiences (R. Lopez, 1997; Wright, 2004). There are differences of opinion regarding public school policies about language instruction. Some policymakers have advocated for English-only school instruction (Purdum, 1998). Others have supported full bilingual instruction that helps students maintain and strengthen their primary language while learning English (Cummins, 1986, 1996). Research findings have supported full bilingual instruction as the best choice for students' long-term educational outcomes (Willig, 1985). Regardless of the instructional policy and program(s) provided in school, educators must be aware of the effect that language proficiency has on school outcomes (E. Lopez, 1997). Students who are still learning English in an English-only school will be at a disadvantage as compared to those who are fluent in English (August & Hakuta, 1997). The same is true for the parents and other family members. If a parent knows little or no English and that is the only language in which school documents are distributed, the parent will have great difficulty participating fully in his or her child's school experience. Similarly, it will be very difficult to have parents participate in the RTI process if the materials and communications are not provided in a common language.

Sometimes it is difficult to assess accurately a student's or parent's English proficiency from observation alone, in part owing to basic differences between two identified levels of language development, basic interpersonal communication skills (BICS) and cognitive academic language proficiency (CALP) (Cummins, 1979). BICs skills develop much more quickly than does CALP. Generally learners can develop BICS in English in about 2 years but need at least 5 years to develop CALP (Cummins, 1979). On the basis of observations with peers, it may appear that a student or parent can communicate effectively in English (Boscardin et al., 2002a) since oral communications with peers in a second language develop more rapidly than formal written language. Watching students and adults talk with others in English about everyday topics may therefore provide a false impression of overall English language development. Nonverbal communication, including gestures and eye gaze, support such use of English by those still learning it. But conversational English is not the same as formal English usage. The ability to talk briefly with classmates and teachers is not the same as reading and writing English. For this reason, educators must not assume that a student or parent is fluent in English on the basis of brief verbal interactions alone. Instead, it is imperative that all those who work in schools be aware of the stages of English language acquisition and provide appropriate supports to those students and their family members who are still learning English.

Race

The United States has a complex racial history. Although recent decades have witnessed policies and practices designed to improve equal treatment of all persons under the law, a long legacy of racial discrimination and segregation cannot be erased overnight. Although all persons have nominal equality according to the U.S. Constitution and its amendments, ongoing evidence of racial inequality still exists. Regarding education, data continue to show that students of color, including African Americans, Hispanics, and Asians, have different educational outcomes than other students, especially Caucasians (National Center for Education Statistics, 2004). Despite evidence that students of all racial backgrounds share similar potential for school success (Helms, 1992), students from certain racial minorities often score lower on school assessment measures. Other evidence has shown that when students from racial minorities are provided with a combination of adequate resources and effective instruction, they perform as well as or better than racial majority students (Chall, 2000). As noted by Carter, Helms, and Juby (2004) and Tatum (1997), racial identity is a powerful factor in individual life experiences, including school. Importantly, racial identity affects all persons, regardless of skin color, and educators need to be aware of how race and racial identity influence students' school experiences.

Some of the seminal work on racial identity was conducted by Kenneth and Mamie Clark (Klein, 2004). This work showed the effects of negative racial identity and was used in the landmark 1954 *Brown v. Board of Education* U.S. Supreme Court case. That case brought attention to the differences in educational outcomes between students of color (primarily African Americans) and Caucasian students. The Brown decision declared that "separate but equal" schools were not allowable because the schools for African-American students were in fact substantially inferior to schools for Caucasian children. Despite many years of efforts to improve educational outcomes for students of color, there remains a racial divide in educational attainment (Carter et al., 2004). Specifically, students of color are less likely that Caucasians students to complete high school and be competitive wage earners (National Center for Education Statistics, 2004). Students of color also are much more likely to be placed in special education as compared a Caucasian student with exactly the same profile.

Knowledge about racial inequality in U.S. schools is important for those who implement RTI policies because many of the students most in need of effective teaching and Tier 2 interventions are students from racial minorities. Being aware of how a student's racial identity has informed his or her mindset about school and personal goals is important. If a student—of any race—has decided that he or she cannot "do" the work expected in school, an additional hurdle on the path to school success is immediately presented. In cases of low self-efficacy among students, educators need to know about and use instructional methods that include frequent reinforcers for the attainment of specific goals. For example, there are ways to identify whether a student has a skill or performance deficit. Sometimes known as a "can't do/won't do" assessment, this process involves determining whether the student has the necessary skills to complete given assignments (VanDerHeyden, 2008). Additionally, educators need to be knowledgeable about the history of racial discrimination in the United States and be willing to confront racism when it is observed in schools. Equally important is equitable and representative coverage of the historical events important to the racial groups in each school setting.

Religion

Religion and religious practice have played a critical role in the history of the United States. All Native American cultures have strong religious traditions that are interwoven into their everyday practices. Similarly, European settlers in North America brought with them specific religious beliefs that defined their communities from the earliest days of settlement. While some early explorers and settlers traveled primarily for commercial reasons, others such as the Pilgrims and Puritans, as well as the Roman Catholic founders of Maryland and the Spanish explorers in the coastal Pacific areas, brought with them various Christian traditions that have shaped North American values ever since. Indeed, the framers of the first 10 amendments to the U.S. Constitution were so concerned about the freedom to practice one's own religious beliefs that such a protection was included in the First Amendment.

Despite constitutional protection of religious practice, schools have not been immune to conflicts and misunderstandings among students and staff of various faiths. Ranging from such matters as which holidays to include in school vacations to whether Christmas carols can be sung by school choirs, there are many ways in which religious beliefs and practices have an effect on school practices. Students who are absent from school owing to religious celebrations may miss out on important events or be viewed by classmates as "outsiders." Specific religious doctrines also have been a source of disputes in schools. For example, in some communities there is widespread support for teaching a "creationist" view of human origins, while textbooks and science teachers generally subscribe to evolutionary principles. Although such issues are normally handled by the courts, there is apt to be a lingering effect from the public debate after the case is settled. For these reasons, educators need to be aware of the ways in which religious beliefs are a universal and significant human tradition.

FAIRNESS AND EQUITY IN EDUCATION

Related to all of the many ways that "diversity" can be interpreted is the issue of equity. As much as an appreciation for and celebration of all backgrounds and cultures may be a desirable goal, public schools have a specific defined task before them, namely, to provide an equitable education for all students who enroll. For this reason, it is imperative that all educators know about and be prepared to work with a wide variety of students, regardless of ability, culture, language, race, or religion. Given the highly mobile and international mixture of students enrolled in U.S. schools in the 21st century, it would be impossible for every teacher to be versed in all aspects of his or her students' backgrounds. Still, educators can be aware of their own expertise and limitations. Some teachers will be able to offer specialized skills such as bilingual instruction, special education, and knowledge about specific cultures. A critical element of what educators know and do to help students from diverse backgrounds relates to assessment practices.

Assessment

High-quality, reliable, and valid assessments are a cornerstone of RTI practices. Without accurate baseline data, it is impossible to know whether a student has made progress as a result of an intervention (Brown-Chidsey et al., 2008; Shinn, Collins, & Gallagher, 1998). *Accuracy* is the key to valid assessment. The extent to which assessment methods designed for majority group students also work with students from diverse backgrounds varies considerably (Boscardin et al., 2002a; Jones, 2009). For example, a student who was born in the United States and grew up speaking, reading, and writing both Spanish and English equally may be able to take tests designed for English-speaking U.S. students. By contrast, a student who immigrated from another country very recently and is still mastering a BICS level of English proficiency should not be expected to participate in testing designed for students fluent in U.S. English and culture. For this reason, three major rules concerning assessment of students from diverse background should be followed during all RTI activities: (1) recognize that ability, culture, language, race, and/or religious variables may influence students' school performance; (2) evaluate a student's mastery of skills in the primary culture and language first; (3) plan and implement RTI activities that focus on attainment of instructional objectives while taking into account each student's unique background and characteristics.

Recognition of Diversity

The first step in conducting RTI practices that are fair and equitable is to identify the features present in students that are unique and diverse. This step seems very simple and yet may take considerable energy and planning. In order to know students' backgrounds, educators need to spend sufficient time with them and their families engaged in activities that enable families to share their experiences. School–community gatherings, family events at school, and informal contact between educators and family members all promote better understanding of the diversity present in the school population.

Background-Specific Assessments

In cases where a student's background is sufficiently unique that assessments using norm-referenced tests are not appropriate, alternative assessment procedures need to be used. A guiding principle for ascertaining whether a student should complete a published norm-referenced assessment is to determine whether students with the same background were included in the norming sample (Salvia & Ysseldyke, 2009). If a student's background characteristics (e.g., language, race, culture, ability) were not represented in the norming sample, decisions about that student's educational performance should not be based on that test. For example, if students with Asperger's syndrome were not included in the norming sample for a given assessment, students with that disorder should not take the test. The same should hold true for students who are recent immigrants. This important principle creates a major challenge for educators whose job it is to teach all students, regardless of background.

The best approach to take regarding assessment of students from diverse cultures is to start with an evaluation of each student's skill in relation to instructional objectives. For example, if it is a stated instructional goal for all students in second grade to learn to subtract while borrowing from columns, then a baseline assessment of this skill is appropriate. In the case of specific assessments, language diversity takes on a prominent role. Even when evaluating a student's math skills, a decision about what language to use in order to conduct the assessment must be made. In general, it is best to identify the student's dominant language as a first step toward RTI instructional planning.

Language learning is a universal aspect of human development. Even among those with hearing and vision impairment, development of functional communication is a primary goal from the time of diagnosis. Once a student's primary language is identified, a decision about which language to use for subsequent instruction must be made. As noted earlier in this chapter, some school districts and states have adopted policies concerning English-only instruction that educators will need to observe. Ideally, students should be allowed to have formal instruction in multiple languages if that is observed to be a culturally or religiously valued goal. However, not all instruction must happen in school, and some language instruction (e.g., in Hebrew or Arabic) may have to occur outside the school setting. In situations where a student's family is fully bilingual and bilingual instruction is both desired and available, this is the optimal solution (Willig, 1985).

In situations where instruction in one language only is permitted, or where there is a time limit for transitional bilingual instruction, RTI procedures and decision making need to take into account the level of the student's current language development, including an estimate of current English proficiency. In many cases such an assessment will require the skills of a bilingual assessment professional. Such individuals are in short supply and may be unavailable for certain regions and languages. When a bilingual assessor is unavailable, a translator may be used, but this method must be noted in all assessment reports and the limitations related to the use of translators described. At a minimum, RTI assessment methods should include an estimate of the student's current skills in the language in which instruction will be provided. This estimate must be taken into account during all RTI procedures. Additionally, progress toward language development goals should be included in all RTI goals and progress monitoring. Given that fluency in standard English is both an explicit and implicit goal in all U.S. educational standards, specifically including English progress monitoring in RTI activities is most likely a good idea.

> *Fair* **and** *equal* **are not the same thing. Some students need different instruction to benefit from public education.**

Appropriate Goal Setting

A related outgrowth of language-specific RTI assessment is goal setting. All RTI procedures involve evaluating students' progress toward certain goals and adjusting instruction to foster the target skill. In some cases, the nature of a student's goals will vary according to that student's unique characteristics. This latter circumstance is most obvious in the case of students with known disabilities. Certain disorders and conditions are likely to influence expected learning outcomes, and a student's goals should reflect these expectations—as should also be the case for students with other diverse backgrounds. For example, in some cultures there may be different expectations for boys and girls. Teachers need to be aware of how family expectations may influence students' school performance, a requirement that especially can be challenging because U.S. education policies focus on equal educational opportunities for boys and girls. Similarly, in some cultures, it may be the norm for multiple generations to participate in child rearing and education decisions. Thus, knowing which family members to invite to meetings is essential.

How RTI Connects Diverse Backgrounds

RTI methods are dynamic and are designed to be used in ways that match the needs of specific students and populations. The choice of what interventions to try at each stage is up to those individuals charged with curriculum decision making in the school or district. The only "rule" that must be followed when selecting specific interventions is that they be research-based. Also central to RTI is trying interventions and using data to determine whether student outcomes are enhanced. There is nothing in RTI to require that the methodology be bound by specific ability, culture, language, race, or religious ideologies. For this reason, interventions can be matched to students' backgrounds and experiences. In many ways RTI methods are preferable to older models for curriculum and instructional decision making that focused primarily on instructional content. RTI focuses on ensuring that *all* students—regardless of ability, culture, language, race, and/or religion—obtain an education. The specific goals and content of the education are up to the local and state policymakers who determine learning standards and goals. In cases where specific learning outcomes are considered to be inappropriate for a student, alternative learning goals need to be set.

Data from studies that have examined the effects of RTI practices for students from diverse backgrounds have shown that RTI can indeed help all students be more successful in school. Most of the data available so far comes from studies of students who are English language learners (ELLs). Linan-Thompson, Cirino, and Vaughn (2007) found that the procedures used to identify English-speaking students at risk of reading problems, as well as to monitor student progress, work equally well for ELL students. Interestingly, when RTI interventions were provided in Spanish and compared with outcomes of those in English, growth in knowledge for both groups of students was observed (Linan-Thompson, Vaughn, Prater, & Cirino, 2006; Vaughn, Mathes, Linan-Thompson, & Francis, 2005). These findings are important because they suggest that the language of instruction is not a barrier to helping students improve their reading skills. Similarly, McIntosh, Graves, and Gersten (2007) found that it was the type of instruction used and not whether the students were ELLs that mattered in student outcomes. McMaster, Kung, Han, and Chao (2008) found that an intervention often used at Tier 1, Peer Assisted Learning Strategies, can also be effective for ELL students.

RTI methods offer educators a systematic and data-driven way to identify whether any given student is meeting specific learning goals. For this reason, RTI can help educators to bridge their various diverse backgrounds by focusing on common goals. In order to create and implement common goals, there need to be planning and development steps based on the backgrounds and experiences of the students involved. The best people to include in such planning are not only teachers but also parents, other family members, and community representatives who are interested in educational planning and growth for all students. Although differences between the school personnel and community members may seem large at first, a commitment to common goals can reduce that divide and foster better outcomes for all students. Other researchers have found similar success with middle school ELL students (Denton, Wexler, Vaughn, & Bryan (2008). Success has also been attained with interventions for emotional disabilities (Harris-Murri, King, & Rostenberg, 2006) and for Alaska Native students (Kashi, 2008).

SUMMARY

This chapter has provided information concerning the use of RTI methods with students of differing abilities, cultures, languages, races, and religions. U.S. schools are becoming more diverse, and all educators need to make themselves aware of the unique backgrounds and experiences among the students and families in their district. As schools seek to improve educational outcomes for all students, they must incorporate practices that recognize and value the abilities, cultures, languages, races, and religions that students bring with them to school. RTI procedures can enhance school outcomes for diverse student populations by focusing on educational goals that reflect community values as well as state or national standards.

CHAPTER 9

Developing RTI Blueprints
Connecting the Dots

PROCESS MATTERS

At about the same time that we were working on the first edition of this book, another team of educators who had been doing RTI for a number of years were working on a book as well. That book, titled *Response to Intervention: Policy Considerations and Implementation* (Batsche et al., 2005), differed from ours in a number of significant ways. While our book focused on the detailed steps needed to implement RTI, theirs offered a comprehensive view of the systems-level changes that must accompany RTI. The Batsche et al. (2005) book is an important contribution to the overall literature on RTI because it provides guidance about the process of making RTI happen. You may have been wondering to yourself, "How can I possibly put all 10 steps of RTI in place in my classroom or school?" *You can't.* No one person can implement RTI alone (Brown-Chidsey, Bronaugh, & McGraw, 2009). This is why guidance about the process that school teams need to follow to make RTI happen is important. This chapter provides information about the overall process that a school, district, or state must follow to make responsive intervention a reality. RTI is a general education initiative but it requires collaboration between general and special education, and many special educators have assisted with developing RTI practices (see Box 9.1).

Batsche et al. provided a very strong framework for how to begin the process of considering and implementing RTI. In that initial work, they encouraged educators seeking to implement RTI to create a *blueprint* for their work. They recommended the blueprint framework because it shows all the underlying plans needed before RTI actions (such as those we have described in Chapter 7) can happen. Just as a builder must have a blueprint before constructing a building, educators need a blueprint for the RTI system they seek to build. The initial blueprint model that Batsche et al. developed has been revised, and there are now three types of blueprint models available, matched to the three main levels of RTI implementation: school, district, and state (Palenchar & Boyer, 2008) (see Box 9.2 for infor-

---

BOX 9.1. If RTI Is a General Education Initiative, Why Are So Many Special Educators Involved?

You might be wondering why so many of the resources related to RTI also have links to special education. After all, we did tell you that RTI is a general education "thing" and that it's not about changing special education. You are right—but there *are* ways that resources once found only in special education can be helpful also in general education.

The transition of a tool from a specialized use to a more general purpose is called *technology transfer*. There are many helpful tools that we use every day that are the result of technology transfer. Look at the following list of items; what do they have in common?

> Radar
> Microwave oven
> Velcro
> Nylon tights or pantyhose
> Cell phones

All of these items are examples of technology transfer. All of these products were originally researched and developed for highly specialized (and sometimes top-secret) military or space purposes. In time, these technologies were supplanted by even fancier ones. The original ones still have great value in everyday life; so the technologies were transferred to commercial applications.

RTI includes a great deal of technology transfer as well. Many of the teaching and assessment methods useful in RTI started out as special education programs and methods. For example, CBM, direct instruction, and PBIS were all initially developed to help students with disabilities. In time, research has shown that these are technologies that can be useful to *all* students; so they have been transferred for use in general education.

---

mation about how to get copies of the blueprint templates). Equally important to the role of RTI blueprints is the role of school-based teams who work together to make RTI happen.

> **RTI blueprints are just like architectural blueprints in that they provide a detailed plan for how a school will construct its RTI supports.**

Next we discuss the importance of these teams and then describe the key features of an RTI blueprint and how it supports the long-term use of RTI.

TEAMWORK IS ESSENTIAL

A variety of different teams play an important role in RTI. The most important teams are those at the school level. Two types of teams that help to support RTI are grade-level teams and problem-solving teams. Importantly, we call them teams because they must work together just like a sports team in order to succeed. Teams must have a common goal and a commitment to sharing the work to achieve that goal. This arrangement is different from other groups that might come together in schools. For example, schools often have many

---

BOX 9.2. School-, District-, and State-Level RTI Blueprints

The initial blueprint publication by Batsche et al. (2005), *Response to Intervention: Policy Considerations and Implementation*, was published by the National Association of State Directors of Special Education (NASDSE). The subsequent school, district, and state blueprints were jointly published by NASDSE and the Council of Administrators of Special Education (CASE). All of these documents can be downloaded from the NASDSE website at *www.nasdse.org*. Once at the site, click on the Publications tab. In the Keyword Search box type "blueprint" and then select *Response to Intervention* as the category. For type, use *any*. This selection will bring up a list of items. The items can be purchased in hard copy, or, if you click on the title of the item, a new screen appears where you can download the blueprint for *free*.

---

committees that are assigned to work on a task. Unlike a team, a committee does not necessarily have a common purpose. Committee members may well not have a common goal, and sometimes they do not even want to be together. By contrast, teams have to share a common goal and must rely on each other to reach that goal.

Grade-Level Teams

Grade-level teams include all the teachers who teach the same grade in a school. If the school has multiage classrooms, the grade-level team can include teachers of more than one grade. Some very small schools have only one teacher per grade, and in such cases teachers of grades near each other (e.g., K–2) can come together to be a grade-level team. In cases where there are a very large number of teachers in a school who teach the same grade (e.g., more than eight), two or more teams can be created. This ensures that all teachers will get a chance to participate fully in the meetings. Grade-level teams play a key role in RTI because they provide a setting where each teacher can get support from colleagues to support students who are struggling. The reason why having teachers meet and use grade-level teams for this work is that teachers of the same, or very close, grade levels know what the grade-level learning expectations are and can suggest ideas for helping students based on those learning goals. Grade-level teams work best if they can meet frequently and long enough to share details about individual students. While there are no data to suggest the best meeting schedule, grade-level teams that meet at least once monthly can offer the best support to participating teachers; some grade-level teams meet twice a month or even weekly.

Once established, grade-level teams can establish their own meeting agendas. For example, a team might decide to talk about one student in detail at each meeting. Alternatively, a team might decide to give each teacher 10 minutes at each meeting. A very effective use of grade-level team meeting time is to review data. At the start of the year, this approach would entail reviewing the screening data for all classes and having teachers identify the students of concern. During the year, teachers can bring and discuss progress data for students participating in Tier 2 interventions. Through the sharing of data from each class, teachers could compare how students in their own classes are doing and discuss what other interventions they might want to try. Through regular meetings and data sharing, grade-level teams strengthen teachers' common goal of supporting all students in their classes.

Problem-Solving Teams

In addition to the grade-level teams, it is important that there be one schoolwide team that helps teachers get additional assistance for students who are not successful with Tier 1 plus Tier 2 interventions. In many schools such schoolwide teams are known as problem-solving teams (PSTs) but other terms used include student support teams, student success teams, child study teams, and teacher assistance teams (Brown-Chidsey, 2005b). Here, the term PST will be used to describe these schoolwide teams. The main purpose of the schoolwide team is to facilitate data-driven decision making, especially at Tier 3 (Tilly, 2002). The exact duties of the PST at each school vary, depending on the size of the school and how long RTI has been in place. Usually the PST has a more precise and closely specified role in larger schools because of the need to ensure consistency. PSTs often also have a major role when RTI is first being initiated because they serve to assure that all staff members know the RTI steps. PST members will get a sense of how RTI is being implemented, and this information can be used to recommend additional professional development to support RTI.

The PST usually meets on a regular basis and has a set schedule of activities at each meeting. Activities generally include reviewing data and considering options for students not making progress. PST members can be selected in a number of different ways. At some schools, there is a representative for each grade as well as for specialists and other staff members. In other cases, PST membership is driven by teacher interest and experience with RTI. It is important for PST members to realize that they are not expected to provide additional instruction, or be "experts," in data review. *All* teachers must actively participate in gathering and reviewing student data. The PST serves the function of making sure that teachers have the resources they need to collect and review data in grade level teams as well as provide additional problem-solving capabilities when an intervention has not resulted in sufficient student progress. For example, after a classroom teacher identified a student with reading difficulties, she worked with her grade-level team to develop and implement two reading interventions during the daily intervention time block. If the progress data showed that the interventions did not work, the teacher would consult with her grade-level team colleagues to see whether another intervention should be tried or whether she should take the case to the PST. If the latter, the PST would then review the data and either recommend a different intervention or initiate a referral to Tier 3 and a comprehensive evaluation.

Both grade-level teams and PSTs play significant roles in creating successful outcomes with RTI. The grade-level teams provide teacher support on a regular basis. When efforts to help students in the classroom and with Tier 2 interventions have not been successful, the PST offers a way for teachers to get additional assistance in meeting student learning needs. The use of these teams ensures that no single teacher—or principal—is running RTI alone. RTI cannot be accompanied by any single individual, but, rather, depends on the collaboration and active teamwork of all the school officials and teachers. These functional teams are typically formed during the RTI planning stage, and they in effect create the blueprints that inform long-term RTI activities in the school, district, and state.

RTI BLUEPRINTS

Blueprints for implementation of RTI—whether at the school, district, or state level—generally must feature three key organizational steps, namely:

1. Consensus building
2. Infrastructure development
3. Process implementation

Next we describe each of these in turn and then discuss how these steps fit together to "connect the dots" for your school, district, or state.

> **RTI requires commitment to a process of school change.**

Consensus Building

Consensus building is the first key organizational step reflected in RTI blueprints because it has such a strong impact on the long-term success of RTI. The *Merriam-Webster Dictionary*'s definition of *consensus* includes three parts: (1a) general agreement, (1b) the judgment arrived at by most of those concerned, and (2) group solidarity in sentiment and belief. When used in terms of RTI, *consensus* refers to the extent that all the educators in the school, district, or state agree that RTI will be helpful for all of its students. This high level of consensus is critical because RTI requires everyone to work together to be effective. As one of us noted in another context "it takes a village" to successfully implement RTI because it is necessarily a *systemic* way of helping students (Brown-Chidsey et al., 2009).

The consensus-building aspect of the blueprint process includes educating peers and colleagues about the core components of RTI (Glover & DiPerna, 2007; Kovaleski, 2007). This education can, and should, take on many forms so that everyone has a chance to ask questions and think over the implications of a universal responsive intervention system. For example, it is important that all key staff members understand that embracing and implementing RTI generally means that they are making a commitment to the following principles:

- All children can learn.
- All children have a right to an efficacious education.
- Not all children have disabilities, but they all might need extra help at various times as they make their way from kindergarten through grade 12.
- Differentiating instruction for individual students is an important part of general education.

- Education outcome data are effective tools for determining what types of extra support a student needs.
- Multi-tier standard protocols and problem-solving methods are effective ways of addressing the learning needs of all students.

The consensus-building phase provides staff members with the opportunity to consider the foregoing statements and decide whether they agree with them. In addition, there need to be conversations about the implications of these ideas and how they will be addressed.

The length of time that the consensus-building phase takes will be depend on the prior experiences with RTI that staff personnel have. If staff members are very familiar with RTI and eagerly embrace the related principles, this step, or phase, may take just a few months. If, however, staff members hold a variety of beliefs about RTI and are not in agreement about its underlying principles, building consensus may take one or more school years to achieve. Having consensus about how to proceed with RTI is important because it is a form of staff "buy-in" or "ownership" of what RTI is all about. Without this "ownership," staff members are unlikely to invest adequate time and energy into making RTI work. Building a genuine consensus may require inordinate time and efforts by key leaders, but that time and effort are very much worth the energy because having a commonly agreed-upon vision for RTI in the school, district, or state will help assure its long-term sustainability.

Infrastructure Development

The second blueprint step or phase is infrastructure development. This phase includes inventorying all the "nuts-and-bolts" materials needed to put RTI firmly into place. This phase is very different from consensus building because it focuses on concrete needs rather than beliefs and ideas. Three main concerns are likely to emerge during this phase: (1) inventories, (2) resource gathering, and (3) professional development. Each concern is very important because adequate provision for all three is crucial to success of the overall RTI plan. Just as an architect needs to know about and specify the right building materials, educators need to know about and use effective instruction and assessment practices. Most of the time, the infrastructure development work is completed by teams of teachers, administrators, parents, specialists, and others. By using goal-specific teams, the work of provisioning inventories, gathering resources, and engaging in professional development is shared equitably among the available personnel.

The inventorying process provides a way for all educators in a school, district, or state to know authoritatively what instructional and assessment materials are currently being used. Instructional materials inventories include lists of all the current instructional tools being used at each grade level, classified according to the specific RTI tier to which they apply. Before starting to gather the inventory information, it is important to think about the types of instructional and assessment tools that the schools are already using; these tools can be grouped by tier according to how they are being used. An organizing tool that can be used to assist teams as they plan an inventory is shown in Form 9.1 at the end of this chapter. This inventory guide includes reminders about how instruction and assessment differ at each tier. For example, Tier 1 calls for the use of scientifically based core curricula in *all* subject areas for *all* students. This requirement means that the Tier 1 inventory process will include identifying all the instructional materials and methods adopted and in use in general education classrooms.

Tier 2 provides *additional* instruction for those students who specifically need it. The inventory of Tier 2 instruction will include instructional materials and methods that are used *in addition to* the Tier 1 core programs. Usually these are materials and methods that work with small groups of students who need to work on the same skill. Tier 3 includes very intensive programs for students who have not been successful with Tier 1 *plus* Tier 2 interventions. The Tier 3 list will include programs that require a very small group typically two students per teacher or one-on-one instruction and that might replace the core program. As seen in Form 9.1, the focus of instruction at each tier becomes increasingly more narrow. *Because this guide may not provide all the room necessary to compile an inventory across both tiers and grade levels, a full-page inventory form can also be used.* A sample reading instruction inventory is shown in Figure 9.1 and the blank inventory form itself is provided as Form 9.2 at the end of the chapter. The instructional materials cited in Figure 9.1 exemplify and were derived from a small elementary school and represent the actual programs in place at that school.

A similar inventory process is used to identify the assessment resources currently in use. Form 9.2 can be used for both instructional and assessment inventories. Figure 9.2 shows a sample math assessment inventory for grades K–5. Also shown on the sample assessment inventory is a description of the type of assessment needed at each tier. At Tier 1, screening assessments are needed to identify which students need help. At Tier 2, progress assessments are essential so that student improvement can be recorded. Tier 2 progress data are the evidence of RTI practices. Tier 3 assessments often include two main elements, but they come under one main heading: diagnostic assessments. These assessments include progress data as well as results from specialized assessments of specific knowledge or skills. Together such Tier 3 data help a team to determine whether a student needs special education. Importantly, for RTI to work, there must be routine assessments at each tier. Without these assessments, it will be impossible to know if the students are meeting their instructional goals.

Once the instruction and assessment inventories are complete, the information gathered is shared with colleagues to identify what other resources are needed. Often the inventories are done by grade-level teams and then shared with the PST to consider what else is needed. The additional resources might include different or additional instructional materials as well as other assessments (Dessof, 2008). Location-specific needs should be considered as well. Schools in urban areas will have different needs than those in rural settings (Dexter, Hughs, & Farmer, 2008). Resources can also include changes in daily schedules and time to meet as colleagues. At the resource gathering stage there are key questions that are likely to come up during discussions, such as:

1. Is anyone really using any of the materials listed in the inventory?
2. Is enough instructional time allocated at each tier?
3. Which staff members are best suited to provide the various levels of instruction?

School: Lincoln Elementary   Subject Area: Reading Instruction

Tier	K	1	2	3	4	5
1	Imagine It			Core Program		
2	Earobics Early Reading Intervention	Early Reading Intervention	Read Naturally Great Leaps	Great Leaps	Read Naturally	Questioning the Author
3	Lindamood–Bell Language for Learning	Language for Learning Reading Mastery	Reading Mastery Sonday	Wilson Sonday	Wilson Spalding	Wilson Corrective Reading

FIGURE 9.1. Sample reading instruction inventory.

School: Lincoln Elementary

Subject Area: Math Assessment

Tier	K	1	2	3	4	5
	Universal: Screening					
1	AIMSweb Tests of Early Numeracy (TEN)	AIMSweb Math	Aimsweb Math	Aimsweb Math	Aimsweb Math G-MADE	Aimsweb Math G-MADE
	Weekly: Progress Monitoring					
2	TEN: selected measure(s)	AIMSweb addition easy CBM	AIMSweb subtraction easy CBM	AIMSweb mixed problems easy CBM	AIMSweb mixed problems easy CBM	AIMSweb mixed problems easy CBM
	In-Depth Assessment: Diagnostic					
3	Survey-Level Assessment Key Math, K-TEA	Survey-Level Assessment Key Math, K-TEA	Survey-Level Assessment Key Math, WIAT	Survey-Level Assessment Key Math, WIAT	Survey-Level Assessment Key Math, WJ-III-ACH	Survey-Level Assessment Key Math, WJ-III-ACH

FIGURE 9.2. Sample math assessment inventory.

Some of these questions can be answered through additional dialogue among team members at both the grade and schoolwide level. Other answers may require additional inventories or professional development. In terms of the long-term RTI blueprint, it is important that staff members be both thoughtful and thoroughgoing about all the resources needed to support instruction and assessment at each tier (Carney & Stiefel, 2008).

> **It's important to encourage team members to be flexible. Occasionally RTI planners will have to go back to the drawing board and perhaps totally revise the blueprint.**

Professional development (PD) is the last major activity within the infrastructure development phase. The reason that it comes at this point is that it serves as a crucial bridge between current and future practices (Kratochwill, Volpiansky, Clements, & Ball, 2007). The inventory and resource gathering stages provide ways to know what has happened in the past and what is needed in the future, but implementation cannot really occur until there is training to equip staff members with the knowledge and skills needed (Danielson, Doolittle, & Bradley, 2007). The specific types of PD that each school, district, and state will need prior to implementation will vary a great deal and may vary for different providers (Nelson & Machek, 2007). The importance of PD in the overall success of RTI cannot be overstated. Teachers need—and deserve—to have the knowledge and skills necessary to provide the instruction and assessment expected of them (Nunn & Jantz, 2009). Just as it is not appropriate to ask a student to demonstrate a skill we have not yet taught him or her, we cannot expect teachers to engage in different instruction and assessment if we do not give them the training needed. Well-designed professional development includes not only the initial training but also frequent "booster" sessions so that teachers can ask questions and practice newly learned skills with supportive feedback from colleagues (Hawkins, Kroeger, Musti-Rao, Barnett, & Ward, 2008). One of the most common complaints that teachers have about any new innovation in schools is that there is not enough PD for them to learn the new practices well. School-level teams must consider carefully what PD will be essential to their local needs and make sure to build it into the RTI blueprint. PD is important at all levels, including state RTI initiatives (Bergstrom, 2008; Palenchar & Boyer, 2008).

Process Implementation

The last step, or phase, of the RTI blueprint process is implementation. This must come after the other phases because only with sufficient consensus and adequate infrastructure can effective implementation be assured. Some staff members may be eager to implement RTI steps right away, but doing so prematurely only results in failure. One of the precautionary elements built into the school, district, and state blueprints is typically a section known as "wisdom from the field." This section normally offers sage advice from those who have been implementing RTI for a while. Examples of how such "wisdom" can help include useful advice on how best to use existing staff in new ways (Hoover & Patton, 2008; Murawski & Hughes, 2009). Such advice based on experience avoids having to "reinvent the wheel" as we make RTI happen. A key part of implementation—and why it needs its own portion of the RTI blueprint—is that it must happen in phases over time. RTI requires a concerted team effort, and, just as "Rome wasn't built in a day," all parts of a blueprint cannot be put into place instantly. A core feature of the implementation section is a detailed plan for what will happen when within a given extended time frame. This plan can be modified over time, if needed, but a schedule for each step is very important so that the right people are in the right place at the right time to make responsive instruction a reality in your setting.

SUMMARY

This chapter has provided information about the importance of long-term planning to support RTI. Templates for school, district, and state RTI blueprints are available for free, and we recommend them as excellent starting points. Creating your own customized blueprints will require staff members to take into account their essential beliefs, resources, and schedules in order to make RTI a functioning reality. In the process of creating the blueprint, staff members will need to create teams, align instructional and assessment practices, and plan for how they can evaluate their own progress toward supporting all students. Much of the day-to-day work in RTI includes teaching well, checking regularly on students' progress, and using performance data to inform subsequent instruction. By having school, district, and state blueprints in place to monitor overall RTI progress, school personnel are positioned to connect the dots generated by student learning so that all students have a greater chance to meet their potential.

Inventory Guide

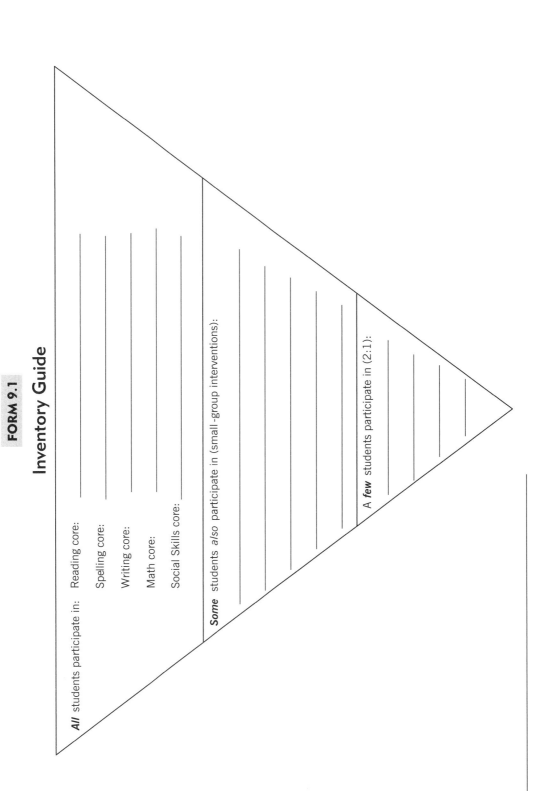

All students participate in: Reading core: _____

Spelling core: _____

Writing core: _____

Math core: _____

Social Skills core: _____

Some students *also* participate in (small-group interventions): _____

A *few* students participate in (2:1): _____

Inventory Form

School: _____   Subject Area: _____

Tier	K	1	2	3	4	5
1						
2						
3						

CHAPTER 10

Case Examples of RTI in Action
Experimental Analysis of Effective Instruction

A more in-depth level of analysis within the RTI model is the experimental analysis of academic difficulties. This type of evaluation is comparable to conducting a functional behavioral assessment (FBA). Two additional resources that address the experimental analysis of academic difficulties and challenging behaviors are briefly described in the accompanying boxes (see Boxes 10.1 and 10.2).

BOX 10.1. Functional Behavioral Assessment

Conducting School-Based Functional Behavioral Assessments: A Practitioner's Guide (2nd Edition)
Mark W. Steege and T. Steuart Watson (Guilford Press, 2009)

Explaining the "whats," "whys," and "how-tos" of functional behavioral assessment, this practical and engaging book is packed with real-world tools and examples. Effective procedures are presented for evaluating challenging behavior in K–12 students, organizing assessment data, and using the results to craft individualized behavior support plans. The authors draw on extensive school-based experience to provide sample reports, decision trees, and reproducible checklists and forms—all in a large-sized format with lay-flat binding to facilitate photocopying.

> ### BOX 10. 2. Locating Reading Intervention Resources
>
> *Interventions for Reading Problems: Designing and Evaluating Effective Strategies*
> Edward J. Daly III, Sandra Chafouleas, and Christopher H. Skinner (Guilford Press, 2005)
>
> This comprehensive user-friendly guide meets a growing need for school psychologists and other practitioners called on to work with struggling readers and their teachers. Presented are a systematic framework and a wealth of step-by-step strategies for targeting such key areas of literacy development as phonological awareness, fluency, and comprehension. Particular emphasis is placed on scientifically based assessment and intervention practices that do not require major curricular change and that can be applied with students of diverse ages and ability levels. Featuring over 35 reproducible assessment and instructional tools—in a large-sized format with lay-flat binding for ease of photocopying and use—the book also offers practical pointers for establishing an effective consultation relationship and documenting student progress over time.

EXPERIMENTAL ANALYSIS OF ACADEMIC SKILLS

Experimental analysis of academic difficulties is typically a two-part process consisting of:

1. Descriptive assessment to identify the types of academic errors the student makes.
2. Comparing intervention strategies to determine the most effective and efficient intervention plan.

Descriptive Assessment

This process involves directing the student to complete academic assignments (e.g., writing samples, math computation worksheets, oral reading probes) with a trained clinician (teacher, special education teacher, school psychologist, consultant, etc.) to observe and record the types of errors the student is making. For example, during a reading assignment the clinician would record (1) words read correctly and reading errors, (2) mispronunciations, (3) substitutions, (4) deletions, and (5) latency (i.e., how long it takes for the student to sound out the word). Likewise, an error analysis of a writing sample might include (1) the number of words written correctly and the writing errors, (2) misspellings, (3) improper capitalization, and (4) incorrect punctuation. Analysis of the descriptive assessment could be used to prescribe student-tailored evidence-based interventions.

Comparing Intervention Strategies

This phase typically includes the use of two types of single-case designs to evaluate interventions: (1) the case study (AB) design and (2) an alternating-treatments design. Detailed

Ed Daly and his colleagues developed the method known as brief experimental analysis (BEA) for comparing academic interventions. It is based on the methods used for understanding the functions of behaviors. BEA can be used to identify one or more interventions likely to be most effective for a student.

information about single-case research designs is found in Chapter 5. The following examples will elucidate three specific cases.

Case Example 1

Consider the case of Billy, a fifth-grade student who has consistently shown delays in reading. So far during fifth grade, Billy has received 3 months of Tier 2 supplemental reading intervention but has not yet demonstrated significant improvement. During problem-solving team meetings, team members expressed opinions about his lack of responsiveness to the additional instruction. Team members' ideas about Billy's reading problems fell into two camps. The motivation camp offered the hypothesis that Billy lacked sufficient motivation and that the results of oral reading fluency probes had underestimated his true reading abilities markedly. In contrast, the skills camp hypothesized that Billy had adequate motivation but did not have sufficient skills to read at benchmark levels. Team members could spend hours debating their respective differences of opinion, or they could test their hypotheses. Here's how. Remember the "can't do/won't do" assessment model described in Chapter 7? The team could use this approach by (1) conducting a brief performance assessment, (2) constructing a baseline plan to determine Billy's preintervention levels of oral reading fluency, and (3) raising the incentive condition to evaluate the degree to which a high-quality reinforcement condition would influence ORF. Figure 10.1 shows the results of this miniassessment.

These data show that the incentive condition resulted in a slightly better reading performance. At this point, most of motivation proponents joined the skills proponents in concluding that a skill deficit was most likely. Next, the PST decided to provide Billy with intensive reading instruction. Specifically, the team decided to evaluate the effectiveness of skills-based instruction. But—wait—team members were divided on the type of reading instruction that would be most effective. Further discussion revealed that the team now split into two new camps, namely, one advocating repeated reading (RR) and the other preferring phase drill error correction (PDEC). Repeated reading is a reading intervention that involves having the student re-read a text 3–5 times in a row to improve fluency. Phrase drill correction procedure is a reading procedure that involves having the student re-read phrases in which errors were made prior to re-reading the passage. Each team presented research evidence that documented the efficacy of its favored method. Again, what to do, what to do? Well, in this example, the PST decided to "test drive" both interventions in a way that the team could compare the *relative effectiveness* of the two interventions (see Chapter 5 on alternating-treatments designs). The team identified 40 grade-level reading passages and randomly assigned 20 to each of the interventions. One classroom teacher was trained to implement both interventions (to rule out the possibility of one teacher being more effective than the other), and the duration of instructional sessions was held constant. Figure 10.2 shows the results of the "comparison trial."

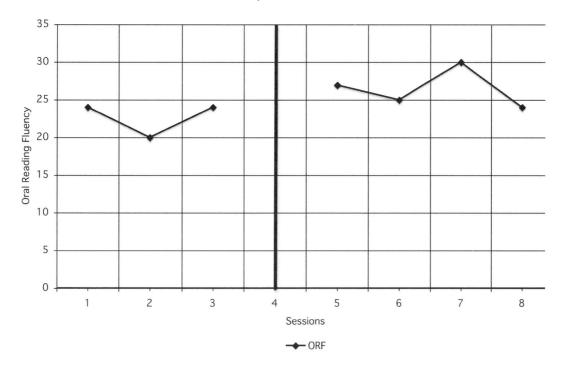

FIGURE 10.1. Comparison of Billy's baseline and incentive condition reading.

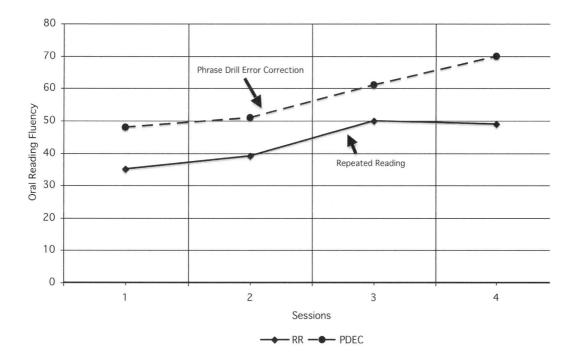

FIGURE 10.2. Results of PDEC versus RR comparison trials.

These data demonstrated that the PDEC procedure was more efficacious than the RR procedure. The team next decided to combine the incentive condition with PDEC. Figure 10.3 depicts the test results obtained when the two most successful interventions were *combined*. These data showed that the intervention package of PDEC correction with rewards resulted in significant improvement in Billy's reading performance.

Case Example 2

Next consider the case of two students, David and Rebecca, with developmental disabilities who exhibited low rates of task completion during functional life skills instruction. Comprehensive FBAs were conducted collaboratively by the school psychologist, speech pathologist, and special education teacher. As part of the FBA, the team conducted a paired-choice preference assessment of leisure activities (e.g., computer games, videos, musical toys) to identify potential reinforcing activities. Team members discussed a variety of intervention options and eventually narrowed their selection to these two:

1. The two students would be prompted to select a preferred leisure activity *prior to* instruction and then reminded of their selection during 5-minute instructional sessions (e.g., "Remember what you are working for"). They would then be provided with the activity following completion of the academic instruction.

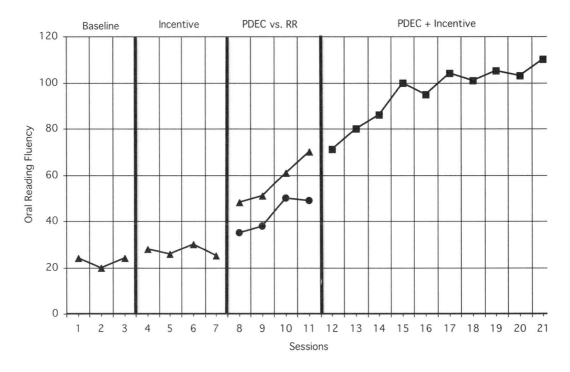

FIGURE 10.3. Comparison of separate and combined reading interventions.

or

2. The students would be provided with tokens contingent on the accuracy of their responses. Upon task completion, the students would be given the opportunity to exchange the tokens for a preferred activity selected from a menu of available options.

The team next decided to "test drive" the two interventions. The "test drive" was constructed to determine which intervention was more effective (i.e., to test the students' differential response to the two interventions). The team selected silverware sorting as the task and the number of items correctly sorted within 5 minutes as the dependent variable. Following a baseline phase (to determine preintervention levels of responding) the team used an alternating treatments design in which the students were asked to sort silverware during (1) the verbal reminder condition ("Remember what you are working for") and (2) the token reinforcement condition. Conditions were reversed sequentially to control for a potential order effect. Figure 10.4 graphs the results from test-driving the two interventions. These data showed that David was more responsive to the token reinforcement intervention while the verbal reminder intervention was more efficacious with Rebecca.

> Preference assessments are conducted to learn what is most rewarding for a student. When teachers know a student's preferred items and activities, they can have them available to ensure that the student remains engaged and motivated in school.

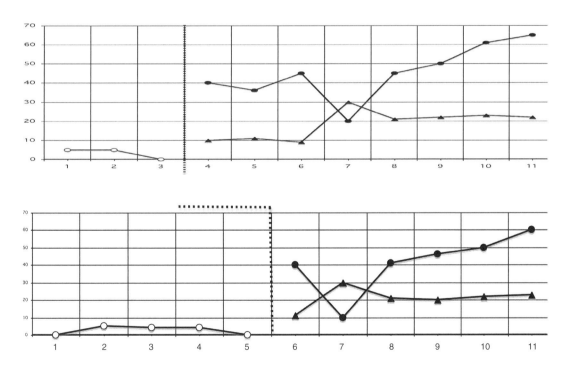

FIGURE 10.4. Sample intervention "test drive."

Case Example 3

Our third case example involves a middle school student, Webster, who displayed interfering behaviors (e.g., verbal opposition, task disruption) during reading instruction. Following a direct reading assessment, the problem-solving team decided to include Webster
in a supplemental reading group that included
daily 30-minute small-group instruction focusing on phonological awareness, oral reading, and
repeated reading exercises. The team also considered providing one-to-one instructional supports
(i.e., during the supplemental reading activity
paraprofession would provide social reinforcement contingent on reading attempts and correct
responses, corrective feedback, and reinforcement of on-task behavior). The team decided to
measure interfering behavior by using a 6-second partial interval recording procedure and
words read correctly (WRC) during 3-minute reading probes two to four times per week.
Figure 10.5 illustrates the results of the intervention.

> For some students, a specific
> problem behavior serves the
> function of avoiding certain difficult
> tasks. By gathering data about
> both academics and classroom
> behaviors, teachers can see how
> these behaviors work together to
> explain a student's performance.

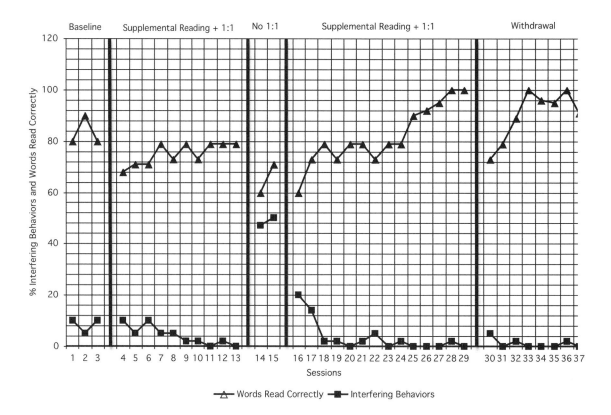

FIGURE 10.5. Behavior reduction through reading improvement.

During the baseline period, Webster exhibited low levels of reading fluency and high rates of interfering behavior. During the initial phase of supplemental reading only, Webster showed an increase in reading fluency and a decrease in interfering behaviors, but both levels were considered by the PST to be unacceptable. Next, the team implemented the intervention package that was composed of both supplemental reading and one-to-one instructional supports. This package resulted in marked decreases in interfering behaviors and increases in reading fluency.

Owing to staffing problems, the one-on-one support was not available for 1 week (sessions 20–21). During that time, in which Webster was provided with supplemental reading only; his interfering behavior increased and reading performance decreased. This development convinced the team that the intervention package was a necessary support, and it was then implemented consistently for several weeks. This course of action resulted in stable levels of responding. The team eventually decided to withdraw the one-to-one support, but Webster was nonetheless able to maintain high levels of reading performance and low levels of interfering behaviors.

SUMMARY

These examples demonstrate that trying out specific interventions and closely graphing how students respond to them is an effective way to learn what works best with individual students. In each case, the most effective intervention or intervention package was selected to be used to support the student's learning needs. These examples show how no one particular intervention will necessarily work with every student. Having a system identify the best interventions for students is a key component in comprehensive RTI implementation. Since each of these students had not responded to less intensive Tier 2 interventions, the PST facilitated trying out (e.g., "test driving") alternative interventions for these students. In all three cases, the students responded to at least one of the intervention conditions, and the new intervention was then implemented for that student. Importantly, none of these students ended up being referred for special education.

CHAPTER 11

RTI Reports

Formal Evidence of Student Progress

Reporting the data collected while implementing RTI interventions is a critical step in the overall process. Chapter 7 includes numerous blank forms that can be used for communicating the results of RTI activities or ongoing progress along the way. Occasionally it is important to summarize RTI data as part of a formal report. This chapter describes several types of RTI reports, including comprehensive evaluation reports that include RTI data, and concludes with several examples of RTI-based reports.

TYPES OF REPORTS

Three main types of reports can be generated from RTI data, namely, brief summary reports, longitudinal data summary reports, and full psychological evaluation reports. We explore each in turn.

Brief Summary Reports

Brief summary reports are those used to communicate the status of a student's academic progress at a given point in time. These can be created and used at a number of different times during the school year. The first appropriate time for brief summary reports is in the fall after benchmark data have been collected. This report generally involves stating each student's performance on the benchmark measures and comparing that performance to local and/or national norms, thereby providing an indicator of the student's relative progress and

> **RTI is a method that should increase the transparency of student performance between teachers and parents. The data collected during RTI activities should be shared frequently with the student, parents, and other educators who are working to support the student's school success.**

standing in the general curriculum. Usually the same format can be used at each of the three normal benchmark data collection time points (i.e., September, January, and May).

Two sample benchmark brief summary reports are shown in Figure 11.1. The first part of Figure 11.1 shows Mark's fall CBM benchmark scores as well as the local and national norms. This brief summary indicates that Mark is off to a good start and should be able to handle the general education instruction planned for the year. The second brief report shown in Figure 11.1 is the winter benchmark report. In this report both Mark's fall and winter benchmark data are included so that his parents can see the improvement he has made and how his scores compare with both local and national norms. The report includes space for a brief teacher summary note explaining what general conclusions may properly be drawn from the data presented. Some parents, or other report readers, may need help in understanding a report like this one the first time it is sent home. With help from teachers and other school personnel, parents can learn to interpret the brief report. Teachers may want to distribute such reports at regular parent–teacher conferences so that explanations

Student: Mark White			Teacher: Mary Brown					
Benchmark Date: September 25, 2009			Grade: 1					
Student Score(s)			District Norms*			National Norms**		
	Reading	Addition	Patterns	Reading	Addition	Patterns	Reading	Addition	Patterns
Fall	14	5	6	2–17	2–8	3–7	2–16	N/A***	N/A
Winter				13–46	5–11	6–9	12–42	N/A	N/A
Spring				31–87	9–15	7–9	26–75	N/A	N/A

*District norms reflect the average range of scores obtained by all students who took the test locally.
**National norms reflect the average range of scores obtained by students throughout the United States.
***National norms are not yet available for addition and patterns tasks.

Notes: Mark is off to a great start in reading and math. His scores indicate that he has the requisite skills to do the first-grade reading and math work we will cover this year.

If you have questions concerning this report, please contact your child's teacher.

Student: Mark White			Teacher: Mary Brown					
Benchmark Date: January 30, 2010			Grade: 1					
Student Score(s)			District Norms*			National Norms**		
	Reading	Addition	Patterns	Reading	Addition	Patterns	Reading	Addition	Patterns
Fall	14	5	6	2–17	2–8	3–7	2–16	N/A***	N/A
Winter	23	9	8	13–46	5–11	6–9	12–42	N/A	N/A
Spring				31–87	9–15	7–9	26–75	N/A	N/A

*District norms reflect the average range of scores obtained by all students who took the test locally.
**National norms reflect the average range of scores obtained by students throughout the United States.
***National norms are not yet available for addition and patterns tasks.

Notes: Mark continues to make good progress in reading and math. His CBM scores reflect that he is learning the knowledge and skills we are covering. He is on track to meet the end-of-year grade-1 expectations.

If you have questions concerning this report, please contact your child's teacher.

FIGURE 11.1. Sample benchmark brief summary RTI reports.

about the report can be provided and any questions from parents can be answered. Some schools include brief summary data in periodically issued report cards and other communications detailing student progress.

Longitudinal Data Summary Reports

The second type of RTI report is a longitudinal data summary. This report consists largely of graphs, such as those we have included throughout this book, that tell the story of a student's progress once a specific intervention has been implemented. In addition to the graphs, such forms as the Student Progress Review and the Referral for Special Education Worksheets (Forms 7.9 and 7.11, respectively, at the end of Chapter 7) provide narrative summaries of student progress. These forms are specifically designed for teachers and other educational personnel to use in determining the effectiveness of interventions for specific students. Forms such as these are normally not sent home to parents but, rather, serve as the starting point for school-based discussions, meetings, and decisions about student progress. For example, Figures 11.2 through 11.4 provide examples of a student's graphs and worksheets used to summarize his or her long-term progress toward specific goals.

> In order for RTI data to be helpful to students, teachers, and family members, it is important that teachers know how to interpret and explain the data. When teachers spend time together reviewing student progress during grade-level team meetings, they build their data analysis skills.

In these figures, data for Guy Wyre are summarized. Guy is a third grader who is currently receiving instruction in a three-student group with Florence McPhee. Ms. McPhee is using the Phonographix reading instruction program. Guy was initially identified as needing additional reading instruction when he moved into the district during the spring of his second-grade year. He participated in the spring reading benchmarks and scored below the 10th percentile as compared with other students in his new district. A Tier 2 small-group instruction program for Guy was implemented during the last few weeks of second grade, and it was resumed when he began the third grade. Guy's progress in the program has been monitored by using the DIBELS Oral Reading Fluency (DORF) measure. As shown in Figure 11.2, Guy obtained scores of 15, 16, and 15 words read correctly during the fall benchmark and follow-up baseline testing in September 2009.

Guy's reading progress is shown in the intervention phase of the graph. His reading fluency increased from 15 words at the last baseline measure to 26 words at the 3-week review of his progress on October 5th. Because 26 words correct is just inside the national norm of 24–73 words per minute and Guy was making progress, it was decided to have Guy remain in the Phonographix program for at least another 3 weeks. The same decision was made on October 26th and November 16th. At each of these points in time, Guy's data indicated that he was making progress toward the next third-grade reading goal of 54. The Student Progress Review Worksheet for October 26th is shown in Figure 11.3. The information in this form summarizes the data on Guy's graph. On December 7th Guy's progress was reviewed again. At this review, a different decision was made because his scores reflected

(text continues on page 162)

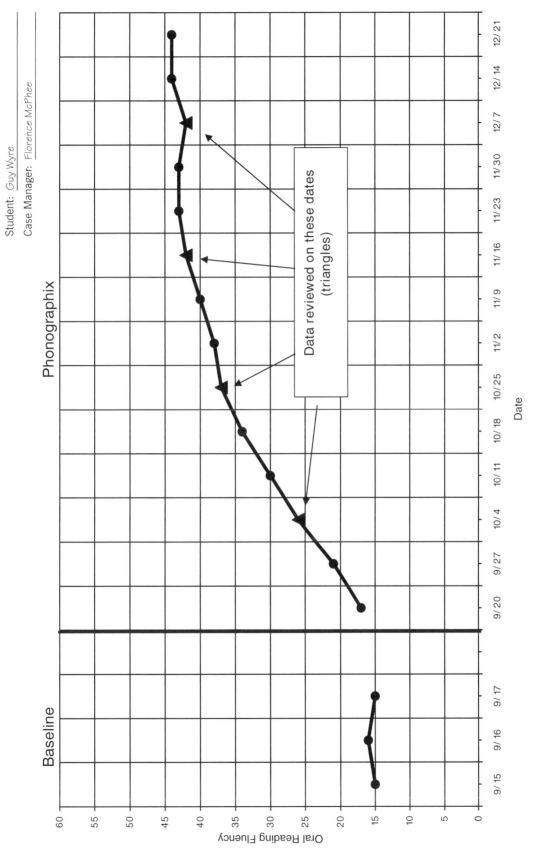

FIGURE 11.2. Example of a completed Progress Monitoring Graph.

Student: *Guy Wyre*   Grade: *3*   Teacher: *Alice Green*

Name of Tier 2 instruction program: *Phonographix*

Who is the teacher? *Florence McPhee*

How many students (total) are in the instruction group? *3*

How often are the instructional sessions held? *Daily*

How long is each session? *40 minutes*

How many sessions has this student attended? *63/65*

Based on the progress monitoring data, how many data points indicate that the student's skills are improving? *6*

Based on the progress monitoring data, how many data points indicate that the student's skills are not improving? *0*

How do the student's current skills compare to typically achieving peers? *Guy's current score of 37 is within the minimum benchmark of 23 for beginning-of-the-year grade-3 students, but below the winter benchmark of 40 words.*

Based on the obtained data, what modifications to the current instructional program will be made? *No modifications will be made. Guy continues to make progress in reading.*

When will the modifications go into effect? *N/A*

When will the student's progress be reviewed again? *Monday, November 16*

ALL PROGRESS MONITORING DATA AND GRAPHS REFERENCED ABOVE MUST BE ATTACHED

Person completing this form: *Florence McPhee, MEd*   Date: *October 26, 2009*

FIGURE 11.3. Example of a completed Student Progress Review Worksheet.

Student *Guy Wyre* Grade *3* Teacher *Florence McPhee*

Describe how student's instructional need was initially identified:

Guy scored in the at-risk range on the 2nd-grade DIBELS at the spring benchmark period last year. This fall, Guy scored in the at-risk range on the fall 3rd-grade reading benchmarks.

Tier 2 instructional methods that were used to improve student's knowledge/skills:

Small-group Phonographix lessons with three students in the group were begun the week of September 21. Guy's progress was monitored, using weekly oral reading fluency probes. Guy made progress in reading for 6 weeks; however, his improvement slowed after December 7, indicating that he is no longer making progress toward better reading skills.

Who provided the Tier 2 instructional program?
Florence McPhee, certified highly qualified special education teacher

Progress monitoring measure used to record student's progress during Tier 2 instruction:
Oral reading fluency probes

Tier 2 program start date *September 21, 2009* Tier 2 program review date(s) *October 5, 26, November 17, 2009*

Describe the student's current instructional need(s):
Guy needs to learn more words and read text more rapidly.

What, if any, additional instruction or supports is this student currently receiving?
Guy is receiving 40 minutes per day of Phonographix 3:1 instruction until a comprehensive evaluation can be completed.

ALL PROGRESS-MONITORING DATA AND GRAPHS REFERENCED ABOVE MUST BE ATTACHED

Person completing this form: *Florence McPhee, MEd* Date: *December 7, 2009*

FIGURE 11.4. Example of a completed Tier 3 Referral for Special Education Worksheet.

little if any growth during the immediately preceding 3 weeks. Due to the slowing in Guy's reading progress, as well as a concern that he would not meet the winter benchmark goal, Guy's small-group teacher referred him for a special education evaluation. The completed referral form is shown in Figure 11.4. Guy remained in the small-group instruction while a comprehensive evaluation was completed.

Full Psychological Evaluation Reports

The third type of RTI report is a comprehensive psychological evaluation report that is similar to other types of reports used in schools. Such reports serve the purpose of describing and documenting a student's school progress and needs. RTI data can easily be integrated into such reports and offer an important source of information concerning what has already been implemented to assist a student. Next we describe the components of full evaluation reports and then provide four examples of such reports.

EVALUATION REPORT COMPONENTS

The best way to write a comprehensive evaluation using RTI data is to base it on the steps of the problem-solving model. Such reports are solution-focused and offer specific ideas for additional instruction (Brown-Chidsey & Steege, 2005). A summary of the key elements of solution-focused RTI reports is presented in Table 11.1. There are three main sections in solution-focused reports: (1) problem identification, (2) problem definition, and (3) exploring

---

TABLE 11.1. Solution-Focused Evaluation Report Outline

1. Identification of the problem
   a. Student's name, age, grade, classroom
   b. Date(s) when problem was observed
   c. Names and positions of those who identified the problem

2. Definition of the problem
   a. Background information about the student
   b. Current educational placement
   c. Present levels of performance
      • Student
      • Typically achieving peers
   d. Magnitude of difference between the student's performance and what is expected
   e. Summary of the problem definition

3. Possible solutions
   a. General education interventions
   b. Special education interventions

Note. From Brown-Chidsey and Steege (2005, p. 272). Copyright 2005 by The Guilford Press. Reprinted by permission.

solutions. These sections correspond to the first three steps of the problem-solving model described in Chapter 1. RTI data should be reported in each of these report sections.

Problem Identification

Problem identification is the first point at which the "problem" appears on the "radar screen." This section includes three major pieces of information: (1) the student's name, age, grade, and classroom; (2) the date(s) when the problem was observed and a basic description of the problem; and (3) the names and positions of those who identified the problem. The identifying information contained in items 1 and 3 is very straightforward. The student's name, age, grade, and current teacher should be listed. If the student has more than one main teacher who has participated in the RTI activities, all the participating teachers should be listed. Item 2 is the place where RTI information can be given. Here the details of the student's performance and the conditions under which the data were collected are provided. For example, this item could be filled in as follows:

> **The goal of a comprehensive evaluation is to provide additional information about a student's learning needs. The evaluation report should tell the story of the student's recent school history, including what interventions were tried and how the student did in each one.**

All third-grade students were screened for reading difficulties, using curriculum-based measures (CBM) of reading, during September 2009. Seth's score of 19 words per minute falls below the 10th percentile, indicating that his current reading skills are lower than 90% of his classmates.

The problem identification section of the report serves the purpose of orienting the reader to the subject and focus of the report and does not need to be long. The next section provides the details about how and why the student's situation is problematic.

Problem Definition

This section of the report contains the essential data concerning the overall circumstances surrounding a student's academic performance. There are five elements in this section:

1. Background information about the student.
2. The student's current educational placement.
3. The student's present levels of performance as well as information about the performance of typically achieving peers.
4. The magnitude (size) of the difference between the student's performance and what is expected.
5. A summary of the problem definition.

Background Information

The background information section includes more detailed aspects of a student's school experience than is covered in the identifying information in section 1. The background section tells the student's "story," from the earliest point of relevance to the current day. In many cases the background section begins with a summary of prenatal, perinatal, and neonatal health obtained from the mother or another family member. In the case of certain disabilities (e.g., cerebral palsy) the presence or absence of symptoms from birth is required for accurate diagnosis. In addition to pregnancy and birth information, a brief summary of any childhood illnesses or medical conditions should be provided. These details are important because chronic medical conditions usually have an effect on a child's performance in school (Brown & Brown, 2005). Similarly, brief histories of the student's social and educational experiences should be included. The social history includes descriptions of the setting(s) in which the child has been raised. Included here would be information about living on- or off-base if a parent is in the military. Also appropriate here would be information about the family composition and the home environment (e.g., siblings, stepparents, grandparents).

The educational history begins at whatever point the student entered out-of-home childcare. For some students, this will occur at the point of kindergarten entry. For those students who attended any kind of out-of-home childcare or preschool program, the basic information about those experiences should be included. After describing preschool experiences, the student's progress in school should be summarized. Even if a student made expected (typical) progress, that should be noted. For students who have previously been identified as having a disability or who have repeated a grade or received other support services, specific mention of those experiences should be made. The educational history section should concompass the entire period of time preceding the current educational placement.

Current Educational Placement

This item in the report is very brief and includes only one or two sentences describing the student's current classroom(s) and teacher(s). If the student participates in multiple classrooms, all subjects, classes, and instructors should be mentioned.

Present Levels of Performance

Once the current educational setting has been described, the report turns to a description of how well the student is doing in the current setting. This is another place in the report where RTI data should be included. In this part of the report, more extensive RTI data can be reported. Specifically, all the scores obtained by the student during Tier 2 instruction should be summarized here. Since it is easiest to understand a student's progress when such data are summarized in a graph, the actual graph used to track the student during Tier 2 RTI activities should be attached to the report and referenced here. In addition, the report should include a narrative summary of the data, indicating under what instructional conditions the student did or did not make progress. If CBM survey-level assessment procedures were conducted in addition to the progress monitoring activities, those data should be reported in this section as well. Similarly, if diagnostic teaching procedures or brief experimental analysis methods were used to learn more about the student's responses to intervention, these data should be reported here as well (Hunley & McNamara, 2010).

In many cases there will be more than RTI data to include in the report. The RTI data should be described first and followed by other data. For example, a student may have been given several standardized, norm-referenced tests as part of the evaluation procedures (Flanagan & Ortiz, 2001). Scores from such assessment tools as the Comprehensive Test of Phonological Processing (CTOPP), the Woodcock–Johnson Tests of Cognitive Abilities, Third Edition (WJ-III/COG), and the Children's Memory Scale (CMS) should be summarized and included in the report. For every standardized score reported, it is important that more than just the standalone score be given, such as, additionally, the confidence interval, the true range of scores, and the percentile rank, if available. There is no need to report age- and grade-equivalent scores, as these are much less reliable than standard scores. The key scores to include are the standard score, the confidence interval, and the percentile rank.

Magnitude of Difference(s)

Once the RTI data are summarized, the extent to which the student's scores differ from those of other students or from expected scores needs to be addressed. It is the magnitude, or size, of the differences between the student's obtained scores and expected or desired scores that really *defines* the problem. This is an important distinction because, while the data might reflect a "problem," it might be one so small as to not merit a major initiative to fix it. Alternatively, of course, the problem could be very large and require intensive and substantial resources to address it properly. For example, a straight-A student who receives a B+ on one history test is not in danger of failing the class or dropping out of school. In contrast, a sixth-grade student who cannot read at all has a huge problem, because virtually all sixth-grade instruction requires reading skills. The large magnitude of that student's problem justifies an intensive remedy. It is important that report authors keep in mind that they are not supposed to determine whether a student is eligible for special education. That decision is reserved for the special education team and the student's parents. However, the report may describe the nature of the student's academic or behavioral needs in terms that match up with certain disability criteria if the data support such a description. Whether to include a specific diagnosis or diagnostic impressions depends on the report audience and whether such information is required by the school district in the state where the student attends school.

> **The beauty of the problem-definition step in problem solving is that it determines whether there is a small or a big problem. Small problems can be solved much more easily and quickly than big problems. The more that schools catch small student problems early, the fewer big problems students are likely to have.**

Report Summary

The final part of this section is a brief summary of the problem definition. This represents the report author's best opportunity to state the nature of the student's school difficulties in clear, unambiguous language. This section should be concise and deliver a solid "take-home" message about the student's needs. For example, the summary could state:

> *Martha is a 10-year-old student who is experiencing difficulty with math assignments. Data collected while Martha participated in additional daily small-group math instruction showed that she made only limited gains in math computation proficiency. Follow-up assessment revealed below-average scores on measures of rapid automatic naming (RAN), short-term memory, and general math achievement. Additional testing showed that she has strong general problem-solving and verbal skills. The data obtained as part of this evaluation suggest that Martha exhibits characteristics consistent with a learning disorder, math subtype.*

Exploring Solutions

Although all parts of an evaluation report are important, the part that is the most useful for the student is exploring solutions, where possible instructional methods that could help the student are given. Not all the methods described will be needed, but they offer important guidance for teachers about what to do next.

The final section of the report involves exploring solutions to the identified problem(s). This section may be divided into two subsections related to the type(s) of intervention(s) considered: general education or special education. While students who are being evaluated for a possible learning disability will have already participated in at least one or more general education intervention(s), it may be the case that the best possible solution for the student still lies in general education. For example, large school districts may offer a wide range of primary grades reading and math support funded by Title I. It may be that a student participated in one or more of these as part of RTI but the ones used were not successful. If the evaluation data suggest that a student is likely to be successful in a different general education intervention, that intervention should be tried—even if the student is identified as having a disability. Alternatively, if the team agrees that the student exhibits a specific disability (e.g., specific learning disability) and that special education instruction is needed, then the next instruction to be used will likely be in special education. In writing the solutions section of the report, authors must keep in mind that they need to explain the type of instruction hypothesized to be helpful for a specific student.

Importantly, the proposed solutions are hypotheses that need to be tested. Until data are collected that verify the efficacy of any given program, the proposed solution is only a hypothesis. Since data about a student's progress in any program will need to be collected, report authors should suggest what progress monitoring instruments would best match the specific instruction proposed. Having the progress monitoring indicator already ready at the time an intervention begins makes it much easier to measure student progress from the first day of the intervention.

REPORT EXAMPLES

The last part of this chapter includes four report examples. The first report reflects a situation in which a student was not identified as a student with a disability. The second shows a student who was identified as having a disability and was subsequently provided with special education services. The third report shows how some evaluations are inconclusive and may lead to additional assessment. The fourth includes an example of how error analysis data were used to identify a student's particular learning need. The "students" in the reports are fictitious but their characteristics and data are drawn from real students we have evaluated. In each case, the student participated in RTI procedures prior to referral for evaluation.

Mary Ann's Math Troubles: No Disability Found

In the first report we show how RTI data were used as a starting point to determine whether a student was eligible for special education services. This report summarizes information about Mary Ann, a third-grade student with poor math performance. Mary Ann's score on the fall CBM math screening was very low; she completed only 3 test items correctly on the mixed addition and subtraction probes. In comparison, the average score for all third graders in Mary Ann's district was 11 digits correct. Because her teacher was concerned about Mary Ann's performance, she implemented small-group math instruction for Mary Ann and two classmates who also scored low in the fall testing. These small-group lessons, conducted each weekday morning for 20 minutes, included direct instruction on addition, repeated practice, and a math facts "game" that featured rapid retrieval of addition facts as the key to winning. Student progress toward benchmark addition skills was monitored with weekly CBM addition probes. Mary Ann's scores on the weekly probes are shown in Figure 11.5. As the graph shows, Mary Ann made limited progress on learning math facts over 3 weeks of the small-group lessons.

Because the other students in Mary Ann's group were ready to move on to subtraction lessons and she was not, her teacher decided to work with Mary Ann and one other student, using the Touch Math program. Again, weekly data were collected. Mary Ann's progress in Touch Math is recorded in the right-hand section of Figure 11.5. As with the earlier intervention, she made only limited progress. Mary Ann's teacher decided to refer Mary Ann for a comprehensive evaluation for special education. The following report integrates the data from Mary Ann's RTI sessions with subsequent additional assessment information.

Student: _Mary Ann Hartwick_   Teacher: _Mrs. Morgan_

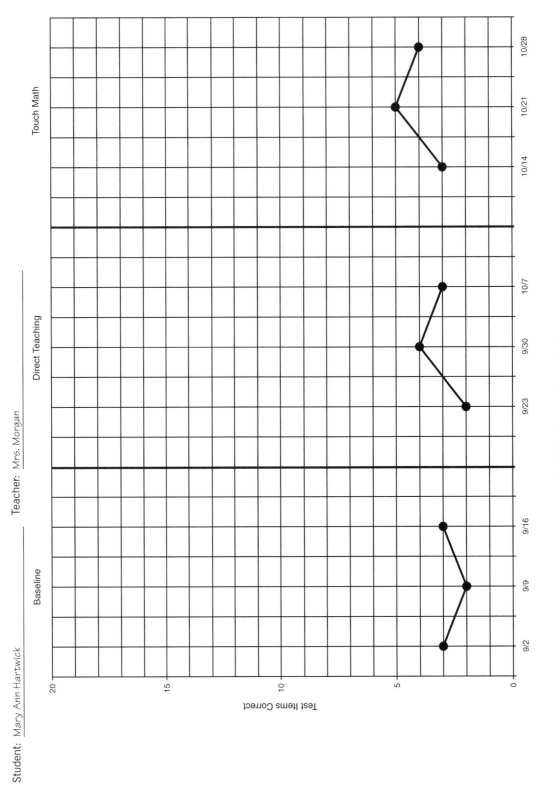

FIGURE 11.5. Mary Ann's math progress.

CONFIDENTIAL
Benson School District
Moose Valley, Alaska
Psychological Evaluation

Name: Mary Ann Hartwick

Date of Birth: 1/17/2001

Age: 9 years, 0 months

Grade: 3rd

Evaluation Dates: 1/18, 1/20, 1/25/2010

Report Date: 2/15/10

IDENTIFICATION OF PROBLEM

On September 15, 2009, all third-grade students in Benson School District were given curriculum-based measures of reading and math proficiency. Mary Ann scored above the target level for reading but scored well below the target for math. Her teacher, Patricia Morgan, identified Mary Ann as a student needing additional math instruction, and small-group math lessons taught by Mrs. Morgan were begun on September 23, 2009.

DEFINITION OF PROBLEM

Background Information about Student

Mary Ann has attended school in the Benson District since kindergarten. An interview with her mother held on January 4, 2010, revealed that Mary Ann reportedly likes the social aspects of school but not the academic work. Mrs. Hartwick reported that Mary Ann was born without complications after a full-term pregnancy. Mary Ann has two younger siblings, Matt (age 6) and Cecily (age 3). Mrs. Hartwick explained that Cecily has cerebral palsy and receives in-home services for her needs under an Individualized Family Service Plan (IFSP). Mrs. Hartwick said that Mary Ann was very healthy as a baby and that her school absences were related to difficulties getting Mary Ann to school and frequent family trips to obtain medical services for Mary Ann's little sister.

Review of Mary Ann's school records showed that she met all milestones at the kindergarten screening and made good progress during her kindergarten year. No problems with overall skill development were noted. Teacher reports from first grade included frequent mention of Mary Ann being absent from school often. Correspondence between the school principal and Mary Ann's parents indicated that these absences were due to complications with Mrs. Hartwick's third pregnancy and the subsequent delivery of Cecily. Similar teacher reports and parent communications from second grade were also found in Mary Ann's file. Mary Ann's benchmark CBM scores from first grade and second grade show initial average performance followed by a decline in scores, starting in the middle of second grade. An interview with Mary Ann's second-grade teacher revealed that he was worried about Mary Ann's progress but decided to wait until third grade to do anything because Mary Ann was absent some part of every week during March, April, and May of the year.

Current Educational Placement

Mary Ann is currently enrolled in a general education third-grade class at Susan Butcher School in Moose Valley, Alaska. Review of Mary Ann's first two report cards for the year showed that she is quiet and withdrawn on the days she is present, but that she was absent 36 out of 68 school days.

Sources of Information

Information concerning Mary Ann's present level of school performance was obtained from the following sources:

> Interviews with Mary Ann, Mrs. Hardwick, and Mary Ann's teachers
> Fall CBM benchmarks
> RTI (Tier 2) progress data
> Key Math Test
> Children's Memory Scale
> Rapid Naming subtests of the Comprehensive Test of Phonological Processing
> Achenbach System of Empirically Based Assessments

The scores obtained from these assessments are summarized in Tables 11.2–11.5. The tables include information that can be used to compare Mary Ann's performance with that of other students her age. The CBM scores show that Mary Ann is reading better than many fourth-grade students, but her math performance is much weaker. Additional math assessment with the Key Math Test showed that Mary Ann's math skills are below-average in all areas. Both her Children's Memory Scale and Rapid Naming test scores are in the average range when compared with norms from a national sample of students her age. These scores suggest that Mary Ann has average memory and retrieval skills for a girl of her age.

Both Mary Ann's mom and teacher provided responses on the Achenbach Child Behavior Checklist indicating that Mary Ann often appears withdrawn and sad. These psychological evaluation data as well as interviews revealed that Mary Ann evidences characteristics associated with a depressed state. An interview with Mary Ann was consistent with the Achenbach scores. Mary Ann reported that she is sad "all the time" and "wished she could make her sister better." Mary Ann also reported that she likes it when she gets to stay home and help her mom because it makes her feel "useful." When asked if she thought that missing so much school might hurt her learning, Mary Ann responded by saying, "Yes, but what good is school anyway if the doctors can't make my sister better?"

Summary of Problem Definition

The combined evaluation information presented here suggests that Mary Ann's math skills are lower than expected for a third-grade student in Benson School District. These apparent dif-

TABLE 11.2. Mary Ann's Curriculum-Based Measurement Scores and Local Benchmark Scores

Test	Mary Ann's score	Local benchmark range
Reading (oral reading fluency)	126	72–122
Math (addition and subtraction fluency)	3	11–15

TABLE 11.3. Mary Ann's Key Math Test Scores

Subtest	Standard score	Percentile rank	Confidence interval
Basic Concepts	81	9	75–87
Operations	78	3	73–83
Applications	73	2	66–80

TABLE 11.4. Mary Ann's Children's Memory Scale Scores

Subtest	Standard score	Percentile rank	Confidence interval
Immediate Verbal Memory	99	49	93–105
Delayed Verbal Memory	98	47	91–105
Immediate Visual Memory	101	51	96–106
Delayed Visual Memory	102	52	96–108
General Memory	100	50	95–105

TABLE 11.5. Mary Ann's Comprehensive Test of Phonological Processing Scores

Subtest	Scaled score[a]	Percentile rank	Confidence interval
Rapid Color Naming	9	48	6–12
Rapid Digit Naming	10	50	7–13
Rapid Letter Naming	11	52	8–14
Rapid Object Naming	12	55	9–15
Rapid Naming Quotient	101	56	95–107

[a]Scaled scores have a mean of 10 and standard deviation of 3; quotients have a mean of 100 and standard deviation of 15.

ficulties have been observed in classroom performance, CBM testing, and on a comprehensive math assessment. While there is a strong consistency in Mary Ann's math scores and performance, evaluation results from assessment of memory skills indicate that the subskills necessary for fluent math computation appear to be intact. Specifically, no deficits or difficulties with rapid automatic naming or other memory skills were observed. The lack of any below-average scores on the memory tests suggests that Mary Ann's school difficulties are related to factors others than memory. Mary Ann did exhibit characteristics associated with a depressive disorder. Her own report, as well as those of her teacher and mother, indicated that she feels sad most of the time.

Taken all together, the evaluation results can be used to generate a hypothesis about Mary Ann's school difficulties. The data suggest that Mary Ann's math problems may be related to her poor school attendance and depressed state. The following suggestions for validating this hypothesis and solving the problem are offered for consideration.

POSSIBLE SOLUTIONS

The following recommendations are based on the current assessment data and are offered for consideration by the team:

1. Increase Mary Ann's attendance and participation in school activities, including math instruction.
2. Reinforce Mary Ann's capability for accurate math work completion.
3. Help Mary Ann's family access family counseling to address the effects of her sister's medical status and needs on the family; Mary Ann may benefit from brief cognitive-behavioral therapy to promote better coping skills. The family may want to consider a referral for additional mental health services for Mary Ann.
4. Provide intensive remedial math instruction to bring Mary Ann's skills up to third-grade level.

Respectfully submitted,
Rachel Brown-Chidsey, PhD, NCSP   2/15/09
Rachel Brown-Chidsey, PhD, NCSP   Date
School Psychologist

Luke: Identification of Disability Using RTI and Cognitive Measures

Luke Walters is a second-grade student with math difficulties. The following sample report shows how RTI procedures were used to identify a learning disability. In Luke's case, RTI methods were used to improve his math skills. When these did not work, he was referred for an evaluation and found to have a specific math disorder.

CONFIDENTIAL
Lincoln School District
Riverside, Oregon
Psychological Evaluation

Name: Luke Walters

Date of Birth: 3/16/2002

Age: 7 years, 8 months

Grade: 2nd

Evaluation Dates: 11/9, 11/12, 11/16/2009

Report Date: 12/01/2009

IDENTIFICATION OF PROBLEM

In September 2009 Luke participated in fall curriculum-based measurement of all students' reading and math skills. While Luke's reading skills were observed to be in the average range, his math scores were well below the expected target for second-grade students.

DEFINITION OF PROBLEM

Background Information about Student

Luke has attended Lincoln Elementary School since kindergarten. He has made suitable progress in most skills areas, but a review of his records indicates that he struggled with math in kindergarten and first grade. In kindergarten, Lincoln students learn counting and quantity skills. By the end of kindergarten, students are expected to be able to count to 100. Luke was able to count only to 52 at the end of his kindergarten year. In first grade Luke again struggled with math and received Title I math instruction. He worked in a small group for 30 minutes each day throughout the year on learning to add single digits up to a sum of 10. By the end of first grade, Luke obtained a score of 8 digits correct on the spring CBM benchmark. At the beginning of second grade Luke again displayed difficulty with math skills. On the fall math CBM benchmark Luke scored only 3 test items correct. The district's CBM data indicated that students who scored below 17 correct items were at risk for ongoing math difficulties.

Current Educational Placement

Due to his score on the fall benchmark, Luke was provided with daily small-group math instruction. This instruction included using the Great Leaps Math program (2004) to build students' fluency with basic computation skills. Progress monitoring data collected during the intervention showed that Luke scored between 4 and 6 test items correct over 3 weeks of the Great Leaps intervention. Due to Luke's limited progress, a new intervention was tried. He moved into a group using the Touch Math program. This program includes direct and sequenced math skills instruction. Progress monitoring data revealed that Luke gained only 2 points after using the Touch Math program for 3 weeks. At the end of October, Luke's teacher referred him for a comprehensive evaluation for special education.

Sources of Information

Information concerning Luke's present level of school performance was obtained from the following sources:

> Interviews with Luke, Mr. Walters, and Luke's teachers
> Fall CBM benchmarks
> RTI (Tier 2) progress data

The scores obtained from benchmark and Tier 2 assessments are summarized in Figure 11.6.

Summary of Problem Definition

Luke's current math computation skills are well below what is expected of grade 2 students at Lincoln Elementary School. Two interventions designed to improve Luke's computation skills resulted in only minimal progress. Given that Luke has made adequate progress in all school areas except math and that he did not respond to two scientifically based math instruction programs, it appears that his math difficulties can best be understood as a specific math learning disability.

POSSIBLE SOLUTIONS

The following recommendations are based on the current assessment data and are offered for consideration by the team:

1. Luke may benefit from more intensive math instruction. He may need individualized daily math instruction that focuses on mastering basic computation fluency.
2. Luke is likely to benefit from short-term counseling and instruction to understand what learning disabilities are and how they affect those who have them.

Respectfully submitted,
Mark W. Steege, PhD, NCSP, BCBA   12/1/2009
Mark W. Steege, PhD, NCSP, BCBA   Date
School Psychologist

Jane: Additional Assessment Is Needed

Sometimes evaluations do not yield the answers that we would like to have. In the case of Jane, the data obtained from the evaluation were inconclusive. When the data obtained as part of an evaluation do not yield a clear answer, then additional assessment should be conducted. It is appropriate to summarize the initial data in a preliminary report so that all team members can be made aware of what evaluation procedures have been conducted as well as what additional

Student: Luke Walters   Teacher: Mrs. Tilton

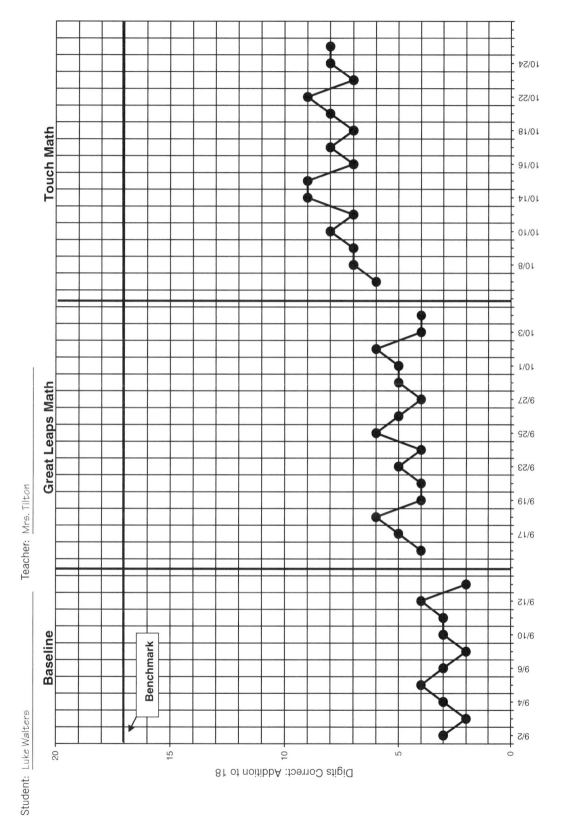

FIGURE 11.6. Luke's math progress.

assessments need to be conducted and when. In such cases, it may be necessary to work closely with the student's parents as well as school staff to ensure that all required parental notification and consultation occur on schedule. In some states, it is possible to have a student qualify for special education services on a temporary or "diagnostic" basis until more assessment data are available to confirm the student's instructional needs. Information from the initial evaluation, such as that given below, provides a starting point for identifying the student's current needs.

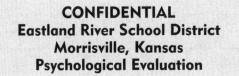

CONFIDENTIAL
Eastland River School District
Morrisville, Kansas
Psychological Evaluation

Name: Jane Murrey
Date of Birth: 7/11/99
Age: 10 years, 4 months

Grade: 5th
Evaluation Dates: 11/2, 11/3, 11/4/2009
Report Date: 11/20/09

IDENTIFICATION OF PROBLEM

Jane was reported by her classroom teacher to have significant reading difficulties.

DEFINITION OF PROBLEM

Background Information about Student

Jane moved to Morrisville in July 2009. Prior to living in Morrisville, her family lived in several towns in central Kansas. No educational records from Jane's prior schools were found in her cumulative folder. Efforts to contact Jane's parents to obtain additional information about Jane's educational history were not successful. Jane scored 34 on the fall CBM reading assessment. The fall reading goal for fifth-grade students is 70 words per minute.

Current Educational Placement

Jane is currently enrolled in Nancy Adams's class at Eastland Elementary. Owing to Jane's low scores on baseline reading assessment measures given in follow-up to the fall benchmark, her teacher implemented the Great Leaps reading program with Jane and several other students. Jane's progress in the Great Leaps program was monitored with oral reading fluency probes twice per week. These scores were graphed and revealed that Jane made no progress in her reading fluency. On October 8th Ms. Adams moved Jane to a new reading group that used the shadow reading procedure. This procedure involves having students read along with and right after the teacher to improve reading fluency. Data collected twice a week during the shadow reading intervention revealed that Jane made only very limited progress.

Sources of Information

Information concerning Jane's present level of school performance was obtained from the following sources:

> Interview with Jane
> Fall CBM benchmarks
> RTI (Tier 2) progress data

The scores obtained from benchmark and Tier 2 assessments are summarized in Figure 11.7. In addition to the intervention data, in an interview with Jane she reported that she has always struggled with reading and that she would like to become a better reader. Jane reported that there are few books at home and that her parents work too late to read to her at night.

Summary of Problem Definition

Jane's current reading skills are well below what is expected of beginning fifth-grade students at Eastland. Efforts to improve Jane's reading skills by using Great Leaps and shadow reading did not result in improved reading performance.

POSSIBLE SOLUTIONS

The following recommendations are based on the current assessment data and are offered for consideration by the team:

1. Additional information about Jane's school history is needed; continued efforts to contact her parents are urged.
2. More specific information about Jane's reading skills is needed. Such information is usually obtained from individualized testing. Parental consent to conduct a detailed evaluation of Jane's reading skills is recommended.

Respectfully submitted,
<u>Rachel Brown-Chidsey, PhD, NCSP</u>   <u>11/21/09</u>
Rachel Brown-Chidsey, PhD, NCSP   Date
School Psychologist

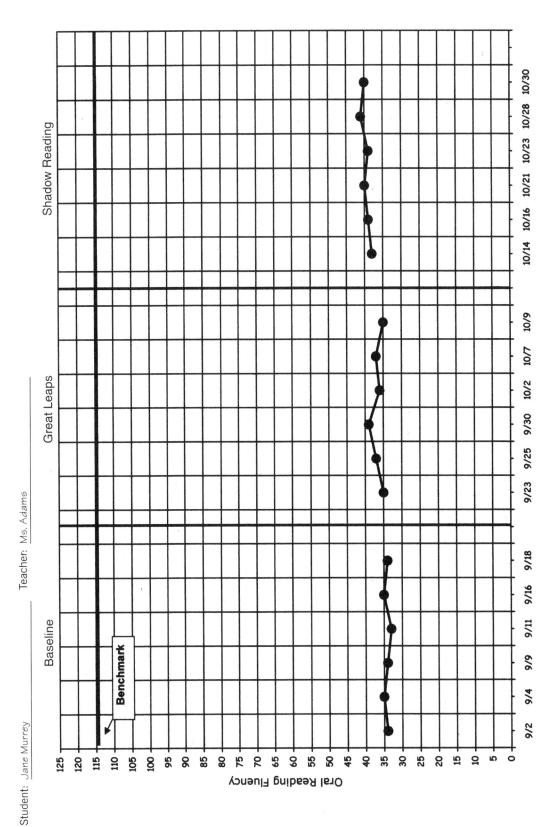

FIGURE 11.7. Jane's reading progress.

Sandy: Error Analysis as Part of Formal Assessment

The final evaluation report includes an example of how error analysis data can be used as part of a comprehensive evaluation. In this case, data for a student named Sandy did not immediately reveal the source of her reading difficulties. The evaluator conducted an error analysis as part of the evaluation to learn more about Sandy's reading difficulties. The error data, along with other sources of useful input, provided the team with enough information to make a decision about special education eligibility and Sandy's instructional needs.

CONFIDENTIAL
Crabapple Cove School District
Crabapple Cove, Maine
Psychological Evaluation

Student: Sandy Beech

Date of Birth: 2/14/01

Age: 8 years, 3 months

Grade: 3

Evaluation Dates: 10/1, 10/2, 10/5, 10/13, 10/19, 2009

Report Date: October 26, 2009

IDENTIFICATION OF PROBLEM

Sandy was referred by the Seal Harbor Elementary School Problem-Solving Team for assessment because of concerns regarding her delays in the area of reading. The team requested comprehensive assessments of Sandy's reading behaviors.

DEFINITION OF PROBLEM

Background Information about Student

Sandy lives with her parents (Jib and Halyard Spinnaker) and younger brother (Seal) in Seaside, Maine. Review of available educational records and interviews revealed that Sandy has attended Seal Harbor Elementary since kindergarten. Although Sandy has struggled in the area of reading, she has otherwise made good progress in meeting expected learning outcomes.

Current Educational Placement

Sandy has participated in screening assessments three times a year since kindergarten. Her scores on these screening assessments as well as the goal scores for each area are shown in Table 11.6. These scores indicate that Sandy started each school year a few points below the goal for the grade. Starting in kindergarten, Sandy has been provided with additional reading instruction on a daily basis. This instruction has included an additional 30 minutes per day in a small-group format with other students who have similar reading skills. The screening data

TABLE 11.6. Sandy's Reading Screening Scores

Grade	Fall Score	Fall Goal	Winter Score	Winter Goal	Spring Score	Spring Goal
Kindergarten						
Initial sounds	9	8	29	25		NA
Letter naming	10	8	30	27	41	40
Phoneme segmentation		NA	15	18	31	35
Nonsense words		NA	10	13	21	25
Grade 1						
Letter naming	39	37		NA		NA
Phoneme segmentation	31	35	38	35	40	35
Nonsense words	22	24	47	50	51	50
Oral reading		NA	12	20	36	40
Grade 2						
Nonsense Words	48	50		NA		NA
Oral Reading	34	44	62	68	87	90
Grade 3						
Oral Reading	68	77		92		110

show that Sandy's scores have improved over the course of each year. Notably, Sandy's fall scores have consistently been below the levels where she scored during the preceding spring.

Sources of Information

Record Review
Interviews:

> Ms. Orten (3rd-grade classroom teacher)
> Ms. Gillingham (reading specialist)
> Mr. and Mrs. Beech (parents)

Anecdotal observations
Descriptive assessment
Error analysis assessment
Brief assessment: Response to intervention
Extended assessment: Response to intervention

Anecdotal Observations

In order to learn Sandy's typical classroom behaviors, she was observed during individual and small-group reading instruction, math instruction, and recess. The results of observation indicated that Sandy was actively engaged in all classroom activities in ways similar to her classroom peers. Following anecdotal observations, direct observations and assessments of reading behaviors were conducted.

Descriptive Assessment

This assessment involved asking Sandy to read sets of leveled passages, starting with third-grade material and working backward to first-grade material. For each grade level, Sandy read three passages, and the middle score for each grade level was used as an indicator of Sandy's skills at that level. Sandy read all the materials orally. Oral reading fluency (ORF) is a measure of the combined accuracy and speed of reading and is reported in words read correctly per minute (WRC). The benchmark ORF is the WRC level that is expected of students in a given grade level in fall, winter, and spring. The results of the descriptive assessment are shown in Table 11.7. For each passage and the median, the number of WRC is shown first and the number of reading errors follows the solidus in each column. The winter ORF benchmarks were used for comparison because that is the reading goal toward which students are currently working.

Sandy's scores show that she did not meet the benchmark goal for any of the third-grade passages, but she did meet the goal for the second-grade passages. She also exceeded the goal for the first-grade passages. These scores suggest that Sandy's current reading performance matches second-grade level material.

Error Analysis Assessment

In order to understand Sandy's reading skills better, an error analysis was conducted. The types of errors that Sandy made during reading were reviewed and coded as one of the following:

1. Omission: not reading a word; skipping a word when reading from the passage.
2. Meaning-based substitution: replacing the word in the passage with another word with a similar meaning.

TABLE 11.7. Sandy's Survey-Level Assessment Scores

| Grade Level | WRC/Errors | | | | Winter Benchmark |
	Passage 1	Passage 2	Passage 3	Median	
1st	91/3	86/2	84/3	86/3	20
2nd	82/5	73/6	77/4	77/5	68
3rd	72/9	68/11	81/8	72/9	92

3. Orthographic substitution: replacing the word in the passage with a word that starts with the same letter.
4. Mispronunciation: not reading the word correctly; decoding error.
5. Latency: word read either after 3-second-delay or after modeling by the evaluator.
6. Insertions: words added to the text by the reader; these are not counted as errors in the total error count.

In addition to the error codes, Sandy's overall reading comprehension was estimated by dividing the number of words read *correctly* by the total number of words read. In order to comprehend text, a reader needs to have about 95% reading accuracy. Sandy's error analysis data is shown in Table 11.8.

The error analysis revealed that Sandy made primarily substitution and mispronunciation errors. Sandy's substitutions included mainly orthographic errors, where she said a word that began with the same letter as the printed word. Such errors typically indicate that a student has not fully mastered the alphabetic principle of sound–symbol correspondence.

POSSIBLE SOLUTIONS

The results of the descriptive assessment and error analysis assessment were shared with members of the problem-solving team. Using a collaborative problem-solving process, the following hypotheses about Sandy's reading difficulties were generated:

1. Sandy has not yet fully mastered the sound–symbol correspondence between letters and the sounds that correspond with them. This lack of mastery is observable in lower-than-expected reading fluency and comprehension.
2. Sandy reads very slowly and makes more errors as the text's difficulty increases. This reading pattern suggests that Sandy has problems with reading fluency.
3. Sandy is very comfortable reading first- and second-grade material and does not seek out more difficult reading material on her own. When given third-grade reading material, Sandy is not able to read rapidly or fluently. She can read such material, but she does not stop to sound out words that are new to her. In such cases her reading accuracy

TABLE 11.8. Sandy's Error Analysis Data

Grade level	Omissions	Substitutions	Mispronunciations	Latency	Insertions	ORF	Comprehension
1st	0	3	0	0	0	86	97%
2nd	1	2	2	0	0	77	94%
3rd	1	4	3	1	0	72	89%

and comprehension are weakened. Although Sandy has the skills to read third-grade material, she does not use these skills as needed.

To test these hypotheses, the team decided to "test drive" interventions with Sandy and measure how she responded to each of the interventions. This process involved asking Sandy to read from graded passages, providing one type of intervention during that passage, and recording the number of words read correctly and the number and types of reading errors. Sandy read the passages according to three reading intervention conditions, matched to the three hypotheses about her reading problems. The three reading conditions were:

1. Reading decodable text that included only words that Sandy had learned to read individually.
2. Repeated reading of a passage.
3. Offering Sandy a prize from a "treasure box" if she reached a preset oral reading goal of 92 words read correctly in 1 minute.

By measuring Sandy's response to each intervention, the team was able to determine which intervention(s) improved Sandy's reading performance over baseline levels of reading and the relative effectiveness of the interventions. In other words, the team was able to answer the question "Which intervention was the *most effective* for Sandy?

Results

Sandy read three passages at the third-grade level during each brief intervention. For each intervention type, Sandy's middle score (median) on the three passages was recorded. The results of these brief interventions are summarized in Figure 11.8. These data indicated that when reading third-grade passages Sandy did best when using a repeated reading intervention. She read 84 words correctly with only two errors during this condition. By comparison, when Sandy read the decodable passages, she read 72 words correctly but still made six errors. Sandy's reading during the incentive condition was the least fluent of the three conditions, as she scored 56 WRC with 6 errors. These results suggest that Sandy is likely to benefit most from a repeated reading intervention to improve her reading skills.

Respectfully submitted,

Mark W. Steege, PhD, NCSP, BCBA   10/26/2009

Mark W. Steege, PhD, NCSP, BCBA   Date

School Psychologist

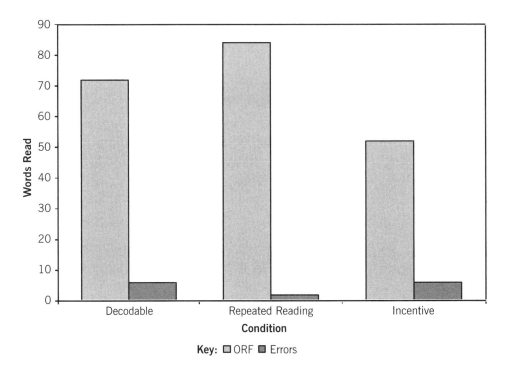

FIGURE 11.8. Brief experimental analysis of reading interventions.

SUMMARY

This chapter has provided a report outline and examples of reports using RTI data. There are three main types of reports used with RTI procedures: brief summary reports, longitudinal data summary reports, and full psychological evaluation reports. Each of these reports provides information about the success of specific RTI procedures. Brief summary reports are designed to be used with all students to share information about general progress. Longitudinal data summary reports provide information that can be used to determine whether an intervention is working. Evaluation reports (often psychological in nature) are used as part of the special education referral process and incorporate RTI data from longitudinal reports but also include other assessment data. To be maximally useful, RTI data must be communicated to those who can best use it to make the critical decisions about students' instructional needs. These report formats offer differentiated ways of sharing RTI data so that teachers, students, and even their parents can participate meaningfully in educational planning aimed at correcting the students' academic deficiencies.

CHAPTER 12

Frequently Asked Questions
Some Answers about RTI

This chapter includes a number of frequently asked questions about RTI, followed by our answers to these questions. Where applicable, we refer readers to the page numbers where more detailed answers to the question may be found.

1. *What is response to intervention?* *Response to intervention* (RTI) is a systematic and data-based method for identifying, defining, and resolving students' academic and/or behavioral difficulties (see pp. 4–5 in Chapter 1). We have defined RTI as a general set of procedures that can be applied to the specific needs of students in schools. RTI is *not* about another form of special education or another "hurdle" that teachers must overcome.

2. *What do I need to know about RTI?* All educators need to know that RTI is a general education initiative that can help all students be more successful in school. RTI includes three tiers of instruction. The first tier is for all students and is the general curriculum. Tier 2 is provided *in addition to* Tier 1 and usually features small-group instruction for about 30 minutes per day. Tier 3 can either be added on to Tiers 1 and 2 or replace Tier 1 if a student needs more intensive instruction.

3. *Who developed RTI?* No single person developed RTI. It is the result of many years of effort to meet the educational needs of all students. A number of researchers contributed to the scientific findings that support RTI. These findings include information about effective instruction and assessment.

4. *How time-consuming is RTI?* When compared to the 10 or more hours often estimated to go into each individualized evaluation conducted for special education eligibility, RTI procedures are not really so time-consuming, at all. While the research steps necessary to review potential Tier 1 and 2 interventions may take several hours, the universal screening is very brief, taking about 10 minutes per student, at most. If CBM is used as the universal screening tool, the only measures requiring individualized testing are DIBELS and oral reading fluency. In the areas of math, spelling, and writing, the assessment items

185

can be administered to entire classes at the same time. Similarly, CBM progress monitoring procedures are very fast, involving weekly testing of 2 minutes or less per student. Most important, several studies (Fuchs et al., 2003; O'Connor, 2003; Tilly, 2003; VanDerHeyden et al., 2007) have shown that RTI methods reduce the overall number of comprehensive evaluations needed; so, there is a net decrease in personnel time expended rather than an increase in the demands placed on staff. Specific data on how many hours are spent on specific RTI procedures need to be collected so that comparisons and cost effectiveness can be more precisely calculated.

5. *How expensive is RTI?* Preventing school failure is always cheaper than paying for remedial education and other supports. The activities in RTI are no more expensive than typical school costs. Since RTI has been found to prevent the need for special education, there are provisions in IDEA 2004 for use of a certain amount of special education funds for joint general–special education services and instruction. Specifically, school districts can spend up to 15% of their special education (IDEA) money on activities that include general education students. Ideal uses for the 15% allocation include materials, training, and support for Tier 2 interventions. Tier 1 activities are clearly general education programs; however, Tier 2 is designed to provide prevention-focused programs for students who are "at risk" for school difficulties. If most of the students who receive Tier 2 supports never need special education, then both the 15% money as well as cost savings from reductions in the number of students with disabilities can be used to fund and strengthen Tier 2 programs and consultation activities by school psychology personnel that support such interventions.

> **Many people have referred to RTI as an "unfunded mandate" by the government. This is not technically true. Except in a few states, RTI is not mandated, and the decision to use RTI methods in a school is made at the local level. Importantly, there is no evidence that schools need more money to implement RTI. Instead, RTI requires changing existing practices rather than adding new ones that cost more money.**

6. *What is the role of general education teachers in using RTI?* General educators are the "first-line" personnel in RTI. They welcome, work with, and know the challenges facing students from the moment they come to school. For this reason RTI—first and foremost—a general education initiative, which means that general education teachers have a critical role in making RTI work. Indeed, far more general educators will be involved in the administration of RTI than all the specialists combined. For this reason, training, materials, and support for general education teachers must be integrated into all RTI planning from the very beginning.

7. *Is RTI useful with general education students or just students with learning disabilities?* RTI is a general education methodology designed to enhance educational outcomes *for all students*. While students with learning disabilities are frequently mentioned in RTI research because they doubtless benefit from its mindful implementation, nevertheless, RTI methods have been shown to help a wide variety of students, regardless of disability.

8. *Does RTI result in an increase in identification of students with LD?* No. Data collected so far have shown that RTI procedures are associated with a decrease in the

number of students identified as learning disabled. Analysis of these data suggests that such reductions are the result of providing students preventive services so that the actual incidence of LD is reduced. This phenomenon is similar to prevention efforts in health care wherein healthy lifestyle factors such as good nutrition and exercise can reduce the actual incidence of such conditions as obesity, diabetes, and hypertension. Some students will still manifest learning disabilities, but the overall numbers are expected to decrease if specific instructional methods are applied at critical early grade levels.

9. *We've been using a discrepancy model for identifying students with LD for years. What's the problem with continuing to use this model?* A number of limitations to the widely used IQ–achievement discrepancy formula for identifying learning disabilities have been documented. Chapter 3 of this volume describes these limitations (pp. 27–28). In sum, the research indicates that IQ–achievement discrepancy formulas are very inaccurate. Given that the goal of special education is to provide children with disabilities a free appropriate education in the least restrictive environment, continuing to use a discrepancy formula known to be inaccurate in determining which students have a learning disability does not fulfill the mission of special education. Some research has shown that use of discrepancy formulas has led to *more restrictive* educational placements for students. Continuing to use a discrepancy formula when more accurate and less restrictive methods are available is not justified.

> **Many researchers have found that IQ–achievement discrepancies are not accurate indicators of whether a student has a learning disability. In many of these studies, discrepancy numbers have been no better than chance in showing which students have a learning disability.**

10. *How does RTI compare with curriculum-based measurement procedures?* RTI involves using a wide array of assessment and instructional methods. In contrast, curriculum-based measurement is one specific type of assessment that can be used for evaluation of students' academic skills. CBM procedures can be used as part of RTI, but they are not one and the same. CBM and RTI do share a common link with a problem-solving model of assessment, in which students' school difficulties (whether academic or behavioral) are understood as being manifestations of person–environment interactions. RTI for academic skills may include use of CBM but will also include many more steps and procedures as well. RTI for problem behaviors would not involve use of CBM but might well include use of functional behavioral assessment procedures.

11. *Does this mean no more IQ testing?* Maybe. But probably not. Although the limitations of IQ scores have been described by many authors over time (Brown-Chidsey, 2005a; Gould, 1981/1996), IQ scores are not likely to disappear immediately. As noted above, there are significant problems with IQ–achievement score discrepancies, but this difficulty is different from problems with IQ scores themselves. Research has shown that IQ scores do provide a general indicator of cognitive ability after about the age of 10 and over one's lifespan. At this time an IQ score is still required for diagnosis of mental retardation; therefore IQ tests will continue to be used for the foreseeable future for certain assessments. Additionally, certain components of IQ tests may be useful for detailed testing of specific cognitive abilities (Flanagan & Harrison, 2005).

12. *Will the RTI model result in the reduction of teaching and other staff positions?* Not necessarily. Although staffing to support RTI varies across the United States, no evidence has surfaced yet attributing a decrease in teaching or other staff positions to RTI initiatives. Indeed, in certain localities the number of teaching and support staff positions has actually increased when RTI methods have been put into place. Such new jobs become possible when RTI procedures result in fewer special education placements, enabling funds to be reallocated from evaluation to prevention and consultation services. These additional staff members can then help maintain the benefits obtained through RTI methods.

13. *If relevant federal legislation does not require use of RTI, why should I use it?* First, it's the right thing to do. A wealth of evidence has documented how past and current special education programs are not meeting students' needs. RTI has been shown to provide an effective mechanism by which students can receive the instruction they need. The old adage "If it ain't broke, don't fix it" does not apply here. There is clear evidence that both general and special education programs in many parts of the United States are definitely broken and need to be fixed. RTI offers a way to repair and improve instruction for all students. Just because IDEA 2004 recommends but does not (yet) require RTI does not excuse professionals who know of its benefits from applying the three tiers to improve educational outcomes for students. Notably ARRA focuses heavily on collecting student data to reflect improvements. It is anticipated that future revisions of IDEA and ESEA will require RTI practices and student outcome data. Those educators who begin using RTI practices now will be well ahead of such future requirements.

14. *What resources are available to support those of us who need additional training in the use of RTI methods?* In addition to this book, a number of RTI training resources exist. Professional associations such as the Council for Exceptional Children, National Association of School Psychologists, National Education Association, and others have materials about RTI methods. State and regional associations also offer workshops and training each year. There is an online RTI resource center known as the National Center on Response to Intervention (*www.rti4success.org*). The U.S. Department of Education has set up a website specifically for information about evidence-based education practices. Known as the What Works Clearinghouse (*www.whatworks.ed.gov*), this resource provides a continuously updated source for information on scientifically based instructional practices. Similarly, the Institute for the Development of Educational Achievement at the University of Oregon (*idea.uoregon.edu*) offers research summaries and technical assistance focusing on educational attainment for all students.

BENEFITS OF RTI

This book has provided a detailed description of the research, model, and steps relating to response to intervention methods. Although RTI is still an emerging methodology, we believe that it offers great promise for increasing the likelihood that *all* students will be successful in school.

Although RTI has been shown to provide needed help to struggling students, it also helps those who were not struggling. It does this by providing a comprehensive and systematic way of ensuring that all students get the help they need as quickly as possible.

PRINCIPLES, SKILLS, AND PRACTICES

RTI is composed of principles, skills, and practices. Alone, each of these components is a modestly useful pedagogical tool. For example, the RTI principle of data-driven systematic instruction can be useful to teachers outside of RTI activities in that it provides a way to organize and structure classroom activities. Similarly, the skills necessary to implement RTI such as benchmark data collection and data interpretation can help teachers review their own past or current assessment and instructional practices. Likewise, applying RTI methods such as creating Tier 2 groups may be helpful for certain students. It is the combination of all three components that makes RTI truly useful. As noted at the beginning of this volume, RTI borrows from a number of scientifically based educational practices that have long been shown to be effective. By combining these techniques, RTI offers a comprehensive prevention-oriented approach to maximizing learning for all students.

RTI APPLICATIONS

There are two major subdivisions into which RTI can be organized. First and foremost it is a general education initiative designed to promote the most effective instruction for all students. Second, RTI provides a set of procedures that can be used in conjunction with other evaluation tools to identify whether a student has a specific LD.

General Education

When used as part of general education, RTI has several distinct advantages. First, RTI facilitates greater communication and consistency in teaching methods among those who teach the same grade or subject. While teachers may share ideas and plans with one another on a collegial basis, there is not a strong history of systematic discussion of progress for all students in the same grade. Second, RTI procedures place emphasis on a belief that all students can learn. By providing all students with high-quality systematic instruction and monitoring their progress, the RTI methodology assumes that most students will be successful. Importantly, even those students who need the extra instruction provided in Tier 2 lessons are included in general education. The goal and expectation is that all students can learn if given the right instruction. A small number of students will not respond to Tier 2 instruction, and comprehensive evaluation of their needs may result in special education services. Still, the mantra covering all aspects of RTI is that students who are not successful at a given tier are those students for whom the right (i.e., effective) intervention has not *yet* been found.

Special Education

RTI also has a role in special education. Specifically, it is mentioned in IDEA 2004 as one of several assessment tools that can be combined to determine whether a student has a learning disability. The nature of the RTI wording in IDEA 2004 documents a strong message that the least restrictive environment (LRE) is an important aspect of educational planning for all students. A similar emphasis is found in the No Child Left Behind Act. Both IDEA 2004 and NCLB include language requiring that schools do everything in their power to provide all students with high-quality, scientifically based effective instruction. Legislative mandates requiring certain procedures are not the same thing as the actual application of the procedures. Only time will tell how well the goals stated in IDEA 2004 and NCLB are met. Still, the policy emphasis is clear: as a society we must do *everything* we can to educate *all* students in certain basic skills. Less explicit in the laws and regulations is the rationale for this universal policy. Unstated is the critical importance of basic skills in reading, writing, and mathematics for basic economic self-sufficiency. Certainly some critics might argue about the merit of this emphasis; however, the emerging economic trends in most world regions support attainment of basic educational skills by all students, or at least as many as possible.

FUTURE DIRECTIONS

Every scientific endeavor requires ongoing research. Scientists continue to refine and verify prior findings even among the most validated and documented practices. When a body of knowledge is no longer studied, it is no longer scientific. The same is true for educational sciences. More study of all aspects of RTI is needed. A variety of research strands need to be explored. However, the three main questions about RTI of greatest urgency are:

1. What are students' long-term outcomes when RTI methods are used?
2. Are there differences in outcomes when RTI methods are used with students from diverse linguistic, racial, religious, cultural, disability, and regional groups?
3. What are the organizational and systems variables needed to promote and sustain effective RTI practices?

RTI researchers are urged to address these questions as part of their scientific endeavors. Other questions will emerge as a result of ongoing RTI practices and research. Only through systematic and long-term investigation will the ultimate relative value and importance of RTI be realized. While such work is ongoing, all educators are encouraged to learn, use, and evaluate those RTI practices most relevant to their area(s) of interest, using the obtained student data to promote academic success for all students. Training slides that summarize the major ideas in this book are available from the publisher's website at *www. guilford.com/rti.*

References

Aaron, P., Joshi, R., Gooden, R., & Bentum, K. (2008, January). Diagnosis and treatment of reading disabilities based on the component model of reading. *Journal of Learning Disabilities, 41*, 67–84.

Ackerman, R. D. (1987). Regular education initiative [Letter to the Editor]. *Journal of Learning Disabilities, 20*, 514–515.

Albrecht, S. F. (2008). Time away: A skill-building alternative to discipline. *Preventing School Failure, 53*, 49–55.

Al Otaiba, S., & Torgeson, J. (2007). Effects from intensive standardized kindergarten and first grade interventions for the prevention of reading disabilities. In S. R. Jimerson, M. K. Burns, & A. M. VanDerHeyden (Eds.), *Handbook of response to intervention: The science and practice of assessment and intervention* (pp. 212–222). New York: Springer.

American Academy of Child and Adolescent Psychiatry. (1993, October 20). Policy statement on facilitated communication. Retrieved from *www.aacap.org/publications/policy*.

American Academy of Pediatrics, Committee on Children with Disabilities. (1998). Auditory integration training and facilitated communication for autism. *Pediatrics, 102*, 431–433.

American Association on Mental Retardation. (2005). Behavioral supports [Position Statement]. Retrieved from *www.aamr.org/Policies/pos_beh_sppts.shtml*.

American Psychological Association. (1994). Resolution facilitated communication. Retrieved from *www.apa.org/about/division/cpmscientific.html#6*.

American Recovery and Reinvestment Act [ARRA]. (2009). Public Law 111–5 and Public Law 111–8. Division A, Title XIV. State Fiscal Stabilization Fund.

American Speech–Language–Hearing Association. (1994). Technical report of the subcommittee on facilitated communication of the ad hoc committee on auditory integration training and facilitated communication. Retrieved from *www.asha.org/NR/rdonlyres/08EAEF85–0EEC-49DF-A4FA-B8F295D6B6DD/0/19454_1.pdf*.

Ardoin, S. (2006). The response in response to intervention: Evaluating the utility of assessing maintenance of intervention effects. *Psychology in the Schools, 43*, 713–725.

Ardoin, S., Roof, C., Klubnick, C., & Carfolite, J. (2008). Evaluating curriculum-based measurement from a behavioral assessment perspective. *Behavior Analyst Today, 9*, 36–49.

Association for Behavior Analysis. (1995). Position statement on students' right to effective education. Retrieved from *www.abainternational.org/sub/membersvcs/journals-pubs/pssree/index.asp*.

August, D., & Hakuta, K. (Eds.). (1997). *Improving schooling for language minority children: A research agenda*. Washington, DC: National Academy Press

Axtell, P. K., McCallum, R. S., Bell, S. M., & Poncy, B. (2009). Developng math automaticity using a classwide fluency building procedure for middle schools students: A preliminary study. *Psychology in the Schools, 46,* 526–538.

Bagnato, S. J., & Neisworth, J. T. (1991). *Assessment for early intervention: Best practices for professionals.* New York: Guilford Press.

Barnes, A., & Harlacher, J. (2008). Clearing the confusion: Response-to-Intervention as a set of principles. *Education and Treatment of Children, 31,* 417–431.

Barnett, D., Daly E., III, Jones, K., & Lentz, F., Jr. (2004). Response to intervention: Empirically based special service decisions from single-case designs of increasing and decreasing intensity. *Journal of Special Education, 38,* 66–79.

Barnett, D., Elliott, N., Wolsing, L., Bunger, C., Haski, H., McKissick, C., et al. (2006). Response to intervention for young children with extremely challenging behaviors: What it might look like. *School Psychology Review, 35,* 568–582.

Barnett, D., VanDerHeyden, A., & Witt, J. (2007). Achieving science-based practice through response to intervention: What it might look like in preschools. *Journal of Educational and Psychological Consultation, 17,* 31–54.

Barth, A. E., Stuebing, K. K., Anthony, J. L., Denton, C. A., Mathes, P. G., Fletcher, J. M., et al. (2008). Agreement among response to intervention criteria for identifying responder status. *Learning and Individual Differences, 18,* 296–307.

Batsche, G., Elliott, J., Graden, J. L., Grimes, J., Kovaleski, J. F., Prasse, D., et al. (2005). *Response to intervention: Policy considerations and implementation.* Washington, DC: NASDSE.

Berg, W., Wacker, D., & Steege, M. (1995). Best practices in the assessment with persons who have severe or profound handicaps. In A. Thomas & J. Grimes (Eds.), *Best practices in school psychology* (pp. 805–816). Washington, DC: National Association of School Psychologists.

Bergstrom, M. (2008). Professional development in response to intervention: Implementation of a model in a rural region. *Rural Special Education Quarterly, 27*(4), 27–36.

Berninger, V. W. (2006). Research-supported ideas for implementing reauthorized IDEA with intelligent professional psychological services. *Psychology in the Schools, 43,* 781–796.

Biglan, A., Mrazek, P. J., Carnine, D., & Flay, B. R. (2003). The integration of research and practice in the prevention of youth problem behaviors. *American Psychologist, 58,* 433–441.

Blachman, B. A., Fletcher, J. M., Schatschneider, C., Francis, D. J., Clonan, S. M., Shaywitz, B. A., et al. (2004). Effects of intensive reading remediation for second and third graders and a 1–year

follow-up. *Journal of Educational Psychology, 96,* 444–462.

Boscardin, M. L., Brown-Chidsey, R., & Gonzalez-Martinez, J. (2002a). Assessment of children from diverse backgrounds. In J. Carey & P. Pedersen (Eds.), *Multicultural counseling in the schools* (2nd ed., pp. 257–279). Boston: Allyn & Bacon.

Boscardin, M. L., Brown-Chidsey, R., & Gonzalez-Martinez, J. (2002b). The essential link for students with disabilities from diverse backgrounds: Forging partnerships with families. *Journal of Special Education Leadership, 14,* 89–95.

Bransford, J. D. (1979). *Human cognition: Learning, understanding, and remembering.* Belmont, CA: Wadsworth.

Bransford, J. D., Brown, A. L., & Cocking, R. R. (Eds.). (2000). *How people learn: Brain, mind experience, and school* (expanded ed.). Washington, DC: National Academy Press.

Brown, G. W., & Brown, C. V. (2005). Physiological factors in students' school success. In R. Brown-Chidsey (Ed.), *Assessment for intervention: A problem-solving approach* (pp. 103–128). New York: Guilford Press.

Brown, J., & Doolittle, J. (2008). A cultural, linguistic, and ecological framework for response to intervention with English language learners. *Teaching Exceptional Children, 40*(5), 66–72.

Brown-Chidsey, R. (2005a). Intelligence tests in an era of standards-based educational reform. In D. P. Flanagan & P. L. Harrison (Eds.), *Contemporary intellectual assessment: Theories, tests, and issues* (2nd ed., pp. 631–641). New York: Guilford Press.

Brown-Chidsey, R. (2005b). Introduction to problem-solving assessment. In R. Brown-Chidsey (Ed.), *Assessment for intervention: A problem-solving approach* (pp. 3–9). New York: Guilford Press.

Brown-Chidsey, R. (2005c). Scaling educational assessments to inform instruction for all students: Response to intervention as essential educational science. *Trainer's Forum, 24,* 1–4, 6–8.

Brown-Chidsey, R. (2007). No more waiting to fail. *Educational Leadership, 65*(2), 40–47.

Brown-Chidsey, R., Bronaugh, L., & McGraw, K. (2009). *RTI in the classroom: Guidelines and recipes for success.* New York: Guilford Press.

Brown-Chidsey, R., Davis, L., & Maya, C. (2003). Sources of variance in curriculum-based measures of silent reading. *Psychology in the Schools, 40,* 363–377.

Brown-Chidsey, R., Seppala, M., & Segura, M. L. (2000). Chapter 766: Massachusetts special education law. *American Education Annual.* New York: Gale.

Brown-Chidsey, R., & Steege, M. W. (2005). Solution-focused psychoeducational reports. In R. Brown-Chidsey (Ed.), *Assessment for intervention: A problem-solving approach* (pp. 267–290). New York: Guilford Press.

Brown-Chidsey, R., Steege, M. W., & Mace, F. C. (2008). Best practices in evaluating the effectiveness of interventions using case study data. In A. Thomas & J. Grimes (Eds.), *Best practices in school psychology V* (pp. 2177–2191). Bethesda, MD: National Association of School Psychologists.

Bryan, T., Bay, M., & Donahue, M. (1988). Implications of the learning disabilities definition for the regular education initiative. *Journal of Learning Disabilities, 21*, 23–28.

Bryant, D., Bryant, B., & Hammill, D. D. (2005). Characteristic behaviors of students with LD who have teacher-identified math weaknesses. *Journal of Learning Disabilities, 33*, 168–177.

Bryant, D., Bryant, B., Gersten, R., Scammacca, N., & Chavez, M. (2008). Mathematics intervention for first- and second-grade students with mathematics difficulties: The effects of tier 2 intervention delivered as booster lessons. *Remedial and Special Education, 29*, 20–32.

Burns, M. K. (2002). Comprehensive system of assessment to intervention using curriculum-based assessments. *Intervention in School and Clinic, 38*, 8–13.

Burns, M. K., Ganuza, Z. M., & London, R. M. (2009). Brief experimental analysis of written letter formation: Single-case demonstration. *Journal of Behavioral Education, 18*, 20–34.

Burns, M. K., & Gibbons, K. A. (2008). *Implementing response to intervention in elementary and secondary schools: Procedures to assure scientific-based practices.* New York: Routledge.

Burns, M. K., Peters, R., & Noell, G. H. (2008). Using performance feedback to enhance implementation fidelity of the problem solving process. *Journal of School Psychology, 46*, 537–550.

Calhoon, M., Al Otaiba, S., Cihak, D., King, A., & Avalos, A. (2007). Effects of a peer-mediated program on reading skill acquisition for two-way bilingual first grade classrooms. *Learning Disability Quarterly, 30*, 169–184.

Caplan, G. (1964). *Principles of preventive psychiatry.* New York: Basic Books.

Carney, K. J., & Stiefel, G. S. (2008). Long-term results of a problem-solving approach to response to intervention: Discussion and implications. *Learning Disabilities—A Contemporary Journal, 6*(2), 61–75.

Carnine, D. (1981). Reducing training problems associated with visually and auditorily similar correspondences. *Journal of Learning Disabilities, 14*, 276–279.

Carnine, D. (1989). Designing practice activities. *Journal of Learning Disabilities, 22*, 603–607.

Carnine, D. (1997a). Bridging the research-to-practice gap. *Exceptional Children, 63*, 513–524.

Carnine, D. (1997b). Instructional design for students with learning disabilities. *Journal of Learning Disabilities, 30*, 130–142.

Carnine, D., & Carnine, L. (2004). The interaction of reading skills and science content knowledge when teaching struggling secondary students. *Reading and Writing Quarterly, 20*, 203–219.

Carnine, D., & Gersten, R. (2000). The nature and roles of research in improving achievement in mathematics. *Journal for Research in Mathematics Education, 31*, 138–142.

Carnine, D., & Granzin, A. (2001). Setting learning expectations for students with disabilities. *School Psychology Review, 30*, 466–472.

Carnine, D., & Jitendra, A. K. (1997). A descriptive analysis of mathematics curricular materials from a pedagogical perspective. *Remedial and Special Education, 18*, 66–82.

Carnine, D., Kame'enui, E., & Maggs, A. (1982). Components of analytic assistance: Statement saying, concept training, and strategy training. *Journal of Educational Research, 75*, 375–377.

Carter, R. T., Helms, J. E., & Juby, H. L. (2004). The relationship between racism and racial identity for white Americans: A profile analysis. *Journal of Multicultural Counseling and Development, 32*, 2–18.

Cartledge, G. (1996). *Cultural diversity and social skills instruction: Understanding ethnic and gender differences.* Champaign, IL: Research Press.

Case, L. P., Speece, D. L., & Molloy, D. E. (2003). The validity of a response-to-instruction paradigm to identify reading disabilities: A longitudinal analysis of individual differences and contextual factors. *School Psychology Review, 32*, 557–582.

Catts, H. W., Petscher, Y., Schatschneider, C., Bridges, M. S., & Mendoza, K. (2008). Floor effects associated with universal screening and their impact on the early identification of reading disabilities. *Journal of Learning Disabilities, 42*, 163–176.

Center for Academic and Reading Skills, University of Texas–Houston Health Science Center, Texas Institute for Measurement, Evaluation, and Statistics, University of Houston. (1999). *Technical report: Texas primary reading inventory.* Retrieved October 12, 2004, from *www.tpri.org.*

Centers for Disease Control [CDC]. (2009). H1N1 recommendations. Retrieved from *www.cdc.gov/h1n1flu/vaccination_qu_pub.html.*

Chall, J. S. (2000). *The academic achievement challenge: What really works in the classroom?* New York: Guilford Press.

Chard, D., Stoolmiller, M., Harn, B., Wanzek, J., Vaughn, S., Linan-Thompson, S., et al. (2008). Predicting reading success in a multilevel schoolwide reading model. *Journal of Learning Disabilities, 41*, 174–188.

Chisholm, D. P. (1988). Concerns respecting the regular education initiative. *Journal of Learning Disabilities, 21*, 487–501.

Christ, T., & Silberglitt, B. (2007). Estimates of the standard error of measurement for curriculum-based measures of oral reading fluency. *School Psychology Review, 36*, 130–146.

Clements, M. A., Bolt, D., Hoyt, W., & Kratochwill, T. R. (2007). Using multilevel modeling to examine the effects of multitiered interventions. *Psychology in the Schools, 44*, 503–513.

Clopton, K. L., & Etscheidt, S. (2009). Utilizing the convergence of data for expedited evaluations: Guidelines for school psychologists. *Psychology in the Schools, 46*, 459–470.

Coates, R. D. (1989). The regular education initiative and opinions of regular classroom teachers. *Journal of Learning Disabilities, 22*, 532–536.

Cognition and Technology Group at Vanderbilt. (1997). *The Jasper Project: Lessons in curriculum, instruction, assessment, and professional development*. Mahwah, NJ: Erlbaum.

Compton, D. L. (2003, December). *RTI: It's all about the nudge*. Paper presented at the Response-to-Intervention Symposium, Kansas City, MO. Retrieved March 9, 2004, from *www.nrcld.org/html/symposium2003*.

Compton, D., Fuchs, D., Fuchs, L., & Bryant, J. (2006). Selecting at-risk readers in first grade for early intervention: A two-year longitudinal study of decision rules and procedures. *Journal of Educational Psychology, 98*, 394–409.

Coyne, M. D., Kame'enui, E. J., & Simmons, D. C. (2001). Prevention and intervention in beginning reading: Two complex systems. *Learning Disabilities Research and Practice, 16*, 62–74.

Coyne, M. D., Kame'enui, E. J., & Simmons, D. C. (2004). Improving beginning reading instruction and intervention for students with LD: Reconciling "all" with "each." *Journal of Learning Disabilities, 37*, 231–240.

Coyne, M. D., Kame'enui, E. J., Simmons, D. C., & Harn, B. A. (2004). Beginning reading intervention as inoculation or insulin: First-grade reading performance of strong responders to kindergarten intervention. *Journal of Learning Disabilities, 37*, 90–105.

Cummins, J. (1979). Cognitive/academic language proficiency, linguistic interdependence, the optimum age question and some other matters. *Working Papers on Bilingualism*, No. 19, 121–129.

Cummins, J. (1986). Empowering minority students: A framework for intervention. *Harvard Educational Review, 56*, 18–36.

Cummins, J. (1996). *Negotiating identities: Education for empowerment in a diverse society*. Los Angeles: California Association for Bilingual Education.

Cummings, K., Atkins, T., Allison, R., & Cole, C. (2008). Response to intervention: Investigating the new role of special educators. *Teaching Exceptional Children, 40*, 24–31.

Daly, E. J., Chafouleas, S., & Skinner, C. H. (2005). *Interventions for reading problems: Designing and evaluating effective strategies*. New York: Guilford Press.

Daly, E. J., Johnson, S., & LeClair, C., (2009). An experimental analysis of phoneme blending and segmenting skills. *Journal of Behavior Education, 18*, 5–19.

Daly, E. J., Martens, B. K., Barnett, D., Witt, J. C., & Olson, S. C. (2007). Varying intervention delivery in response to intervention: Confronting and resolving challenges with measurement, instruction, and intensity. *School Psychology Review, 36*, 562–581.

Daly, E. J., Persampieri, M., McCurdy, M., & Gortmaker, V. (2005). Generating reading interventions through experimental analysis of academic skills: Demonstration and empirical evaluation. *School Psychology Review, 34*, 395–414.

D'Alonzo, B. J., & Boggs, E. T. (1990). A review of the regular education initiative. *Preventing School Failure, 35*, 18–24.

Danielson, L., Doolittle, J., & Bradley, R. (2007). Professional development, capacity building, and research needs: Critical issues for response to intervention implementation. *School Psychology Review, 36*, 632, 637.

Davis, G., Lindo, E., & Compton, D. (2007). Children at risk for reading failure. *Teaching Exceptional Children, 39*, 32–37.

Delpit, L.. & Kohl, H. (2006). *Other's peoples children: Cultural conflict in the classroom*. New York: The New Press.

Deno, E. (1970). Special education as developmental capital. *Exceptional Children, 37*, 229–237.

Deno, S. L. (2002). Problem solving as "best practice." In A. Thomas & J. Grimes (Eds.), *Best practices in school psychology IV* (pp. 37–56). Bethesda, MD: National Association of School Psychologists.

Deno, S. L. (2005). Problem-solving assessment. In R. Brown-Chidsey (Ed.), *Assessment for intervention:*

A problem-solving approach (pp. 10–40). New York: Guilford Press.

Deno, S., Reschly, A., Lembke, E., Magnusson, D., Callender, S., Windram, H., et al. (2009). Developing a school-wide progress-monitoring system. *Psychology in the Schools, 46,* 44–55.

Denton, C. A., Fletcher, J., Anthony, J., & Frances, D. (2006). An evaluation of intensive intervention for students with persistent reading difficulties. *Journal of Learning Disabilities, 39,* 447–466.

Denton, C. A., Wexler, J., Vaughn, S., & Bryan, D. (2008). Intervention provided to linguistically diverse middle school students with severe reading difficulties. *Learning Disabilities Research and Practice, 23,* 79–89.

Dessof, A. (2008, May). Resources to support disabled learners. *District Administration,* 49–52.

Dexter, D., Hughes, C., & Farmer, T. (2008, Fall). Responsiveness to intervention: A review of field studies and implications for rural special education. *Rural Special Education Quarterly, 27,* 3–9.

Doll, B., & Haack, K. M. (2005). Population-based strategies for identifying schoolwide problems. In R. Brown-Chidsey (Ed.), *Assessment for intervention: A problem-solving approach* (pp. 82–102). New York: Guilford Press.

Drame, E. R. (2002). Sociocultural context effects of teachers' readiness to refer for learning disabilities. *Exceptional Children, 69,* 41–53.

Duhon, G. J., Mesmer, E. M., Gregerson, L., & Witt, J. C. (2009). Effects of public feedback during RTI team meetings on teacher implementation integrity and student academic performance. *Journal of School Psychology, 47,* 19–37.

Dykeman, B. (2006). Alternative strategies in assessing special education needs. *Education, 127,* 265–273.

Eber, L., Breen, K., Rose, J., Unizycki, R. M., & London, T. H. (2008). Wraparound. *Teaching Exceptional Children, 40*(6), 16–22.

Ehren, B., & Nelson, N. (2005). The responsiveness to intervention approach and language impairment. *Topics in Language Disorders, 25,* 120–131.

Elliott, S. N., & Fuchs, L. S. (1997). The utility of curriculum-based measurement and performance assessment as alternatives to traditional intelligence and achievement tests. *School Psychology Review, 26,* 224–233.

Elliott, S. N., Huai, N., & Roach, A. T. (2007). Universal and early screening for educational difficulties: Current and future approaches. *Journal of School Psychology, 45,* 137–161.

Engelmann, S. (1999). The benefits of direct instruction: Affirmative action for at-risk students. *Educational Leadership, 57,* 77–79.

Evans, R. (1990). Making mainstreaming work through prereferral consultation. *Educational Leadership, 48,* 73–78.

Fairbanks, S., Sugai, G., Guardino, D., & Lathrop, M. (2007). Response to intervention: Examining classroom behavior support in second grade. *Exceptional Children, 73,* 288–310.

Feifer, S. (2008). Integrating response to intervention (RTI) with neuropsychology: A scientific approach to reading. *Psychology in the Schools, 45,* 812–825.

Fiorello, C., Hale, J., Holdnack, J., Kavanagh, J., Terrell, J., & Long, L. (2007). Interpreting intelligence test results for children with disabilities: Is global intelligence relevant? *Applied Neuropsychology, 14,* 2–12.

Fiorello, C., Hale, J., & Snyder, L. (2006). Cognitive hypothesis testing and response to intervention for children with reading problems. *Psychology in the Schools, 43,* 835–853.

Flanagan, D. P., & Harrison, P. L. (Eds.). (2005). *Contemporary intellectual assessment: Theories, tests, and issues* (2nd ed.). New York: Guilford Press.

Flanagan, D. P., & Ortiz, S. (2001). *Essentials of cross-battery assessment.* New York: Wiley.

Flanagan, D., Ortiz, S., Alfonso, V., & Dynda, A. (2006). Integration of response to intervention and norm-referenced tests in learning disability identification: Learning from the Tower of Babel. *Psychology in the Schools, 43,* 807–825.

Fletcher, J. M. (2003, December). *Validity of alternative approaches to the identification of LD: Operationalizing unexpected underachievement.* Paper presented at the Response-to-Intervention Symposium, Kansas City, MO. Retrieved March 9, 2004, from *www.nrcld.org/html/symposium2003.*

Fletcher, J. M. (2005). Predicting math outcomes: Reading predictors and comorbidity. *Journal of Learning Disabilities, 38,* 308–312.

Fletcher, J. M., Coulter, W. A., Reschly, D. J., & Vaughn, S. (2004). Alternative approaches to the definition and identification of learning disabilities: Some questions and answers. *Annals of Dyslexia, 54,* 304–331.

Fletcher, J. M., Foorman, B. R., Boudousquie, A., Barnes, M. A., Schatschneider, C., & Francis, D. J. (2002). Assessment of reading and learning disabilities: A research-based intervention-oriented approach. *Journal of School Psychology, 40,* 27–63.

Fletcher, J., Francis, D., Morris, R., & Lyon, G. (2005). Evidence-based assessment of learning disabilities in children and adolescents. *Journal of Clinical Child and Adolescent Psychology, 34,* 506–522.

Fletcher, J. M., Morris, R. D., & Lyon, G. R. (2003). Classification and definition of learning disabilities: An integrative perspective. In H. L. Swanson, K. R. Harris, & S. Graham (Eds.), *Handbook of learning disabilities* (pp. 30–56). New York: Guilford Press.

Foorman, B. R. (2003). *Preventing and remediating reading difficulties: Bringing science to scale.* Baltimore, MD: York Press.

Foorman, B. R., Breier, J. I., & Fletcher, J. M. (2003). Interventions aimed at improving reading success: An evidence-based approach. *Developmental Neuropsychology, 24,* 613–640.

Foxx, R. M. (1999). Long term maintenance of language and social skills. *Behavioral Interventions, 14,* 135–147.

Francis, D. J. (2003, December). *Response to intervention (RTI): A conceptually and statistically superior alternative to discrepancy.* Paper presented at the Response-to-Intervention Symposium, Kansas City, MO. Retrieved March 9, 2004, from *www.nrcld.org/html/symposium2003.*

Freeman, P. J. (1994). National health care reform minus public health: A formula for failure. *Public Health Policy, 15,* 261–282.

Fuchs, D., & Fuchs, L. S. (1994). Inclusive schools movement and the radicalization of special education reform. *Exceptional Children, 60,* 294–300.

Fuchs, D., & Fuchs, L. S. (2008, October). Implementing RTI. *District Administration, 44*(11), 73–76.

Fuchs, D., Fuchs, L. S., Mathes, P. G., Lipsey, M. E., & Eaton, S. (2000). A meta-analysis of reading differences between underachievers with and without the disability label: A brief report. *Learning Disabilities, 10,* 1–4.

Fuchs, D., Mick, D., Morgan, P. L., & Young, C. L. (2003). Responsiveness to intervention: Definitions, evidence, and implications for the learning disabilities construct. *Learning Disabilities: Research and Practice, 18,* 157–171.

Fuchs, L. (2003). Assessing intervention responsiveness: Conceptual and technical issues. *Learning Disabilities: Research and Practice, 18,* 172–186.

Fuchs, L. S., Compton, D. L., Fuchs, D., Paulsen, K., Bryant, J. D., & Hamlet, C. L. (2005). The prevention, identification, and cognitive determinants of math difficulty. *Journal of Educational Psychology, 97,* 493–515.

Fuchs, L. S., & Deno, S. L. (1994). Must instructionally useful assessment be based in the curriculum? *Exceptional Children, 61,* 15–24.

Fuchs, L. S., Fuchs, D., Compton, D. L., Bryant, J. D., & Hamlet, C. L., & Seethaler, D. M. (2007). Mathematics screening and progress monitoring at first grade: Implications for response to intervention. *Exceptional Children, 73,* 311–330.

Fuchs, L. S., Fuchs, D., Compton, D. L., Powell, S. R.,

Seethaler, P. M., Capizzi, A. M., et al. (2006). The cognitive correlates of third-grade skill in arithmetic, algorithmic computation, and arithmetic word problems. *Journal of Educational Psychology, 98,* 29–43.

Gersten, R., & Carnine, D. (1986). Direct instruction in reading comprehension. *Educational Leadership, 43,* 70–79.

Gettinger, M., & Stoiber, K. (2007). Applying a response-to-intervention model for early literacy development in low-income children. *Topics in Early Childhood Special Education, 27,* 198–213.

Gibb, G. S., & Wilder, L. K. (2002). Using functional analysis to improve reading instruction for reading instruction for students with learning disabilities and emotional/behavioral disorders. *Preventing School Failure, 46,* 152–157.

Gilbertson, D., & Ferre, S. (2008). Considerations in the identification, assessment, and intervention process for deaf and hard-of-hearing students with reading difficulties. *Psychology in the Schools, 45,* 104–120.

Glover, T. A., & Albers, C. A. (2006). Considerations for evaluating universal screening assessments. *Journal of School Psychology, 45,* 117–135.

Glover, T. A,, & DiPerna, J. (2007). Service delivery for response to intervention: Core components and directions for future research. *School Psychology Review, 36,* 526–540.

Glutting, J. J., McDermott, P. A., Watkins, M. M., Kush, J. C., & Konold, T. R. (1997). The base rate problem and its consequences for interpreting children's ability profiles. *School Psychology Review, 26,* 176–188.

Good, R. H., & Kaminski, R. A. (Eds.). (2002). *Dynamic Indicators of Basic Early Literacy Skills* (6th ed.). Eugene, OR: Institute for the Development of Educational Achievement. Retrieved November 8, 2004, from *dibels.uoregon.edu.*

Good, R. H., III, Simmons, D. C., & Kame'enui, E. J. (2001). The importance and decision-making utility of a continuum of fluency-based indicators of foundational reading skills for third-grade high-stakes outcomes. *Scientific Studies of Reading, 5,* 257–289.

Goodman, G., & Webb, M. (2006). Reading disability referrals: Teacher bias and other factors that impact response to intervention. *Learning Disabilities—a Contemporary Journal, 4,* 59–70.

Gould, S. J. (1996). *The mismeasure of man.* New York: Norton. (Original work published 1981)

Graham, S., & Harris, K. R. (1997). It can be taught, but it does not develop naturally: Myths and realities in writing instruction. *School Psychology Review, 26,* 414–425.

Graner, P., Faggella-Luby, M., & Fritschmann, N. (2005). An overview of responsiveness to intervention: What practitioners ought to know. *Topics in Language Disorders, 25*, 93–105.

Great Leaps Math. (2004). Retrieved November 8, 2004, from *www.greatleaps.com*.

Green, G. (1996). Evaluating claims about treatments for autism. In C. Maurice, G. Green, & S. Luce (Eds.), *Behavioral intervention for young children with autism: A manual for parents and professionals* (pp. 15–27). Austin, TX: Pro-Ed.

Gresham, F. (2004). Current status and future directions of school-based behavioral interventions. *School Psychology Review, 33*, 326–343.

Gresham, F. (2005). Response to intervention: An alternative means of identifying students as emotionally disturbed. *Education & Treatment of Children, 28*, 328–344.

Griffiths, A. J., VanDerHeyden, A. M., Skocut, M., & Lilles, E. (2009). Progress monitoring in roal reading fluency within the context of RTI. *School Psychology Quarterly, 24*, 13–23.

Gutkin, T. B. (2002). Evidence-based interventions in school psychology: State of the art and directions for the future. *School Psychology Quarterly, 17*, 339–340.

Haager, D. (2007). Promises and cautions regarding using response to intervention with English language learners. *Learning Disability Quarterly, 30*, 213–218.

Hale, J., Kaufman, A., Naglieri, J., & Kavale, K. (2006). Implementation of IDEA: Integrating response to intervention and cognitive assessment methods. *Psychology in the Schools, 43*, 753–770.

Hallahan, D. P., Keller, C. E., McKinney, J. D., Lloyd, J. W., & Bryan, T. (1988). Examining the research base of the regular education initiative: Efficacy studies and the adaptive learning environments model. *Journal of Learning Disabilities, 21*, 29–35, 55.

Halperin, S. (1979). ESEA comes of age: Some historical reflections. *Educational Leadership, 36*, 349–353.

Hardy, L. (2008, March). Children at risk. *American School Board Journal, 195*(3), 24–27.

Harris-Murri, N., King, K., & Rostenberg, D. (2006). Reducing disproportionate minority representation in special education programs for students with emotional disturbances: Toward a culturally responsive response to intervention model. *Education and Treatment of Children, 29*, 779–799.

Harry, B., & Klingner, J. (2007, February). Discarding the deficit model. *Educational Leadership, 64*(5), 16–21.

Hart, B., & Risley, T. R. (1995). *Meaningful differences in the everyday experience of young American children*. Baltimore, MD: Brookes.

Hawkins, R., Kroeger, S., Musti-Rao, S., Barnett, D., & Ward, J. (2008). Preservice training in response to intervention: Learning by doing an interdisciplinary field experience. *Psychology in the Schools, 45*, 745–762.

Hayes, S. C., Barlow, D. H., & Nelson-Grey, R. O. (1999). *The scientist-practitioner: Research and accountability in the age of managed care*. Boston: Allyn & Bacon.

Helms, J. E. (1992). Why is there no study of cultural equivalence in standardized cognitive ability testing? *American Psychologist, 47*, 1083–1102.

Holdnack, J., & Weiss, L. (2006). IDEA 2004: Anticipated implications for clinical practice—integrating assessment and intervention. *Psychology in the Schools, 43*, 871–882.

Hoover, J. J., Patton, J. R. (2008). The role of special educators in a multitiered instructional system. *Intervention in School and Clinic, 43*, 195–202.

Hunley, S., & McNamara, K. (2010). *Tier 3 of the RTI model: Problem solving through a case study approach*. Thousand Oaks, CA: Corwin/National Association of School Psychologists.

Individuals with Disabilities Education Act [IDEA]. (1997). Public Law 105–17.

Individuals with Disabilities Education Improvement Act [IDEA 2002]. (2004). Public Law 108–446 (20 U.S.C. 1400 *et seq.*).

Institute of Medicine, Committee on the Evaluation of Vaccine Purchase Financing in the United States. (2004). *Financing vaccines in the 21st century: Assuring access and availability*. Washington, DC: National Academies Press.

Intervention Central. (2010). Your source for RTI resources. Retrieved from *www.interventioncentral.org*.

Jenkins, J., Hudson, R., & Johnson, E. (2007). Screening for at-risk readers in a response to intervention framework. *School Psychology Review, 36*, 582–600.

Jenkins, J. R., Pious, C. G., & Jewell, M. (1990). Special education and the regular education initiative: Basic assumptions. *Exceptional Children, 56*(6), 479–491.

Jenkins, J., Zumeta, R., Dupree, O., & Johnson, K. (2005). Measuring gains in reading ability with passage reading fluency. *Learning Disabilities Research and Practice, 20*, 245–253.

Jones, J. (Ed.). (2009). The psychology of multiculturalism in the schools: A primer for practice, training, and research. Bethesda, MD: National Association of School Psychologists.

Jones, K., Wickstrom, K. E., Noltemeyer, A. L., &

Brown, S. M. (2009). An experimental analysis of reading fluency. *Journal of Behavioral Education, 18,* 35–55.

Justice, L. (2006). Evidence-based practice, response to intervention, and the prevention of reading difficulties. *Language, Speech, and Hearing Services in Schools, 37,* 284–297.

Kame'enui, E. J., & Carnine, D. W. (1998). *Effective teaching strategies that accommodate diverse learners.* Upper Saddle River, NJ: Prentice-Hall.

Kame'enui, E. J., & Simmons, D. (2002). *Early reading intervention.* Upper Saddle River, NJ: Pearson/Scott Foresman.

Kaminski, R. A., & Good, R. H., III. (1998). Assessing early literacy skills in a problem-solving model: Dynamic Indicators of Basic Early Literacy Skills. In M. R. Shinn (Ed.), *Advanced applications of curriculum-based measurement* (pp. 113–142). New York: Guilford Press.

Kansas Department of Education. (2009). State assessment results show continued growth by Kansas students. Retrieved from *www.ksde.org.*

Kashi, T. (2008). Response to intervention as a suggested generalized approach to improving minority AYP scores. *Rural Special Education Quarterly, 27,* 37–44.

Kavale, K. A. (2001). Decision making in special education: The function of meta-analysis. *Exceptionality, 9,* 245–269.

Kavale, K. A. (2002). Mainstreaming to full inclusion: From orthogenesis to pathogenesis of an idea. *International Journal of Disability, Development and Education, 49,* 201–215.

Kavale, K. A., & Forness, S. R. (2000). History, rhetoric, and reality. *Remedial and Special Education, 21,* 279–297.

Kavale, K., Kauffman, J., Bachmeier, R., & LeFever, G. (2008). Response to intervention: Separating the rhetoric of self-congratulations from the reality of specific learning disability identification. *Learning Disability Quarterly, 31,* 135–150.

Klein, W. (2004). *Toward humanity and justice: The writings of Kenneth B. Clark, scholar of the 1954 Brown v. Board of Education decision.* New York: Praeger.

Koutsoftas, A., Harmon, M., & Gray, S. (2009). The effect of tier 2 intervention for phonemic awareness in a response-to-intervention model in low-income preschool classrooms. *Language, Speech, and Hearing Services in Schools, 40,* 116–130.

Kovaleski, J. F. (2003, December). The three-tier model for identifying learning disabilities: Critical program features and system issues. Paper presented at the Response-to-Intervention Symposium, Kansas City, MO. Retrieved March 9, 2004, from *www.nrcld.org/html/symposium2003.*

Kovaleski, J. (2007). Response to intervention: Considerations for research and systems change. *School Psychology Review, 36,* 638, 646.

Kranzler, J. H. (1997). Educational and policy issues related to the use and interpretation of intelligence tests in the schools. *School Psychology Review, 26,* 150–163.

Kratochwill, T. R., & Stoiber, K. C. (2002). Evidence-based interventions in school psychology: Conceptual foundations of the procedural and coding manual of Division 16 and the Society for the Study of School Psychology Task Force. *School Psychology Quarterly, 17,* 341–389.

Kratochwill, T. R., & Stoiber, K. C. (2002). *Procedural and coding manual for review of evidence-based interventions.* Retrieved from *www.eric.ed.gov.*

Kratochwill, T., Volpiansky, P., Clements, M., & Ball, C. (2007). Professional development in implementing and sustaining multitier prevention models: Implications for response to intervention. *School Psychology Review, 36,* 618–631.

Kroeger, S. D., & Kouche, B. (2006). Using peer-assisted learning strategies to increase response to intervention in inclusive middle math settings. *Teaching Exceptional Children, 38*(5), 6–13.

Kubicek, F. C. (1994). Special education reform in light of select state and federal court decisions. *Journal of Special Education, 28,* 27–43.

Lichtenstein, R., & Klotz, M. B. (2007). Deciphering the federal regulations on identifying children with specific learning disabilities. *NASP Communique, 36*(3), 1, 13, 15.

Linan-Thompson, S., Cirino, P., & Vaughn, S. (2007). Determining English language learners' response to intervention: Questions and some answers. *Learning Disability Quarterly, 30,* 185–195.

Linan-Thompson, S., Vaughn, S., Prater, K., & Cirino, P. (2006). The response to intervention of English language learners at risk for reading problems. *Journal of Learning Disabilities, 39,* 390–398.

Lopez, E. (1997). The cognitive assessment of limited English proficient and bilingual children. In D. P. Flanagan, J. L. Genshaft, & P. L. Harrison (Eds.), *Contemporary intellectual assessment: Theories, tests, and issues* (pp. 503–516). New York: Guilford Press.

Lopez, R. (1997). The practical impact of current research and issues in intelligence test interpretation and use for multicultural populations. *School Psychology Review, 26,* 249–254.

Lyon, G. R., Fletcher, J. M., Shaywtiz, S. E., Shaywitz, B. A., Wood, F. B., Schulte, A., et al. (2001). *Learn-*

ing disabilities: An evidence-based conceptualiza-tion. Washington, DC: Fordham Foundation.

Lyon, G. R., Shaywitz, S. E., & Chhabra, V. (2004). Evidence-based reading policy in the United States: How scientific research informs instructional practice. In D. Ravitch (Ed.), *Brookings papers on education policy: 2005* (pp. 198–216). Washington, DC: Brookings Institution.

Machek, G., & Nelson, J. (2007). How should reading disabilities be operationalized?: A survey of practicing school psychologists. *Learning Disabilities Research and Practice, 22,* 147–157.

Marston, D. (2005). Tiers of intervention in responsiveness to intervention: Prevention outcomes and learning disabilities identification patterns. *Journal of Learning Disabilities, 38,* 539–544.

Marston, D., Muyskens, P., Lau, M., & Canter, A. (2003). Problem-solving model for decision-making with high-incidence disabilities: The Minneapolis experience. *Learning Disabilities: Research and Practice, 18,* 187–200.

Martens, B. K., & Gertz, L. E. (2009). Brief experimental analysis: A decision tool for bridging the gap between research and practice. *Journal of Behavioral Education, 18,* 92–99.

Mastropieri, M., & Scruggs, T. (2005). Feasibility and consequences of response to intervention: Examination of the issues and scientific evidence as a model for the identification of individuals with learning disabilities. *Journal of Learning Disabilities, 38,* 525–531.

Mather, N., & Kaufman, N. (2006). Introduction to the special issue, part one: It's about the what, the how well, and the why. *Psychology in the Schools, 43,* 747–752.

McBride, G., Dumont, R., & Willis, J. O. (2004). Response to intervention legislation: Have we found a better way, or will we be just as confused as we have been for the last ten years? *The School Psychologist, 58,* 86–91.

McCardle, P., & Chhabra, V. (Eds.). (2004). *The voice of evidence in reading research.* Baltimore, MD: Brookes.

McComas, J. J., Wagner, D., Chapffin, M. C., Holton, E., McDonnell, M., & Monn, E. (2009). Prescriptive analysis: Further individualization of hypothesis testing in brief experimental analysis of reading fluency. *Journal of Behavioral Education, 18,* 56–70.

McIntosh, A., Graves, A., & Gersten, R. (2007). The effects of response to intervention on literacy development in multiple-language settings. *Learning Disability Quarterly, 30,* 197–212.

McLeskey, J., & Skiba, R. (1990). Reform and special education: A mainstream perspective. *Journal of Special Education, 24,* 319–326.

McMaster, K., Kung, S., Han, I., & Cao, M. (2008). Peer-assisted learning strategies: A tier 1 approach to promoting English learners' response to intervention. *Exceptional Children, 74,* 194–214.

Menzies, H., Mahdavi, J., & Lewis, J. (2008). Early intervention in reading: From research to practice. *Remedial and Special Education, 29,* 67–77.

Mesmer, E., & Mesmer, H. (2008). Response to intervention (RTI): What teachers of reading need to know. *Reading Teacher, 62,* 280–290.

Moore, J., & Whitfield, V. (2009). Building schoolwide capacity for preventing reading failure. *Reading Teacher, 62,* 622–624.

Murawski, W. W., & Hughes, C. E. (2009). Response to intervention, collaboration, and co-teaching: A logical combination for systemic change. *Preventing School Failure, 53,* 267–277.

Murphy, D. M. (1996). Implications of inclusion for general and special education. *Elementary School Journal, 96,* 469–494.

National Association of School Psychologists. (2000). *Professional conduct manual: Principles for professional ethics and guidelines for the provision of school psychological services.* Bethesda, MD: Author. Retrieved from *www.nasponline.org/pdf/ProfessionalCond.pdf.*

National Association of School Psychologists. (2002). *Rights without labels* [Position paper on the provision of services to students with disabilities]. Bethesda, MD: Author.

National Association of School Psychologists. (2003). *NASP recommendations: LD eligibility and identification for IDEA reauthorization.* Bethesda, MD: Author.

National Autism Center. (2010). National standards project. Retrieved from *www.nationalautismcenter.org/about/national.php.*

National Center for Education Statistics. (2004). *The condition of education 2004.* Washington, DC: U.S. Department of Education.

National Center on Response to Intervention. (2009). Response to intervention. Retrieved from *www.rti4success.org.*

National Joint Committee on Learning Disabilities. (2002). Achieving better outcomes—maintaining rights: An approach to identifying and serving students with specific learning disabilities. *NASP Communiqué, 31,* 1, 5, 7.

National Reading Panel. (2000). *Teaching children to read: An evidence-based assessment of the scientific research literature on reading and its impli-*

cations for reading instruction. Washington, DC: National Institute for Literacy.

Nelson, J. R., Hurley, K. D., Synhorst, L., Epstein, M. H., Stage, S., & Buckley, J. (2009). The child outcomes of a behavior model. *Exceptional Children, 76,* 7–30.

Nelson, J., & Machek, G. (2007). A survey of training, practice, and competence in reading assessment and intervention. *School Psychology Review, 36,* 311–327.

Newell, M., & Kratochwill, T. R., (2007). The integration of response to intervention and critical race theory–disability studies: A robust approach to reducing racial discrimination in evaluation decisions. In S. R. Jimerson, M. K. Burns, & A. M. Jimerson (Eds.), *Handbook of response to intervention: The science and practice of assessment and interventions* (pp. 65–79). New York: Springer.

No Child Left Behind Act [NCLB]. (2001). Public Law 107–15.

Nunn, G. D., & Jantz, P. B. (2009). Factors within response to intervention implementation training associated with teacher efficacy belief. *Education, 129,* 599–609.

O'Connor, R. (2003). Tiers of intervention in kindergarten through third grade. Paper presented at the Response-to-Intervention Symposium, December 4–5, 2003, Kansas City, MO. Retrieved March 9, 2004, from *www.nrcld.org/html/symposium2003.*

Odegard, T., Ring, J., Smith, S., Biggan, J., & Black, J. (2008). Differentiating the neural response to intervention in children with developmental dyslexia. *Annals of Dyslexia, 58,* 1–14.

Ofiesh, N. (2006). Response to intervention and the identification of specific learning disabilities: Why we need comprehensive evaluations as part of the process. *Psychology in the Schools, 43,* 883–888.

O'Malley, K. J., Francis, D. J., Foorman, B. R., Fletcher, J. M., & Swank, P. R. (2002). Growth in precursor and reading-related skills: Do low-achieving and IQ-discrepant readers develop differently? *Learning Disabilities Research and Practice, 17,* 19–35.

Ortiz, S., & Flanagan, D. P. (2002). Best practices in working with culturally diverse children and families. In A. Thomas & J. Grimes (Eds.), *Best practices in school psychology IV* (pp. 337–352). Bethesda, MD: National Association of School Psychologists.

Palenchar, L., & Boyer, L. (2008). Response to intervention: Implementation of a statewide system. *Rural Special Education Quarterly, 27,* 18–26.

Pearson Education, Inc. (2008). *AIMSweb.* Retrieved from *www.aimsweb.com.*

Peltier, G. L. (1993). The regular education initiative

teacher: The research results and recommended practice. *Education, 114,* 54–61.

Peterson, K. M. H., & Shinn, M. R. (2002). Severe discrepancy models: Which best explains school identification practices for learning disabilities. *School Psychology Review, 31,* 459–476.

Polaha, J. A., & Allen, K. D. (1999). A tutorial for understanding and evaluating single-subject methodology. *Proven Practice, 1,* 73–77.

Powers, K., Hagans, K., & Miller, M. (2007). Using response to intervention to promote transition from special education services. In S. R. Jimerson, M. K. Burns, & A. M. Jimerson (Eds.), *Handbook of response to intervention: The science and practice of assessment and interventions* (pp. 418–427). New York: Springer.

Prasse, D. (2006). Legal supports for problem-solving systems. *Remedial and Special Education, 27,* 7–15.

President's Commission on Excellence in Special Education [PCESE]. (2002). *A new era: Revitalizing special education for children and their families.* Washington, DC: Author. Retrieved from *www. ed.gov/inits/commissionsboard/whspecialeducation/reports/index.html.*

Pressley, M., Duke, N. K., & Boling, E. (2004). The educational science and scientifically based instruction we need: Lessons from reading research and policymaking. *Harvard Educational Review, 74,* 30–62.

Purdum, T. S. (1998, June 3). California passes measure to limit bilingual schools. *New York Times, 147*(51177), p. A1.

Reschly, D. J. (1997). Utility of individual ability measures and public policy choices for the 21st century. *School Psychology Review, 26,* 234–241.

Reynolds, C. R., & Shaywitz, S. E. (2009). Response to intervention: Ready or not? Or, from waiting to fail to watch them fail. *School Psychology Quarterly, 24,* 130–145.

Riley-Tillman, T., & Burns, M. K. (2009). *Evaluating educational interventions: Single-case design for measuring response intervention.* New York: Guilford Press.

Riley-Tillman, T., Chafouleas, S., & Briesch, A. (2007). A school practitioner's guide to using daily behavior report cards to monitor student behavior. *Psychology in the Schools, 44,* 77–89.

Rinaldi, C., & Samson, J. (2008). English language learners and response to intervention. *Teaching Exceptional Children, 40,* 6–14.

Salvia, J., & Ysseldyke, J. E. (2004). *Assessment in special and inclusive education* (9th ed.). Boston: Houghton Mifflin.

Sanetti, L. H., & Kratochwill, T. R. (2005). Treatment

integrity assessment within a problem-solving model. In R. Brown-Chidsey (Ed.), *Assessment for intervention: A problem-solving approach* (pp. 304–325). New York: Guilford Press.

Sattler, J. M. (2001). *Assessment of children: Cognitive applications.* San Diego, CA: Author.

Schatschneider, C., Francis, D. J., Carlson, C. D., Fletcher, J. M., & Foorman, B. R. (2004). Kindergarten prediction of reading skills: A longitudinal comparative analysis. *Journal of Educational Psychology, 96,* 265–283.

Schmitt, A., & Wodrich, D. (2008). Reasons and rationales for neuropsychological tests in a multitier system of school services. *Psychology in the Schools, 45,* 826–837.

Semmel, M. I., & Abernathy, T. V. (1991). Teacher perceptions of the regular education initiative. *Exceptional Children, 58,* 9–24.

Semrud-Clikeman, M. (2005). Neuropsychological aspects for evaluating learning disabilities. *Journal of Learning Disabilities, 38,* 563–568.

Severson, H. H., Walker, H. M., Hope-Doolittle, J., Kratochwill, T. R., & Gresham, F. M. (2007). Proactive early screening to detect behaviorally at-risk students: Issues, approaches, emerging innovations, and professional practices. *Journal of School Psychology, 45,* 193–223.

Shapiro, E. S. (2005). *Academic skills problems: Direct assessment and intervention* (3rd ed.). New York: Guilford Press.

Shaywitz, S. (2003). *Overcoming dyslexia.* New York: Knopf.

Sheehan, G. (2009). Biography. Retrieved from *www.georgesheehan.com/welcome/bio.html.*

Shernoff, E. S., Kratochwill, T. R., & Stoiber, K. C. (2002). Evidence-based interventions in school psychology: An illustration of task force coding criteria using single-participant research design. *School Psychology Quarterly, 17,* 390–422.

Shinn, M. R. (1989). *Curriculum-based measurement: Assessing special children.* New York: Guilford Press.

Shinn, M. R. (1998). *Advanced applications of curriculum-based measurement.* New York: Guilford Press.

Shinn, M. R. (2005). Identifying and validating academic problems in a problem-solving model. In R. Brown-Chidsey (Ed.), *Assessment for intervention: A problem-solving approach* (pp. 219–246). New York: Guilford Press.

Shinn, M. (2007). Identifying students at risk, monitoring performance, and determining eligibility within response to intervention: Research on educational need and benefit from academic intervention. *School Psychology Review, 36,* 601–617.

Shinn, M. R., Collins, V. L., & Gallagher, S. (1998). Curriculum-based measurement and its use in a problem-solving model with students from minority backgrounds. In M. R. Shinn (Ed.), *Advanced applications of curriculum-based measurement* (pp. 143–174). New York: Guilford Press.

Siegel, L. (2003). IQ–discrepancy definitions and the diagnosis of LD. *Journal of Learning Disabilities, 36,* 2–4.

Siegel, L. S., & Himel, N. (1998). Socioeconomic status, age, and the classification of dyslexics and poor readers: The dangers of using IQ scores in the definition of reading disability. *Dyslexia, 4,* 90–105.

Silberglitt, B., & Hintze, J. (2007). How much growth can we expect?: A conditional analysis of R-CBM growth rates by level of performance. *Exceptional Children, 74,* 71–84.

Simmons, D., Coyne, M., Kwok, O., McDonagh, S., Harn, B., & Kame'enui, E. (2008). Indexing Response to Intervention. *Journal of Learning Disabilities, 41,* 158–173.

Snow, C. E., Burns, M. S., & Griffin, P. (Eds.). (1998). *Preventing reading difficulties in young children.* Washington, DC: National Academy Press.

Spear-Swerling, L., & Sternberg, R. J. (1996). *Off track: How poor readers become "learning disabled."* Boulder, CO: Westview Press.

Spectrum K12 School Solutions. (2009). *Response to Intervention (RTI) adoption survey 2009.* Retrieved from *www.spectrumk12.com/thankyourtisurvey.*

Speece, D. L., Case, L. P., & Molloy, D. E. (2003). Responsiveness to general education instruction as the first gate to learning disabilities identification. *Learning Disabilities: Research and Practice, 18,* 147–156.

Sprague, J., Cook, C. R., Wright, D., B., & Sadler, C. (2008). *RTI and behavior: A guide to integrating behavioral and academic supports.* Palm Beach, FL: LRP Publications.

Stage, S. A., Abbott, R. D., Jenkins, J. R., & Berninger, V. W. (2003). Predicting response to early reading intervention from verbal IQ, reading-related language abilities, attention ratings, and verbal IQ–word reading discrepancy. *Journal of Learning Disabilities, 36,* 24–34.

Stanovich, K. E. (1991). Discrepancy definition of reading disability: Has intelligence led us astray? *Reading Research Quarterly, 26,* 7–29.

Stanovich, K. E. (1993). It's practical to be rational. *Journal of Learning Disabilities, 26,* 524–533.

Stanovich, K. E. (2000). *Progress in understanding reading: Scientific foundations and new frontiers.* New York: Guilford Press.

Stanovich, P. J., & Stanovich, K. E. (2003). *Using re-*

search and reason in education: How teachers use scientifically based research to make curricular decisions. Washington, DC: The Partnership for Reading.

Stecker, P. (2007). Tertiary Intervention: Using progress monitoring with intensive services. *Teaching Exceptional Children, 39,* 50–57.

Stecker, P., Fuchs, D., & Fuchs, L. (2008, Fall). Progress monitoring as essential practice within response to intervention. *Rural Special Education Quarterly, 27,* 10–17.

Steege, M. (1997). Encopresis and enuresis. In G. Baer, K. Minke, & A. Thomas (Eds.), *Children's needs III: Development, problems and alternatives* (pp. 879–885). Washington, DC: National Association of School Psychologists.

Steege, M. W., Brown-Chidsey, R., & Mace, F. C. (2002). Best practices in evaluating interventions. In A. Thomas & J. Grimes (Eds.), *Best practices in school psychology IV* (pp. 517–534). Bethesda, MD: National Association of School Psychologists.

Steege, M. W., Davin, T., & Hathaway, M. (2001). Reliability and accuracy of a performance-based behavioral recording procedure. *School Psychology Review, 30,* 252–262.

Steege, M. W., & Wacker, D. (1995). Best practices in evaluating the effectiveness of applied interventions. In A. Thomas & J. Grimes (Eds.), *Best practices in school psychology III* (pp. 625–636). Washington DC: National Association of School Psychologists.

Steege, M. W., & Watson, T. S. (2009). *Conducting school-based functional behavioral assessments* (2nd ed.). New York: Guilford Press.

Stein, M., Carnine, D., & Dixon, R. (1989). Direct instruction: Integrating curriculum design and effective teaching practice. *Intervention in School and Clinic, 33,* 227–235.

Stein, M., Stuen, C., Carnine, D., & Long, R. M. (2001). Textbook evaluation and adoption. *Reading and Writing Quarterly, 17,* 5–24.

Stuebing, K. K., Barth, A. E., Molfese, P. J., Weiss, B., & Fletcher, J. M. (2009). IQ is not strongly related to response to reading instruction: A meta-analytic interpretation. *Exceptional Children, 76,* 31–51.

Stuebing, K. K., Fletcher, J. M., LeDoux, J. M., Lyon, G. R., Shaywitz, S. E., & Shaywitz, B. A. (2002). Validity of IQ–discrepancy classifications of reading disabilities: A meta-analysis. *American Educational Research Journal, 39,* 469–518.

Swanson, H. L., Harris, K. R., & Graham, S. (Eds.). (2003). *Handbook of learning disabilities.* New York: Guilford Press.

Swanson, H. L., & Sachse-Lee, C. (2000). A meta-analysis of single-subject-design intervention research for students with LD. *Journal of Learning Disabilities, 33,* 114–137.

Sweet, R. W. (2004). The big picture: Where we are nationally on the reading front and how we got here. In P. McCarde & V. Chhabra (Eds.), *The voice of evidence in reading research* (pp. 13–46). Baltimore, MD: Brookes.

Task Force on Evidence-Based Interventions in School Psychology [sponsored by Division 16 of the American Psychological Association and the Society for the Study of School Psychology]. (2003, June). *Procedural and coding manual for review of evidence-based interventions.* Retrieved from *www.sp-ebi.org/_workingfiles/EBImanual1.pdf.*

Tatum, B. D. (1997). *Why are all the black kids sitting together in the cafeteria? and other conversations about race: A psychologist explains the development of racial identity* (rev. ed.). New York: Basic Books.

Taylor, R. L., & Richards, S. B. (1997). Teacher perceptions of inclusive settings. *Teaching Exceptional Children, 29,* 50–55.

Telzrow, C. F., McNamara, K., & Hollinger, C. L. (2000). Fidelity of problem-solving implementation and relationship to student performance. *School Psychology Review, 29,* 443–461.

Tilly, W. D., III. (2002). Best practices in school psychology as a problem-solving enterprise. In A. Thomas & J. Grimes (Eds.), *Best practices in school psychology IV* (pp. 21–36). Bethesda, MD: National Association of School Psychologists.

Tilly, W. D., III. (2003, December). *How many tiers are needed for successful prevention and early intervention?: Heartland Area Education Agency's evolution from four to three tiers.* Paper presented at the Response-to-Intervention Symposium, Kansas City, MO. Retrieved March 9, 2004, from *www.nrcld.org/html/symposium2003.*

Tilly, W. D., III. (2008). The evolution of school psychology to science-based practice: Problem-solving and the three-tiered model. In A. Thomas & J. Grimes (Eds.), *Best practices in school psychology V* (pp. 17–36). Bethesda, MD: National Association of School Psychologists.

Torgeson, J. K. (2003, December). *Operationalizing the response to intervention model to identify children with learning disabilities: Specific issues with older children.* Paper presented at the Response-to-Intervention Symposium, Kansas City, MO. Retrieved March 9, 2004, from *www.nrcld.org/html/symposium2003.*

Twyman, J. S., & Sota, M. (2009). Identifying research-based practices for response to intervention: Scientifically based instruction. *Journal of Evidence-Based Practices for Schools.* 9, 86–101.

U.S. Department of Education. (2002a). *Guidance for the reading first program.* Retrieved October 12, 2004, from *www.ed.gov/programs/readingfirst/ guidance.doc.*

U.S. Department of Education. (2002b). *No Child Left Behind: A desktop reference.* Washington, DC: Author.

U.S. Department of Education. (2005). *Scientifically based research.* Retrieved from *www.ed.gov/nclb/ methods/whatworks/research/index.html.*

U.S. Department of Education. (2008). *Reading First state APR data, 2003–2007.* Washington, DC: Author. Retrieved from *www.ed.gov/programs/read-ingfirst/data.html.*

U.S. Department of Education. (2009). *Early Reading First: Annual performance data.* Washington, DC: Author. Retrieved from *www.ed.gov/programs/ earlyreading/performance.html.*

U.S. Department of Education, Institute of Education Sciences. (2004). *What Works Clearinghouse.* Retrieved April 27, 2004, from *www.w-w-c.org.*

VanDerHeyden, A. M., & Burns, M. K. (2009). Performance indicators in math: Implications for brief experimental analysis of academic performance. *Journal of Behavioral Education, 18,* 71–91.

VanDerHeyden, A., & Snyder, P. (2006). Integrating frameworks from early childhood intervention and school psychology to accelerate growth for all young children. *School Psychology Review, 35,* 519–534.

VanDerHeyden, A., Snyder, P., Broussard, C., & Ramsdell, K. (2007). Measuring response to early literacy intervention with preschoolers at risk. *Topics in Early Childhood Special Education, 27,* 232–249.

VanDerHeyden, A. M., & Witt, J. C. (2008). Best practices in can't do/won't do assessment. In A. Thomas & J. Grimes, *Best Practices in School Psychology V* (pp. 131–139). Bethesda, MD: National Association of School Psychologists.

VanDerHeyden, A. M., Witt, J. C., & Gilbertson, D. (2007). A multi-year evaluation of the effects of a response to intervention (RTI) model on identification of children for special education. *Journal of School Psychology, 45,* 225–256.

Vaughn, S., & Fuchs, L. S. (2003). Redefining learning disabilities as inadequate response to instruction: The promises and potential problems. *Learning Disabilities: Research and Practice, 18,* 137–146.

Vaughn, S., Mathes, P., Linan-Thompson, S., & Francis, D. (2005). Teaching English language learn-

ers at risk for reading disabilities to read: Putting research into practice. *Learning Disabilities Research and Practice, 20,* 58–67.

Vaughn, S., Wanzek, J., Murray, C. S., Scammacca, N., Linan-Thompson, S., & Woodruff, A. L. (2009). Response to early reading intervention: Examining higher and lower responders. *Exceptional Children, 75,* 165–183.

Vellutino, F. R., Scanlon, D. M., & Lyon, G. R. (2000). Differentiating between difficult-to-remediate and readily remediated poor readers: More evidence against the IQ–achievement discrepancy definition for reading disability. *Journal of Learning Disabilities, 33,* 223–238.

Vellutino, F. R., Scanlon, D. M., Small, S., & Fanuele, D. (2006). Response to intervention as a vehicle for distinguishing between children with and without reading disabilities: Evidence for the role of kindergarten and first-grade interventions. *Journal of Learning Disabilities, 39,* 157–169.

Vellutino, F. R., Scanlon, D. M., & Zhang, H. (2007). Identifying reading disability based on response to intervention: Evidence from early intervention research. In S. R. Jimerson, M. K. Burns, & A. M. Jimerson (Eds.), *Handbook of response to intervention: The science and practice of assessment and interventions* (pp. 185–211). New York: Springer.

Villa, R. A., & Thousand, J. S. (1996). Teacher and administrator perceptions of heterogeneous education. *Exceptional Children, 63,* 29–46.

Walker, D., Carta, J. J., Greenwood, C. R., & Buzhardt, J. F. (2008). The use of individual growth and developmental indicators for progress monitoring and intervention decision making in early education. *Exceptionality, 16,* 33–47.

Wanzek, J., & Vaughn, S. (2008). Response to varying amounts of time in reading intervention for students with low response to intervention. *Journal of Learning Disabilities, 41,* 126–142.

Watson, T. S., & Steege, M. W. (2003). *Conducting school-based functional behavioral assessments: A practitioner's guide.* New York: Guilford Press.

Weisz, J. R., & Hawley, K. M. (1999). Finding, evaluating, refining, and applying empirically supported treatments for children and adolescents. *Journal of Clinical Child Psychology, 27,* 206–217.

Wilber, A., & Cushman, T. (2006). Selecting effective academic interventions: An example using brief experimental analysis for oral reading. *Psychology in the Schools, 43,* 79–84.

Williams, P. B., & Carnine, D. W. (1981). Relationship between range of examples and of instructions and attention in concept attainment. *Journal of Educational Research, 74,* 144–148.

Willig, A. (1985). A meta-analysis of selected studies on the effectiveness of bilingual education. *Review of Educational Research, 55,* 269–317.

Willis, J. O., & Dumont, R. (2006). And never the twain shall meet: Can response to intervention and cognitive assessment be reconciled? *Psychology in the Schools, 43,* 901–908.

Witsken, D., Stoeckel, A., & D'Amato, R. (2008). Leading educational change using a neuropsychological response-to-intervention approach: Linking our past, present, and future. *Psychology in the Schools, 45,* 781–798.

Wodrich, D., Spencer, M., & Daley, K. (2006). Combining RTI and psychoeducational assessment: What we must assume to do otherwise. *Psychology in the Schools, 43,* 797–806.

Wright, W. E. (2004). What English-only really means: A study of the implementation of California language policy with Cambodian-American students. *International Journal of Bilingual Education and Bilingualism, 7,* 1–23.

Xu, Y., & Drame, E. (2008). Culturally appropriate context: Unlocking the potential of response to intervention for English language learners. *Early Childhood Education Journal, 35,* 305–311.

Ysseldyke, J. (2005). Assessment and decision making for students with learning disabilities: What if this is as good as it gets? *Learning Disability Quarterly, 28,* 125–128.

Zirkel, P. A. (2006). What does the law say? *Teaching Exceptional Children, 38*(5), 67–68.

Zirkel, P., & Krohn, N. (2008). RTI after IDEA. *Teaching Exceptional Children, 40*(3), 71–73.

Index

Page numbers followed by an *f* or a *t* indicate figures or tables.